CATHOLIC RECORD SOCIETY PUBLICATIONS

RECORDS SERIES
VOLUME 81

Portrait of Mary Ward. School of Rubens, c.1621. Rubens was the court painter to the Infanta Isabella Clara Eugenia at this time. From the CJ house at Augsburg.

Mary Ward

(1585–1645)

A Briefe Relation … with Autobiographical Fragments and a Selection of Letters

Edited by

CHRISTINA KENWORTHY-BROWNE CJ

PUBLISHED FOR

THE CATHOLIC RECORD SOCIETY

BY

THE BOYDELL PRESS

2008

First published 2008

ISBN 978-0-902832-24-4

A Catholic Record Society publication
published by The Boydell Press
an imprint of Boydell & Brewer Ltd
PO Box 9, Woodbridge, Suffolk IP12 3DF, UK
and of Boydell & Brewer Inc.
668 Mt Hope Avenue, Rochester, NY 14620, USA
website: www.boydellandbrewer.com

A CIP catalogue record for this book is available
from the British Library

Information about the Catholic Record Society
and its publications may be obtained from the Hon. Secretary,
c/o 114 Mount St, London W1X 6AH

This publication is printed on acid-free paper

Printed in Great Britain by
CPI Antony Rowe, Chippenham, Wiltshire

CONTENTS

List of Illustrations   vi

Acknowledgements   vii

Abbreviations   ix

Introduction   xi

MARY WARD, THE *ENGLISH VITA*, KNOWN ALSO AS   1
THE *BRIEFE RELATION* ...

AUTOBIOGRAPHICAL FRAGMENTS
AB 1.	Early childhood 1585–1594	103
AB 7.	Fire at Mulwith 1595	110
AB 2.	A case of conscience (undated) c.1601–1605	111
AB 3.	Life with the Babthorpe family at Osgodby 1600–1605	112
AB 4.	Religious vocation c.1600	117
AB 5.	Entry as a lay sister with the Poor Clares in St Omer 1606	119
AB 6.	The *Italian Autobiography*, covering the period 1600–1609	121

SELECTED LETTERS AND DOCUMENTS
L 1.	Mary Ward to John Gerard SJ, April 1619	141
L 2.	Mary Ward to the Nuncio Antonio Albergati, c.1621	143
L 3.	Petition to Pope Urban VIII and the Cardinals, 25 March 1629	148
L 4	Mary Ward's final appeal to Pope Urban VIII, 28 November 1630	155
L 5.	Mary Ward to the Superiors and Members of her Society, 2 February 1631	157
L 6.	Mary Poyntz to Barbara Babthorpe, 3 February 1645	158

Time Line for Mary Ward's Life   163

Select Bibliography   167

Index of People   171

Index of Places   174

ILLUSTRATIONS

Frontispiece
Portrait of Mary Ward c.1621.

Plates 1–8 appear between pp. 74 and 75

1. First page of the *English Vita*, known also as the *Briefe Relation*.
2. (a) Portrait of Mary Poyntz.
   (b) Portrait of Winefrid Wigmore.
3. Mary Ward's First Word. Panel No. 1 of the seventeenth century Painted Life of Mary Ward.
4. Mary's Vocation to the Religious Life. PL No. 9.
5. The Spilling of the Chalice. PL No. 14.
6. The First Companions and the Departure for Saint-Omer. PL No. 22.
7. Near Munich, January 1627. PL No. 45.
8. (a) Mary Ward's gravestone in the Church of St Thomas, Osbaldwick.
   (b) Mary's signature, at the end of one of her letters.

The frontispiece and plates 2(b) to 7 are reproduced by kind permission of Geistliches Zentrum Maria Ward, Augsburg, and Photo Tanner Nesselwang.

ACKNOWLEDGEMENTS

My foremost expression of gratitude must be to the late Sister Gregory Kirkus, Archivist of the CJ English Province and well known in the world of historical scholarship, who first asked me to undertake this edition of the earliest biography of Mary Ward. She dismissed my diffidence, recommended the project to the Catholic Record Society, and encouraged me at every step of the way. It was hoped that she would provide a foreword on Mary Ward for this volume, but she died before this could be completed. Her draft has been expanded and incorporated into the first part of the Introduction. I must also thank our Provincial, Sister Jane Livesey, for making this project possible; the members of both branches of Mary Ward's foundation, CJ and IBVM in England and in other provinces, for their interest and support; and my own community at the Bar Convent for their understanding and forbearance.

As editor, I am greatly indebted to Sr Ursula Dirmeier CJ for her generosity in making available to me the texts from her edition of the entire Mary Ward archive, recently published in Germany by Aschendorff Verlag, Münster, and for obtaining permission from the publishers for the use of these texts, with part of the textual criticism, for a selective edition for English readers. I acknowledge with thanks the permission given by the editor of *The Way* to use the English translation of Mary Ward's letter of 2 February 1631, previously published in *Mary Ward under the Shadow of the Inquisition* by Immolata Wetter CJ (Way Books, Oxford 2006); and also the permission given by Geistliches Zentrum Maria Ward, Augsburg, and Photo Tanner Nesselwang for the use of the Painted Life images.

I am very grateful to Dr Peter Doyle and the CRS publications committee for advice and guidance, and to Professor Alan McClelland for his interest and encouragement. Professor David Wallace of the University of Pennsylvania urged me on, lamenting the complete lack of a scholarly edition of the Mary Ward primary sources for English speaking students and researchers.

I would also like to thank Sr Patricia Harriss CJ for her patience and time spent on the translations from German, and for amending two earlier translations of the seventeenth century Italian texts; Elizabeth Lowry for some additional help with German translation; Mrs Beryl Helps for typing the English translation of a long text; Alison Jones for assisting with the checking of introductions and footnotes; Chris Weston, whose expert rebinding (in the style of the seventeenth century) of the oldest extant manuscript of the *Briefe Relation* has made it one of the greatest treasures of the Bar Convent Archives. Finally I would like to express my gratitude again to Sr Ursula Dirmeier CJ for sharing with me her deep knowledge of Mary Ward, and to Sr Manuela Wiesheu CJ who made it possible for me to spend time in the archives of the Congregatio Jesu at Munich/Nymphenburg, the home of so many of the precious seventeenth century Mary Ward manuscripts.

ABBREVIATIONS

AB	Autobiographical Fragment.
ACDF	Archivum Congregationis Doctrinae Fidei.
AIB	Archives CJ, Bamberg.
AIM	Archives CJ, Munich/Nymphenburg.
AIMan	Archives IBVM, Manchester.
AIY	Archives CJ, The Bar Convent, York.
Allison/Rogers	*Contemporary Printed Literature of the English Counter-Reformation 1558–1640*, Vol II, 1994.
AV	Archivio Segreto Vaticano.
BayHStA	State Archives for Upper Bavaria, Munich.
BV	Biblioteca Apostolica Vaticana.
Chambers	*Life of Mary Ward*, 1883, 1885.
DNB	*Dictionary of National Biography*, 1917 onwards.
Foley	*Records of the English Province of the Society of Jesus*, 1875–1883.
Fridl	*Englishe Tugend-Schul ... Maria Ward*, 1732.
Grisar *MW*	*Maria Wards Institut vor Römischen Kongregationen, 1616–1630*, 1966.
Kirkus	*IBVM/CJ Biographical Dictionary*, 2001 and 2007.
L	Letter.
Morris	*The Troubles of our Catholic Forefathers*, 1872–1877.
Peters	*Mary Ward, A World in Contemplation*, trans. 1994.
PL	Painted Life of Mary Ward.
Vita E	Mary Ward *English Vita*.
Vita I	Mary Ward *Italian Vita*.
Wetter	*Mary Ward under the Shadow of the Inquisition*, 2006.
Wright	*Mary Ward's Institute, The Struggle for Identity*, 1997.

INTRODUCTION

Who was Mary Ward?

The source texts in this volume bring us very close to Mary Ward, the remarkable seventeenth century English woman who felt herself called by God to found a new religious congregation where women could take part in the apostolic work of the Church, and girls could receive the education they needed for their future, whether in religious or lay life. In a world where the only way for women to live the religious life was in isolated, dependent convents, cut off from the rest of the world by strict cloister, the religious society she founded was to be modelled on the Society of Jesus but not dependent on it: it was to be mobile, free from the barriers of enclosure, governed by one of its own members, and subject directly to the Pope. This has become the recognised way of life for women's apostolic congregations, but Mary Ward's vision was not understood or accepted by the Church of her day. Her story can only be outlined here, but for the interested reader there are several full biographies now available.

Mary Ward's life must be seen against the background of the English Reformation. The sixteenth century was an age of religious intolerance, when all deviation was brutally repressed by whichever faith tradition was in the ascendant. In Mary's time it was the Catholic Church which was suffering persecution in England. The first ten years of her life witnessed a savage acceleration of persecution, and twenty-two martyrs, including Margaret Clitherow, were put to death in York alone. Others suffered imprisonment, or loss of property, privilege and liberty. Mary's father moved his family from place to place to avoid the crippling fines, or worse, meted out to recusants and in her youth Mary dreamt of martyrdom for herself.

Mary Ward was born in 1585 near Ripon in Yorkshire, of staunchly recusant parents. Her maternal uncles, John and Christopher Wright, were prominent 'Gunpowder Plotters'. Much of her childhood was spent with relatives, where her spirituality matured in these devout Catholic households and where, at the age of fifteen, she received her religious vocation. This brought her into opposition with her father, to whom she was devoted, but once his permission was obtained the way forward seemed clear. In 1606 Mary took ship for Flanders, where she entered a convent of Poor Clares in St Omer.

At a time when the world was alive with exploration and discovery, while astronomers swept the heavens with Galileo's telescopes and mariners charted the oceans, this high-spirited young woman was content to write, 'I would no more nor other than His will.' It might seem a modest ambition, but it made immense demands on her as she journeyed on foot through Europe, setting up foundations, conferring with Popes and princes, and experiencing achievement accompanied by opposition, calumny and failure. First she learnt that she was not to be a Poor Clare, nor to join any other established religious order, but was to do 'some other thing' that was to be to the greater glory of God. In 1609, with a group of seven like-minded companions, she set up a household and school in Saint-Omer and for several years they lived very austerely in order to discover the details of God's will. The answer, when it came in 1611 'by an interior voice', would have daunted any heart less courageous than Mary's. She was told to 'Take the same of the Society'. It seemed an impossible task, for the Council of Trent (1545–1563) had confirmed and strengthened the rule of enclosure for women religious and St Ignatius had made it clear that there were to be no women Jesuits. With many twists and turns of fortune, Mary spent the rest of her life attempting to fulfil this divine intimation. She made foundations without enclosure in Saint-Omer, Liège, Trier and Cologne, sent members on the English Mission to support the hard-pressed priests, and attempted to gain papal approval for her new form of religious life by accomplishing an astonishing journey from Flanders to Rome on foot, in order to lay her pleas before the Holy Father. Both Gregory XV and his successor Urban VIII received her kindly, but Mary, with her forthright Yorkshire outlook and lack of experience of the elaborate diplomacy of the Papal court, mistook the papal affability for acquiescence. Pope Gregory XV passed her written memorials and plans on to the Congregation of Bishops and Superiors of Religious Orders, and then to the newly established Congregation of Propaganda Fide for scrutiny. Endless delays and frustrations followed, and Mary's Italian foundations and schools in Rome, Naples and Perugia, though promising, were short-lived.

In central Europe her aims were better understood and for a time fortune shone on communities and schools alike. In 1627 the Elector Maximilian of Bavaria offered her the Paradeiserhaus in Munich and supported what became a very flourishing foundation. The Emperor Ferdinand II himself invited her to Vienna and saw her installed in the Stoss im Himmel mansion, while in Pressburg (now Bratislava) her Institute was under the aegis of Cardinal Pázmány. But Mary had many opponents and not all her powerful patronage could withstand them. The Jesuit General, Muzio Vitelleschi, was greatly impressed by her personality and holiness, but, following the directives of St Ignatius, he felt unable to support her plans. Though some Jesuits assisted her, many others were hostile. Memorials with complaints from the English secular clergy, many of whom were bitterly opposed to the Jesuits and to anyone connected with them, had been reaching Rome since 1622; to these were added the spiteful accusations of one Mary Alcock, a former member who had left the Institute some years previously. Religious conservatives, ecclesiastics who felt threatened by the activities of these young women, and *bona fide* supporters of the enclosure decrees of the Council of Trent, all raised their voices in protest against the 'galloping girls', but Mary and her companions, who were never allowed to see the written statements, were unable to defend themselves. Nor did they know, apart from leaked information and rumours, what was being discussed in secret by the Cardinals in Congregations which were often chaired by the Pope himself. From the beginning the Cardinals declined to approve a religious order of women which was not enclosed, and on 7 July 1628 they decreed its suppression. But although Mary Ward had been able to present her case personally before the ecclesiastical authorities on various occasions, she was not informed of this decision, nor of the decrees which followed it.

The dismantling of the Institute began with closure of the northern houses in 1630. Mary Ward, bewildered and ignorant of the authority that lay behind the acts of suppression, advised her Superiors in Flanders to disregard the decree. Her letter fell into the hands of the Inquisition and disaster followed disaster as Winefrid Wigmore, her closest companion whom she had sent as Visitor to Liège, tried to reverse the suppression and came into conflict with the Papal Nuncio. In January 1631 Pope Urban VIII signed the Bull *Pastoralis Romani Pontificis*, condemning the Institute in the harshest possible terms and suppressing it for ever, and in February Mary was arrested, charged with heresy and rebellion, and imprisoned in the Anger Convent in Munich. It was the nadir of her career, but she was neither dispirited nor discouraged. 'Never be given to sorrow, therefore be merry, not sad', she wrote from her horrid cell. And again, 'We will pray and hope the best, and not be troubled at what we cannot mend, but confide in God.'

After her release from prison she was summoned to Rome. There the Pope received her kindly, and allowed the members in Rome to live together as lay persons, under his special protection. Mary herself was cleared of the charge of heresy, but she was obliged by the Inquisition to live in Rome under strict surveillance. Only in 1637, when she was seriously ill, did she receive permission to leave the city and seek a cure in Spa, near Liège. With extended leave she travelled on to London, still under orders eventually to return to Rome. But the perils of the English Civil War took her back to her native Yorkshire, where she lived with a small group of companions at Heworth, a village outside York, until her death on 30 January 1645. The impoverished vicar of nearby Osbaldwick offered a place of burial in his obscure little country churchyard; there is now no trace of her grave, but the large tombstone, with its enigmatic inscription, has been given a place of honour inside the church.

Subsequent history of the Mary Ward foundation

Mary Ward's great venture was over. It had ended in failure and there
seemed little to show for it, just small groups of lay women living and
working together in Munich and Rome, a few more running a little school
in Yorkshire, and perhaps some individuals ploughing lonely furrows
in other parts of England or northern Europe. But Mary had never lost
hope that her plans would be approved, and these faithful companions
were already reviving the Institute. *The same*[1] became a code word for
the Ignatian model, which was never lost sight of, though it took four
hundred years to achieve. From the fragments came new growth, but
slow and with many setbacks. The companions lived as lay persons for
fifty years. Following the first diocesan recognition in 1680,[2] the Institute
in its modified form was tolerated, even without canonical enclosure,
but the Bull of Suppression was not rescinded. Mary Ward herself was
still regarded with suspicion, and many books on her life and work were
placed on the Index Librorum Prohibitorum. In 1749 Pope Benedict XIV
in his Apostolic Constitution *Quamvis Justo* approved the office of Chief
Superior, but he described the English Virgins as a new Institute, and
forbade the acknowledgement of Mary Ward as foundress.

It was not until 1877, by which time Mary Ward's foundation had
spread to every continent, and there were many other orders of women
operating under papal blessing, yet governed by women and knowing no
enclosure, that the congregation received full ecclesiastical confirmation
by Pope Pius IX. In 1909 the petition for Mary Ward's rehabilitation,
fittingly presented by Cardinals Gasquet and Merry del Val on the initiative of English sisters, received the approval of Pope Pius X, and the
Bar Convent in York proudly holds in its archives the telegram dated
8 April with the words, 'Foundress recognised by Pope. Silence except to
community till decree is issued. Gasquet.'

Mary Ward's foundation: its name and its branches

The history of the names applied to Mary Ward's institute is long and
complex, reflecting many of the travails experienced by her movement.
Mary understood the name of *Jesus* to be part of the founding vision,
expressing the identity and charism of this new venture for women in
the history of the Church. Neither the name nor the apostolic role for
women were acceptable in her day, and after the Suppression the order
had no official title, being known by friends as 'English Ladies' or later

---

[1]   See letters to John Gerard and the Nuncio Albergati.
[2]   Chambers II pp. 522–524.

as the 'Institute of Mary', and by enemies as 'Jesuitesses' or 'Galloping Girls'.

In the nineteenth century the name *Institute of the Blessed Virgin Mary* emerged in York, to become the official title in 1900. This name was taken to Ireland by Frances (Teresa) Ball,[3] who in 1821 set up in Dublin the IBVM Loreto branch of the Mary Ward Institute, with further foundations in five continents. This branch retains the title *Institute of the Blessed Virgin Mary*. In 2004 the Roman branch of the Mary Ward foundation, with permission from the Church, adopted the full Jesuit Constitutions (laicised and feminised), with the name *Congregation of Jesus*, thus fulfilling after four hundred years the vision of its foundress Mary Ward.

The source texts

Most of the source texts for the life of Mary Ward have previously been available only in manuscript, or in extracts quoted in later biographies. They have recently been published in Germany as *Mary Ward und ihre Gründung. Die Quellentexte bis 1645*, edited by Ursula Dirmeier CJ, 4 vols, Münster, Aschendorff Verlag 2007. This contains all the Mary Ward source texts up to 1645 in their original languages, with introductions and notes in German.

By kind permission of the editor and publishers, some of the same texts and textual criticism have been used in this volume. It contains the earliest biography of Mary Ward, known as the *English Vita* or the *Briefe Relation*, with the *Autobiographical Fragments*, which offer Mary Ward's own view of her early life and vocation up to 1609, and some related *Letters and Documents* to enlarge the picture. The *Italian Vita*, the second early biography of Mary Ward, thought to have been written in Rome by Mary Poyntz at a later date, has been omitted for reasons of space. It can be found in the full edition of the source texts.

A further source for the life of Mary Ward is the series of fifty pictures known as *The Painted Life*. These paintings, commissioned in the seventeenth century by Mary Ward's early companions, and probably executed somewhere between Flanders and the Tyrol, are kept by the Congregation of Jesus at Augsburg. They are selective, focussing on Mary's faith journey and the fulfilment of her vocation rather than on a series of events. Some of these pictures have been chosen to illustrate

---

3   Wright pp. 100ff. See also Kirkus pp. 36–37. Sister Gregory Kirkus' *Biographical Dictionary*, Catholic Record Society Vol. No. 78, now in its second edition (details in the Select Bibliography) is to be recommended as a most useful source of information about the history and personalities of the English Province of Mary Ward's congregation.

this volume, and the notes contain references to all the relevant panels from this series of paintings.

Authorship of the *English Vita*

Although many of Mary Ward's followers left her society after its suppression, her closest companions remained faithful. The letter of Mary Poyntz to Barbara Babthorpe in Rome, written four days after Mary's death, is evidence of their love for 'our dearest Mother of blessed memory, Mrs Mary Ward', as the *English Vita* begins. This *English Life* was the first of the early biographies, written only a few years after her death. It is thought to have been completed at Heworth between 1645 and 1650, before the community moved to Paris.

The manuscript of the *English Vita* has no title page or named author, but according to tradition it was the work of Mary's two closest companions, Mary Poyntz[4] and Winefrid Wigmore.[5] Later research on the internal and external evidence assigns the actual authorship to Mary Poyntz, with the assistance of Winefrid. A note written on the Manchester manuscript by Canon Toole[6] says,

> I have been informed by Sr M Thecla of the Convent of the Institute at Bamberg, in a letter dated April 10 – 1880, that Winefrid Wigmor to whom this "Briefe Relation" is attributed, was not the author of it; that it was written by Mary Poyntz and copied by Winefrid Wigmor on account of her better handwriting. Lau Toole

According to Marcus Fridl[7] (1732) Winefrid 'made several copies in beautiful handwriting'. Before her death in Paris in 1657 she had also translated the biography into French, with some small additions and the insertion of extra superlatives. Several copies of both the French and the English manuscripts of this biography were made by Winefrid and others.

---

[4] Mary Poyntz 1603/4–1667. Kirkus pp. 150–152. There is some confusion about the date of birth and early years of this lifelong companion of Mary Ward, who succeeded Barbara Babthorpe in 1653 as the third 'Chief Superior' of the Institute.

[5] Winefrid Wigmore 1595–1657. Kirkus pp. 175–176.

[6] Canon Lawrence Toole c. 1812–1892, parish priest of St Wilfrid's Manchester, an admirer of Mary Ward who received the Manchester Manuscript B of the *English Vita* from the Benedictine nuns of Hammersmith and gave it to the IBVM Loreto community whom he had invited to Manchester in 1851.

[7] Marcus Fridl, parish priest of Moorenweis in Schwäbia, author of *Englische Tugende-Schule … Maria Ward*, 1732. See Sources.

Purpose of the *English Vita*

The aim of the author seems to have been twofold. In her letter describing Mary Ward's death, Mary Poyntz tells the community in Rome of Mary's wish that all her companions could have been present, and her final instruction for them to cherish and remain faithful to their vocation. Till her life ended Mary Ward had held together the remaining companions, perhaps about fifty in number in the years following the suppression, but what now? In their position of continuing instability, living in small groups as lay women without ecclesiastical approval, the distribution of a portrait in words might help, enabling Mary's followers to keep in their minds and hearts their great foundress and leader, faithful till death to the call she had received from God. So the biography was written to strengthen the fidelity of companions who, like their foundress, had never lost hope that the Church would one day approve her plans. For this reason the author takes every opportunity of underlining Mary's good relationships with the Pope and the Cardinals, and in particular her submission to the suppression of her Institute and her obedience to the Church authorities.

The first part of the book is a narration of the events of Mary Ward's life: her infancy and childhood in Yorkshire described as a preparation for her future vocation; a period of search for her future mission; and finally her fidelity in carrying out what she considered to be God's will. This is followed by a word-portrait of the character and virtues of the foundress, narrated in an uncoordinated succession and illustrated with events from her life. The purpose may be a defence of Mary Ward against the accusations disseminated first by the English secular clergy, and then by others in Flanders, Bohemia and Vienna. The final impression is not that of the traditional nun, cloistered, silent, praying. Human qualities such as friendship, courage, and respect for learning find a place, as well as humility, obedience, and love of enemies. This is the new religious woman, engaged in strenuous apostolic activity while centred above all on a personal search for union with God. Throughout the biography there are insights into Mary's deep personal relationship with God, and a view of a woman with an inner peace and conviction, these being the driving force of all she does.

Historical value of the *English Vita*

The value of such a biography may be judged partly by its aim, but a critical appraisal is also necessary. First, the credentials of the author. As a contemporary and an early companion, Mary Poyntz was well qualified; she had been attracted to the new institute by Mary Ward herself, and from 1623 onwards she had lived almost continuously with her. From

1654, when she was unanimously chosen as the third 'Chief Superior', till her death in 1667, Mary Poyntz moved between Rome and Munich, founding a new house at Augsburg in 1662. She had taken part in the events she narrates, and tradition says that she also drew on the memories of Winefrid Wigmore and perhaps those of other companions. Given the probable dates for the composition of the biography as 1645–1650, when the companions were living in the village of Heworth, it is unlikely that written documents were used, but the events described can usually be substantiated by other texts now available to us. There are a few mistakes in the dating of the early part of the story, which covers the years before Mary Poyntz joined Mary Ward in Rome in 1623.

Mary Poyntz was writing immediately after the death of the foundress, for whom she had the greatest regard and admiration. In comparison with the extreme baroque style of much seventeenth century religious biography, the *English Vita* is simple, plain and unadorned. However, in an age when holiness was confused with perfection and it was not customary to include personal failures in the written lives of holy persons, Mary Ward's companions could not be impartial about the mother whom they loved so much and whose aspirations and suffering they had shared. The foundress is idealised, and each decision and action is defended, even when it was clear that mistakes had been made. To redress the balance, the reader must turn to Mary Ward's own writings, her autobiography (included in this volume) and the corpus of letters and spiritual notes, which refreshingly reveal a woman whose holiness developed slowly, conscious of her own sinfulness, no different from other human beings in weaknesses, errors and failures. The same zeal to show that the companions were also faultless led Mary Poyntz to disregard the serious misjudgement shown by Winefrid Wigmore,[8] sent as Visitor to Liège in 1630, which was an important factor in the severity with which Mary Ward's institute was suppressed in 1631.

Like Mary Ward, her companions in their youthful enthusiasm gave no thought to the impact which their new kind of religious order would have on the Church of the Counter Reformation in southern Europe. Although there had been opposition in the countries where Mary had made foundations, she had the support of important religious and civil authorities: Bishop Jacques Blaes of Saint-Omer, the Archduchess Isabella, ruler of the Spanish Netherlands, the Elector Maximilian I of Bavaria and his brother the Prince Bishop Ferdinand of Cologne, the Emperor Ferdinand II, and the internationally revered Carmelite P. Dominicus a Jesu Maria. But in Rome, where the authorities were engaged in stiffening the rules for the enclosure of women religious in accordance with the decrees of

---

[8] See Introduction to *Letters and Documents* L 4, and for the full story, Wetter Chs. II, III, VII and VIII.

the Council of Trent, it was unthinkable that a women's religious order should ask for freedom from enclosure, self-government, and a share in the pastoral work of the Church. Mary Ward's companions understood no better than Mary herself that such expectations were considered to be extremely dangerous, and in Rome these opinions were supported by the accusations made against Mary Ward, originating from the English secular clergy. These allegations, which included distortions of actual events as well as slander and prejudice, can perhaps be summed up in the sentence, 'Up to now it has never been known that women undertake apostolic work. They are not capable of it.'[9]

The deliberations of the Roman Curia were held in secret, and it was only in 1998 that the Vatican archives holding the records of the Holy Office (the Inquisition) were opened to researchers. Under the diplomatic conventions of the time, the Pope and many of the Cardinals received their visitors, including Mary Ward, with an elaborate courtesy which belied their real attitude to the English women. Mary was received in audience several times by the Popes Gregory XV and Urban VIII, and was able to plead her own cause before congregations of Cardinals. She knew well that she had enemies, but she had little idea of what was really going on, and her childlike trust that the Pope himself would favour her plans was sadly misplaced. Today, with the records of the meetings of the Congregations of Propaganda Fide and the Holy Office and copies of the Vatican correspondence at our disposal, our view is very different from what could be known and recorded by Mary Ward and her companions at the time.

We may question what readership the *English Vita* was intended for. There was probably no extensive distribution, but the original English manuscript version and the translations made from it were widely circulated among the members of Mary Ward's institute. The members in York possessed both the English and French versions, and a letter from Elizabeth Nason[10] to Dorothy Pendrill[11] dated 17 June 1792 shows that copies of both were sent to the sister house at Hammersmith:[12]

> I am sorry the life of Mrs Ward is lost. I directed it to you, Madam, by Ann Ford's coach and Mrs Banks assures us she sent it. It is providential we did not

---

9   Peters p. 340, translated from the Latin *Copia informatio ...*, Vatican Library Capponi 47, ff. 68r–72r.

10   Elizabeth Nason 1764–1812. Bar Convent community. Kirkus pp. 138–139.

11   Dorothy Pendrill. c. 1735–1795. Hammersmith community. Kirkus p. 146.

12   The Hammersmith community and school were founded by Frances Bedingfield in 1669. The community, which in 1703 had separated itself from the main body of the Mary Ward foundation, was so diminished in 1795 that the house was offered to the Benedictine nuns from Dunkirk, who remained there until they transferred to Teignmouth in 1865. Kirkus pp. 3–5.

send the French one. I have it safe and will return it back to you, Madam, with an English one like that which is lost, at the first opportunity.[13]

The English copy which was sent to Hammersmith is probably the manuscript which is now in the archives of the IBVM Loreto English Province. The French manuscript was given back to the Bar Convent in 1879. The lost English copy may be the one which was found in the library of the Canonesses of the Holy Sepulchre at New Hall, who generously gave it to the Congregation of Jesus English Province in 1972.

However, for those without access to the other contemporary sources, the *English Vita* is not easy to understand. In 1878 Dame Mary English OSB wrote from St Scholastica's Abbey, Teignmouth,

> ... I have been occupied for some time ... in copying an old French Vita of Mrs Mary Ward. It is a manuscript, and came into our possession from our previous dear sisters of your Institute, who received us in Hammersmith ... It is, all the same, a disappointing work, evidently written for those who know well the principal events of the holy Mother's life, and so it only refers to these, so that the account is obscure and incomplete for those who do not have the same knowledge of the facts. The manuscript has no title, pagination and writer's name, but has only this heading: 'Breve relation de la vie exemplaire et de la Sainte Mort de notre chère Mère Mademoiselle Marie de Ward.' Presumably it is a translation of the English Vita by Winefrid Wigmore ...[14]

There are other obscurities which must be understood in the context of the *Vita*'s seventeenth century origin. At this time the persecution of English Catholics was still very severe. Spies were everywhere, and documents could easily fall into the wrong hands, both in England and in parts of Europe. The companions were accustomed to aliases and coded letters, and the author applied the necessary safeguards: some events are described in a way which would have prevented the identification of living persons, and no one closely connected with Mary Ward's society is named. Within the Church Mary Ward had lived in hope that her plans would one day be approved, but as she and her Institute remained under suspicion for over two centuries, the companions had to be equally cautious. The revelation of 1611, 'Take the same of the Society [of Jesus]' is described only in the most general terms: 'she understood intellectually but distinctly in precise words what Institute she was to take'. We have to turn to Mary Ward's earlier letters[15] to John Gerard (1619) and the Nuncio Antonio Albergati (c. May/June 1621) to find the exact words and a fuller description of this fundamental revelation, so controversial at the time.

13 AIY 2A/35
14 AIY Provincial Archives.
15 See L 1 and L 2 in this volume.

Apart from its primary purpose, the *English Vita* has added value for the modern social historian for the light it throws on Catholic recusant life of the period, especially on its difficulties and dangers, and the devotions practised at the time. Mary Ward travelled extensively, and her journeys and the trials inherent in them are related in considerable detail. We are also given an external view of the complex workings of the Roman Curia and its Congregations, as seen by Mary Ward and her companions, but without access to their confidential meetings and subsequent decrees.

Editorial policy

At the request of many scholars the English texts are printed in their original form, including the seventeenth century spelling, syntax and punctuation, but without the textual abbreviations. The *Italian Autobiography* and three of the *Letters and Documents* have been translated from the Italian; the originals can be found in the larger source book described above.

Each text has been given its own special preface. The preface to the *English Vita* contains further information on the manuscripts and the early translations which were made from the English original. As neither the English original nor the seventeenth century copies made from it have survived, the text used for this edition is the earliest English version, dated 1716 and held in the archives of the Bar Convent, York.

The aims of this publication are as follows: first, to edit and make available an important part of the Mary Ward source material, which up to now has been available only in manuscripts kept in private archives; secondly, to set this material in context for the interested reader, while providing archival references for students and researchers. Many of the primary texts are scattered throughout Europe, at present difficult to access. They will remain so for some English speaking readers until the four volume edition of source texts described above has been published in an English edition. The editor has therefore taken a route which may invite criticism. Rather than overload this edition with a multitude of exact but inaccessible references, the reader has frequently been referred to the major biography by Henriette Peters, *Mary Ward, a World in Contemplation*, 1991, translated by Helen Butterworth, Gracewing 1994. Here an event can be seen in its broader context, and reference can be made to the primary sources which are all carefully listed at the end of each chapter. Peters had access to the major archive, which in 1991 contained copies of all the source documents except those of the Holy Office and a few other recently discovered texts. For this later material the reader is referred to the recent translation of M Immolata Wetter's *Mary Ward under the Shadow of the Inquisition,* Oxford, Campion Hall, Way Books 2006. The editor feels that this compromise will ease the path of the general reader, while providing access to archival references for the serious researcher.

A note on the names used in this volume for the Mary Ward foundation is needed. In St Ignatius and in the documents of the Society of Jesus the term *Institute* (*Institutum*) sums up everything constituting the Society: its nature, spiritual principle, activities, and written constitutions. It is in this sense that Mary Ward and the author of the *English Vita* use the word *Institute* as the way of life they are presenting to the Holy See for confirmation. Informally they speak of their *Society/society, Company/company*, keeping this indefinite because the full title *Societas Jesu*, which they used among themselves until 1631, was not approved. *Institute/institute*, with an indefinite meaning also occurs sometimes in the texts. The editor has adopted the same policy, with the addition of *congregation* for later history, and hopes that this will not make for confusion. These terms are not used as titles in the canonical sense of the word; this would be inappropriate for a congregation which was nameless, with its members living as lay persons, at the time when the *English Vita* was written.

Use of the *English Vita* in subsequent biographies

As the first biography, the *English Vita* is the source on which the later biographies draw. Internal evidence shows that it was known to almost all the other seventeenth and eighteenth century biographers. It was used extensively by Marcus Fridl in 1732 and by M. Catherine Chambers, the scholarly author of the two volume Life of 1882 and 1885. Later writers have also used it, but generally in paraphrase rather than quotations. Like many modern researchers who discover Mary Ward, most of these writers find her personality attractive, and share the views of Leo Hicks SJ, author of *Mary Ward's Great Enterprise*, a trenchant six part series published in *The Month* from February 1928 to March 1929. It seems fitting to end with a few words from a contemporary letter of his to M Salome Oates at the Bar Convent:

> She seems to me remarkable – even among the saints – for the rare combination of qualities, indomitable courage and strength allied with such very human tenderness and gentleness.[16]

---

[16] AIY MW 17A/6. Letter dated 26 October 1927.

Mary Ward, The *English Vita* (Vita E).

Written by Mary Poyntz.
Known also as the *Briefe Relation*.

Copies:
A. AIY 113 ff. English: A Briefe Relation of the holy Life, and happy Death, of our dearest Mother, of blessed memory, Mistress Mary Ward;
B. AIMan 107 ff. English: A Briefe Relation of the holy Life, and happy Death, of our dearest Mother, of blessed memory, Mistress Mary Ward;
C. AIY 112 pp. French: Briefve Relation de la Sainte Vie et Mort de nôtre chere Mere Mademoiselle Marie de Ward;
D. AIY 226 pp. French: Breve Relation de la Vie Exemplaire et de la Sainte mort de Nostre chere Mere Mademoiselle Marie de Ward;
E. AIB 201 pp. German: Ein Kürtze Relation deß Heilligen Lebens, unnd Seelligen Ableibens Unnßerer Allerliebsten Frauen Muetter Hochseelligister Gedechtnüs La Signora Donna Maria Della Guardia, alias Ward.

Authorship
Traditionally considered to be Mary Poyntz, one of Mary Ward's first companions who was present at many of the events which she describes in the first person. Written soon after Mary Ward's death, probably between 1645 and 1650, when the group of early companions, which included Mary Poyntz and Winefrid Wigmore, were living at Heworth, York. Winefrid co-operated in the writing of the Life, and an early tradition related that the first copies were made by her 'because of her better handwriting'. In 1650 the community left York and went to Paris, where Winefrid translated the Life into French.

The Early Manuscripts
Neither the original manuscript nor the seventeenth century copies of the English version have survived. The earliest manuscripts extant are as follows:

A. **English. New Hall/York manuscript.** Formerly in the possession of the Canonesses of the Holy Sepulchre, New Hall, who gave it to the Congregation of Jesus in 1972. It was transferred from Ascot to the Bar Convent, York, c.1988. A note from the copyist dates it to 1716, which accords with the eighteenth century script. There is a large omission (c. April 1630 to February 1631) which is made good by pages, in the handwriting of an earlier period (two separate hands), inserted at the end of the manuscript.
This is the text which has been used for this edition. Divergences in B and C will be noted in the apparatus criticus.
B. **English. Hammersmith/Manchester manuscript.** Formerly in the possession of the Benedictine nuns of Hammersmith, who had taken over the convent of the Mary Ward sisters in 1795. In the nineteenth century they gave it to Fr Lawrence Toole, who transferred it to the IBVM Loreto Sisters in Manchester. From the nature of the variations and the same omission (1630–1631) in each, it appears that manuscripts A and B are twins, dependent on a common older

copy. Manuscript B, written in a different hand from A, was probably also made in the early eighteenth century. It does not have the additional pages which in A supply for the omission.

C. French. Ascot/York. Inscription on the inside leaf of the cover: 'C.P.A. Comberbach 1850'. The handwriting, spelling and parchment binding suggest a date in the seventeenth century. Transferred from Ascot to York c.1988 when the archives and manuscript books of the Congregation of Jesus were centralised there.

D. French. Hammersmith/York. The handwriting, spelling and binding suggest a date in the mid or later seventeenth century. Given in 1879 to the Bar Convent, York by the Benedictine nuns who were moving from Hammersmith to Teignmouth.

E. German. Bamberg. From the first quarter of the eighteenth century. The house at Bamberg was founded from Augsburg in 1717.

F. English AIY 19th C. There is also a nineteenth century English manuscript (155 ff.) in York, prepared by Dr Daniel Henry Haigh (1819–1879) uncle of M Hilda Haigh and a friend of the Bar Convent, York. This is a copy of the Hammersmith/Manchester manuscript which Dr Haigh borrowed from Fr Lawrence Toole. He used the French manuscript C to make good the long missing passage and other omissions in the Manchester manuscript.

The early English and French manuscripts are continuous texts, without paragraphs. In this edition section headings and sub-headings have been added for reasons of clarity. The original pagination is contained in [ ].
[ ] is also used to supply missing words or explain lacunae in the manuscript. Additionally, this text contains some textual criticism to show the differences between the two English manuscripts A and B and the earliest French manuscript C.

[1r] A Briefe Relation.
Of the holy Life, and happy Death, of our dearest Mother, of blessed memory, Mistress Mary Ward.

1. Early years.

Mary Ward's family. Infancy: 'Jesus' her first word.

Our dearest Mother of happy memory Mistress Mary Ward, was eldest Daughter[1] of Mister Marmaduke Ward of Ghendall,[2] in the County of Yorke: Mullwith and Newby were Maner houses of his, his name is to this day famous in that Countrey, for his exceeding comelynes of Person, sweetness and beauty of face, agility and activenes, constancy and courage in Catholicke Religion, admirable charity to the poore, so as in an extreame dearth, never was poore denyed at his gate, commonly 60, 80 and sometimes 100 in a Day, as yet is also famous his valour and fidelity to his friend and my selfe have heard it spoken of by severall and with much feeling by Mister William Mallery the Eldest, and best of that Name[3] who was neere of [1v] kinne to our Mother, both by Father and Mother. Her Mother was Mistress Ursula Wright, eldest Daughter to Mister William Wright of Pluland,[4] first marryed to Mister Constable of Hatfield[5] (as I take it) by whom she had noe child, her first by Mister Ward, was this blessed child our dearest Mother, who at the Font was called Jane, and by Confirmation Mary.[6] From the Nurses breast as it were marked out for heaven, before the time Babes use to speake, hearing her Mother forth of a sudden apprehension the child might fall, say, JESUS blesse my Child, turned with a sweet smile and sayd distinctly, JESUS: which was the first, and all the words she spooke of many Months after.[7]

---

1   Mary Ward was born on 23 January 1585 (AB 1) traditionally at Mulwith near Ripon. See Peters Chs I and II, text and archival references, for Mary's childhood and youth.
2   Ghendall: Givendale, the original seat of the Ward family. This Manor was not owned by Marmaduke Ward.
3   The Mallory connection was through marriage with the Ward family.
4   Ursula Wright, the daughter of Robert Wright of Ploughland (Holderness) by his second wife; William was her half-brother.
5   John Constable of Great Hatfield, in the East Riding of Yorkshire.
6   Mary probably received the sacrament of Confirmation in Flanders in 1606, as there was no Catholic Bishop in England. The change of name is not recorded elsewhere; Mary makes no mention of it in her autobiographical writings.
7   PL No. 1 records this incident.

Childhood. First proposal of marriage. God's providence in Mary's life.

Her very childish years were not onely exempt from displeasing actions which commonly accompany those Years, but adorned with such graces as rendred her amiable and aggreable to all, never gave offence, but allways sought out occasions to pleasure the very Servants, though to her owne incommodity, as [2r] when in the Yeare 42 I[8] being at Newby with this sayd our dearest Mother of happy memory, the Lady Blakestone recounted with great feeling, the memory was to that Day kept in that Towne of her goodnes, meekenes, and gratiousnes amongst her Father his Servants, and Neighbours.

Her being the Eldest, so beautifull and of such expectation was cause her Parents were seeking her a marriage,[9] when she was but ten yeares old, and for that end a Youth, her equall, ritch and very handsome was found out, and especially proposed by her Kinsman the Earle of Northumberland.[10] God having not yet prevented her litle Hart with his extraordinary Love, she innocently mean'd the said Party should be her Husband; but with so great modesty and care of her honour, as she was wont to alleadge passages of those Times, as condemnations of her preferring humane respects before her care of avoiding God's offence.

The Devine Providence having designed this [2v] selected Soule for a higher State, would not let this Love though so innocent have longer place in her Hart reserved to himselfe; disposed that this hopefull Youngman was on urgent affaires concerning his owne Estate, to goe to London, and so home. God whose workes are ever admirable weaned her from this beginning Love, by an apprehension of some Lacke of constancy and fervour in her pretended Spouse, his respects to her selfe, which yet really was not so, for he both loved and honored her till his Death, which in few Monthes after happened.

Though God be the beginning, middle and End of all our good, yet that goodnes so admirable in his operations in the Soule of Man seemeth as it were not to move, but as we will, or as one may say, give him leave, by leaving occasions, and corresponding with meanes offred. This blessed Child, thus farre prevented by grace, began to have such feelings of God and Vertue as was rare, yet conversable, and agreable to all, not in a manner to startle or amaze one, but [3r] as if God[a] would by her make appeare the Lovelynes of vertue, with the force and sweetness of it, and as if by her his Devine designe was to draw many to him selfe their finall End, not with violence or Strife, but as an apparant and satisfying truth. The foundation thus laid in her tender Years, so grew with her and encrease of vertue as gave to admire, and indeed unexpresable. The efficacy of her words and Letters, and even her presence and gestures hath in them to dampe vice, weane from all sensible Love, and those meane things the fancy of Man useth to houver[b] about, and in a sweet manner, forcibly with truth to put a Soule into God as its center, that made one as it were say to themselves, What have I done hitherto?

a A: illegible deletion. B: an empty space | b F: know

8   Mary's companion was her biographer, Mary Poyntz (1603–1667). The visit to Newby would have taken place c.1642. Newby was leased from 1640 to 1647 to Lady Blakestone and her husband Sir Ralph Blakestone. West Yorkshire Archives, Leeds, 5013/890 and 892.
9   PL No. 2 names a young man called Redshaw.
10 Henry Percy, 9th Earl of Northumberland (1564–1632).

Invocation of the Name of Jesus.

But to returne to our matter, this Servant of God yet not above 9 or 10 Yeares old, forth of play[a] (and as may be supposed, designed by the Ennemy of all good to cutt of her Life) would needs make one of

her Mothers Maides carry her [3v] on her[b] Shoulders whence she fell
her owne and the Maides height, and lighting on her Head was wholly
stunted, and lost her speach: the Maide extreamely terrifyed laid her
in Bed, it was Bed time, and she had nothing but her Linnen on: she
had her understanding good, and thought with her selfe, could she but
once say JESUS she would willingly dy; which sacred Name she at last
pronounced, and it brought her so much sweetnes and Love, as all her
Life after she was most sensible of, and in that instant restored to her
former health without any the least harme.[11]

a in A superscript; missing in B | b missing in B

---

[11] PL No. 3 records this incident.

Years spent at Harewell (1595–1599). First Communion September 8th 1598.

A great persecution a rising in that Countrey her Parents were forced
to quitt it, and transport themselves into Northumberland: and fearing
the ayre there might not aggree with her, it being much ruder then her
owne, left her with a Kinswoman of theirs, a Widdow of rare and proved
Vertue, by name Mistress Ardington of Harewell.[12] In this place, God
[4r] Allmighty did this his beginning Servant many graces which she
herself understood not, yet corresponded with, not knowing. She tooke
from the feast of our Blessed Lady her Assomption 15 of August, till her
sacred Nativity 8th of September to prepare for her first Communion,[13]
in which interim one evening, neare Supper time, whilst yet light, one of
the Servants came and told her, there was a Gentleman at the gate from
her Father in great hast to speake with her, she surprised with joy to
heare of her Father (whom she loved entirely deare) without reflection it
was against the civill and ordinary way, ranne without delay or reply: the
Man on horsebake on one side of the pale, and she on the other, tooke
out of his poket a Letter which he said was from her Father, and he was
to reade it to her, but not to deliver it, the contents were, that her Father
commanded her on his blessing, not to proceed in the [4v] Way she was
for matter of communicating[14] (it was afterwards found her Father never
sent such a Man or message) for he had a match in hand for her, greatly
advantagious, one of the Talbots of Graften, and so tooke Leave. She
as above said, loving so tenderly her deare and deserving Father, felt
pangs as of Death to disobey him, on the other side, not to communicate, caused her such remorse and griefe, as betweene both her Life was
unconsolable, nor would she discover it to any, partly out of a secresy
and closenes of nature, and greatly because she esteemd it against the
reputation of the Catholicke Zeale, her Father had ever had fame of; and
oft her griefe was such as she could not contayne her teares, when urged

to tell the cause, she made an excuse. In this time and after, she never came to the Chapell, but she seem'd to feele a loving reproach from God Allmighty for her ingratitude. [5r] She continued in this conflict, till she resolved to communicate the first opportunity she should have.

---

12   Catherine Ardington, daughter of Sir William Ingleby of Ripley Castle, married to Sir William Ardington.
13   PL No. 7.
14   PL No. 6.

Relatives and friends. Another proposal of marriage.

She was much loved by a Kinsman of hers, Sir William Ingleby of Ripley, whither he often invited her, and where she gave such excellent Example, as old Servants of that House keepe things given them by her, as holy; a Gentleman who had an ivory Image given him by a depender of Sir William Ingleby, told my selfe this particular; much more of this Nature might be sayd, of the particular veneration she was in even to our first coming into the North, especially by the Mallerges, Inglebys, Plumptons, and Midletons.[15]

At thirteene she was againe very much urged to marry, the Person and Estate being competently advantagious, but her mind was so much an other Way, as the very greefe had like to have putt her into a mortall Sickenes,[16] that for meere[17] compassion, her[a] [5v] dear and noble harted Father broke it off, esteeming it an[b] aversion she had from that particular Person, and that it would not be hard, to find her her choyce. But her heavenly Father had higher designes on this his blessed Child, and drew her by the Wayes he pleased, and she knew not.

a in A: her repeated | b A: *as* changed to *an* in a different ink. B: as

---

15   Mallerges = Mallorys. These were families connected with the Wards, or living in neighbouring properties in Yorkshire.
16   PL No. 8. Mary Ward's third suitor, named Ralph Eldrington.
17   more (Haigh Manuscript F).

2. Vocation to religious life.

Desire for religious life; dreams of martyrdom; spiritual direction and reading.

At Sixteene[18] she earnestly desired Religion in generall, nothing then satisfying, but what tended that way, she wou'd retyre herselfe alone in her Chamber, with an old Catholicke Woman,[19] and[a] heare her tell storyes of Religious Women[a], particularly one, who for having comitted a frailety, was severly punished for it,[20] which gave her such Light of the excellency of a Religious state, as all her Life she had a feeling of it, and upon occasions would speake to us concerning that Light. She was wont also to spend much time in reading the Lifes of Saints, particularly Martyrs, which so enflammed her well prepared [6r] Hart, as nothing cou'd satisfy her, but a Living or dying Martyrdome.[21]

In some of these fervours, she would needs make a generall Confession, the Devine Providence disposing that she light on a discreet Confessour who finding her at that time enclining to Scrupulosity would not permit her, but gave her that litle, but excellent Booke, the Spirituall Conflict,[22] and bidd her reade and practise that litle Booke in place of her generall Confession, which this devine Schollar so punctually performed, as she made it the fondation of her whole Spirituall Life, and had it by hart, as to the very last hower of her Life, she cou'd tell without looking on the Booke the substance of every Chapter.

a–a missing in B; C du logis à qui elle ecoutoit raconter des histoires des religieuses, particulierement d'une certaine qui

---

[18] Mary Ward was then in her sixteenth year: cf. AB 3.
[19] Margaret Garrett at Osgodby, one of the Babthorpe houses south of York. Mary lived with the Babthorpes from late 1599 till 1605. Cf. AB 3 and 4.
[20] PL No. 9. Cf. AB 3.
[21] PL No. 10 and 11. Cf. AB 6.
[22] Cf. AB 6, note 6. The English translation of the *Spiritual Combat* by John Gerard SJ was first published secretly in London as the *Spiritual Conflict* in 1598. This book may have been given to Mary by John Gerard himself or by Richard Holtby SJ.

With the Babthorpe family (1599–1605).

Betweene this, and the first time of her going over Seas, she lived in the House of an other Kinsman[a] of hers,[23] where her great modesty and rare discretion, rendred her not onely admirable, but greatly helpefull to [6v] that Family, which by an unfortunate match of the eldest Sonne, was in eminent danger to ruine,[24] as it did soone after her leaving it; whilst she was there, her power was so prevalent with the young cupple, as she kept all in a good meane.

Her desires encreasing, so did her practice of solid vertue in an eminent measure, so as her Life was a perpetuall prayer, her Examines, and frequenting the Sacraments so exact, as even from one Communion she began to prepare for the other. For mortification her care was, to find out what was most against her, and that to doe: For Example finding in her selfe (as all noble harts naturally doe) great Love to her owne ranke and degree by birth, when she had seene strangers, who knew her not, nor cou'd know the truth of what she did, wou'd trusse up her Sleeves, put on an Apron, take a broome[b] in her hand, and so passe through the hall where the strangers [7r] were, that they might thinke she lived there in the nature of a Servant, which many did and the poore divell hath since served himselfe of it, with hope to lessen her, at least in the Eyes of the foolish, who envy what they as little possesse as capable to understand it. She being of herselfe in the highest degree neat and daintly, thought necessary to curbe it, which she did by lying in Bed with one of the Maides that had the Itch, and gott it; to accomplish her mortification, she resolved never to doe what might ease or cure her, but that goodnes for whose sake she did it, did that part, for in a short Time she was perfectly well. Every roome in the house[25] was dedicated to a severall devotion and notes to herselfe to gayne and keepe the presence of God: Many graces God did her in those her young Yeares, which after her coming over, and speaking of them as ordinary things to Men of great Learning and Spirit, they admired in [7v] her the speciall solid and secure guidance she had found from the holy Ghost.

a C: un autre sein Parent | b C: un balet et un bassin d'eau

---

23 Sir Ralph and Lady Grace Babthorpe. Cf. AB3.
24 William Babthorpe, married to Ursula (née Tyrwhitt). There were ten children of this marriage, two of whom entered Mary Ward's Society in 1630. Financial difficulties caused by recusant fines forced William to sell both Babthorpe and Osgodby Manors, and to go abroad.
25 Cf. AB6.

Opposition to Mary's vocation from her father. Edmund Neville's proposal of marriage.

She tooke opportunity to make knowne to her deare Father, her great desire to be Religious, and to have his permission,[26] but he on noe tearmes wou'd heare of it. It was not now with her as it had beene, having learned to follow the councell of her heavenly Father and gained such courage as little to value the words before so deare and powerful, that they not at all daunted her, or gave her the least difficulty in this her devine undertaking; she resolved to embrace the first opportunity to passe the Seas, and sayd in her selfe, I will see him noe more, and that with joy, so as what had beene above thousands of Worlds deare to her, when in ballance with her best pleasing God, was as nothing. But this endeavering for her Father's good will lasted seaven yeares,[27] with her noe smal toile anxiety, conflict, prayers and [8r] Pennances, and that noe tryall might be wanting in the last yeare of this conflict came to her acquaintance a noble Man, and Catholicke;[28] in vertues and Qualityes compleate, farre out of her thought (which was wholly on God) who sought her in Marriage, but so liked and approved by all as each one vehemently urged her, and above all her Confessour,[29] so farre as to say, were she a Novice in any Religion she would doe God more Service to come out and marry this party, then to proceede: and particularly he resolving never to marry if she would not have him; nor did he, but became a Religious Man and a Priest, and from him the Title went to Heretikes, so as by his absence the Catholickes lost a great support.

26 Cf. AB 6.
27 From 1599 when Mary went to Osgodby/Babthorpe, to 1606 in London, when her father and her confessor finally gave permission. Cf. AB 6.
28 Edmund Neville, 1563–1648, claimant to the title of Earl of Westmorland, was the final suitor for Mary Ward's hand. PL Nos. 12–13 and Peters p. 49. After Mary had left England, he was ordained a priest in 1608, entered the Society of Jesus, and spent many years on the English Mission. Following arrest and imprisonment, he died at the age of eighty-five. Foley I, pp. 220–223, 669–670.
29 Traditionally Richard Holtby SJ, Superior of the Jesuits working in the north of England, who is known to have visited Osgodby and Babthorpe; possibly Fr John Mush.

Opposition from Mary Ward's confessor: the spilling of the chalice.

This assault of her Ghostly Fathers was beyond measure sensible, carrying the colours of Religion and Zeale,[30] in so much that she, as it were in an agony, cast her self at the feete of her deare Lord, and said it was he [8v] must answer for her, then holy quiet from noyse and motion of any exterior thing rested in her selfe united with God: this was a litle before Masse in the Chappell in Lodgings in Bauldwins Gardens in London:[31] in this manner she remained, not minding at all what passed there, till the Priest[32] after his recollection which had beene longer then ordinary washing his hands she forth of her wonted great respect to all Priests, especially her ghostly Father arose to give him the towell, she perceaved he had wept much, then sighing said, shall I live to offend my God? and to her, I will never more hinder your Religious designe, but further you all I can, which was to her an unspeakable Jubily. By what meanes God changed this good Priest his Hart, he alone knoweth that wrought it, but in that Mass after Consecration the Chalice was spilt,[33] this priest was a very Exemplar and Religious Man.

30 Cf. AB 6.
31 In 1605 or early 1606 Mary Ward and her father were staying in lodgings, with a chapel, in Baldwin Gardens, Holborn. Baldwin Gardens are shown in Richard Baldwin's plan of London, 1589.
32 Traditionally Richard Holtby SJ. Following the execution of Henry Garnet SJ, he was in London in the spring of 1606.
33 PL No. 14. The inscription on this picture reads, 'When Mary Ward's confessor was saying Mass in London in 1605, it happened by divine permission that he inadvertently spilt the chalice. This wrought such a change in him that when Mary, after Mass, respectfully handed him a towel to dry his hands, he said to her with tears streaming from his eyes: "I will never more hinder your religious design, but further you all I can." '

3. With the Poor Clares in Saint-Omer and Gravelines.

To Saint-Omer. Entry to the Poor Clares as an extern sister (1606–1607).

How[a] the blessed Servant of God was as if [9r] Chaynes had beene taken of her, thus freed she even flew in the pursuite of her holy designes, insensible of whatsoever else.[34] Crossing the seas,[35] arrived at Saint Omers a citty of Artoise, and not assured of the particular Order God would have her embrace, she put her selfe into the direction of her ghostly Father,[36] confident that God for whom she did it, would guide her by him, as in effect he did in the sense of Diligentibus Deum etc.[37] but as by following effects it appeard, there was in that occasion much for her to suffer, God permitting this good Religious Man to be drawn to the interest of others, to her great disadvantage he assured her, it was God's will she should be a Lay Sister amongst the french poore Clares in that Towne: saying it was the will of God, was of such high force, as to overcome whatsoever inclination, or feelings of her owne and embrace what was so contrary to her as[b] that I have heard her say it had beene sweeter to her[b] to have entred into a Caldron of boyling oyle, then put herselfe into a Life of so great distraction, she wholly [9v] enclining to retyrement, and had practised it more exactly in her Fathers House, then that place afforded her meanes for. Notwithstanding (as I have sayd), her ghostly Father saying it was Gods will, she without reply or resistance put on the habit, and without the least regard to what her selfe would or wou'd not, did exactly what the strongest and meanest borne amongst them did, carryed burthens, going into the Countrey to begg, faired rudely, and lodged worse which though it could not master her heroicall and gallant mind, did in few Monthes her young and delicate Body: Those labours and over heatings caused an impostume in her knee, which confined her for some time to her Bed which her mind a litle tyrannicall to her selfe could not brooke long: wherefore rising she went about her worke as if nothing had ayled her, yet was she fayne to carry for many Monthes after, a powltisse at her Knee. I have oft heard her speake of those times with great [10r] Content and satisfaction, saying she shou'd never dy with more assurance of Heaven then, then as a time when she least sought her selfe, but very sincearly God.

Her dearest and best Master did at once please himselfe in her faithfull suffrance, and revenge her quarrell for that Religious Man her Confessour, as[c] also the English Religious Woman,[38] who had proceeded indirectly in that matter, fell both of them into desperate Sickenesses, with such remorse of Conscience, as her remaining in that state, seemed their torture and where as he had before say'd it was Gods will she should enter now that it was Gods will she should come out. But this Champion was not so lightly waved to quit, what once he while actually her Confessour had so oft and oft avered to be God's will, and this without knowledge of what she was to doe, wherefore discreetly answer'd by order she entred, and by order she would goe out, or dy a thousand deaths there: not that [10v] the practise had rendred it sweet or easy to her but before she entred, she had noe guide but her Confessour, now the Superiours of the Order were hers, and were to dispose of her, accept, or send her away.

a A Corrected from Now to How; C: Ce fut pour lors que | b–b in A: inserted in the margin | c repeated in A

---

34   Cf. AB 5 and 6.
35   PL No. 15 and AB 6. Mary travelled as one of the daughters of Mrs Catherine Bentley (née Roper), a great-granddaughter of St Thomas More.
36   George Keynes SJ, Professor of Moral Theology at the English seminary at Saint-Omer.
37   Romans 8:28.
38   Mary Stephen Goudge, Superior and Novice Mistress of the extern sisters of the Poor Clares in Saint-Omer, later Abbess of the English Poor Clare foundation at Gravelines.

St Gregory's Day, March 12th 1607.

On Saint Gregory the great his day,[39] her speciall Advocate and Patron towards the End of her Noviship, working with the rest of the Religious as the custome was on their habits, and what belonged to them, she offred up certaine devotions for the conversion of England, remembering the Saint the graces he on Earth had done to the sayd Countrey, begging he wou'd not forget them now, and obtain for her, that she might live and dy in Gods will. Scarcely had she ended her prayers, when the bell rung to call them all togeather, to receave their Generall[40] his blessing, he happening at that time to make his visitt there, which falls out but once in six yeares: when he had done, he called for the English, there being none of the Nation but she,[41] she presented her selfe to him, who said: My Child [11r] you are not for this state of Life, you are capable to serve God in what soever order, make your choyce, I will serve you in what soever I can. This was the most unexpected newse to her in the World, who had put herselfe and whole rest into the hands of the devine Providence, not casting her thought on any particular, but allwayes had an unspeakable Zeale for the good of England. Being returned to her Cell, she putt her selfe to prayer, and made an entyre offer of herselfe to God, begging to know and doe his will: she would recount to us, as she was pleas'd to tearme it her simplicity, thinking wherein this good father his assistance might contribute to Gods service. She concluded he might put two Monasteryes in one, and leave one for the English Nation, and this with great sincerity she proposed to the Generall,[42] who said, that was a thing he could not doe, but all in his power he would etc.

39   St Gregory the Great, Pope 590–604. In AD 596 he sent St Augustine with 40 monks
to preach the gospel in England.
40   The Spanish Franciscan Andreas de Soto, appointed as General Visitor. Besides
holding other positions in the Order, he was confessor to the Archduchess Isabella. Peters
p. 81.
41   Anne Campian is named in AB 5 as an English lay sister; she entered the new foundation at Gravelines.
42   Cf. AB 6. Mary Ward writes that the Visitor had left, and she did not see him.

Foundation of an English Poor Clare Convent at Gravelines; temporary housing at Saint-Omer.

Who can heare expresse the courage with which [11v] this holy
Amazon undertooke this second encounter, wholy confident in God,
thus young and beautyfull put her selfe to negotiate in the Arch-Duke
his Court,43 for a Foundation of a Monastery of Saint Clares Order
for the English Nation: in which times and occasions she used great
prayer, much fasting and pennance, living with admirable edification,
and gave to all sorts of Persons to admire in her her modesty, courage,
Prudence, and perseverence. Her ayme being not to have it under the
Order,44 had them all to oppose herᵃ, and which was immediately the
worst the Comissary Generall living in the Court, and Confessor to the
Arch-Dutches:45 notwithstanding all these difficultyes she obtained her
pretensions, to the admiration of as well opposers as friends, and this in
the space of six Months. After this she obtained the House of Gravelin,
where now the English poore Clares are,46 had Leave of the Bishop to
take Mother Googe47 out of the Waloon Monastery, but the place of
Gravelin not being [12r] yet ready, they tooke a place in Saint Omers,48
where they lived regularly in the sevearest rule of Saint Clare extant in
the Church of God, which this blessed Woman used all diligence under
heaven to get, and had it from the Dutches of Feria.49
     As she was wont to recount, tearming it selfe-love, how glad she
was to be at rest, and out of the noyse and negotiation of the World, and
what content she had to thinke, the time would come, when it should
be a mortall sinne for her to put her foot over the thresheld, which
motion caused her, contrary to her humility and relyane on the devine
Providence, to aske the Abbesse to be professed50 some Months after
her cloathing, and that the Bishop had urged to have beene done, the
very day of her taking the Habitt, but the Abbes would not admitt of
it, to the Bishop his much discontent. This might and was by diverse
interpreted to evill sense in the Abbesse, but doubtles it was gods devine
Providence, who had his blessed and high designes, in this his deare
and singularly [12v] selected servant, for as herselfe oft recounted to
us she had certaine glimpesᵇ and hoverings in her mind that God would
some what else with her, which ever gave her trouble, and she was easy

to persuade her selfe that it was a temptation, and to prevent it, would
have made sure by her Profession. But God having ordained her for
an other end, would that this should be but as the meanes to prepare
her, and for other secrett judgments knowne to himselfe, and perhaps,
as herselfe was wont to say, to take a way a temptation, had she not^c
proved, she might have conceaved^c as all commonly doe, she zealous of
the best; that perfection is measured by the practise of austerityes, and
consequently not have had that entire satisfaction in her owne blessed
state.

a B: to her | b B: glimpses | c–c C: [Dieu] peut-être permit-il qu'elle fit épreuve de cét
austere genre de vie, car autrement

---

43 Archduke Albrecht of Austria and his wife, Archduchess Isabella Clara Eugenia,
daughter of Philip II of Spain, who had received the Spanish Netherlands from her father
as a wedding gift. They kept court in Brussels. After the death of Albrecht in 1621,
Isabella governed alone until her own death in 1633. See Peters, passim.

44 Mary placed her new foundation under the jurisdiction of Bishop Blaes (see note 68)
of the Order of Friars Minor. It was her wish that the Jesuits should take on the spiritual
guidance of the community. After the death of Bishop Blaes in 1618 the convent remained
under the jurisdiction of the local Bishop, but was later (c.1628) returned to the jurisdiction of the Franciscan Order. Peters pp. 97–101.

45 Note 40.

46 Other manuscripts in AIM contain information about the difficulties of the two years
spent in founding the Poor Clare convent at Gravelines. The community finally took
possession of the newly built house at Gravelines on 15 September 1609. They remained
there until the French Revolution, when they moved to England and settled at Darlington,
North Yorkshire. (Gravelines Chronicles, St Clare's Abbey, Darlington, England. pp. 6–
7).

47 Pope Paul V gave the Bishop of Saint-Omer permission to transfer three choir-nuns
and two lay-sisters from the Saint-Omer convent to the new house. Peters p. 89.

48 Cf. AB 6. From 7 November 1608 to 15 September 1609 the community rented a
house belonging to the Cathedral Chapter. Mary and her younger sister Frances were
among the postulants. Peters p. 89.

49 Jane Dormer (1538–1612) wife of the Duke of Feria, the Spanish ambassador to
England. DNB V, 1150–51.

50 In AB 6 Mary Ward says that this initiative came from Bishop Blaes alone.

The revelation of St Athanasius' Day, May 2nd 1609, and its consequences.

As the custome of those good Religious is, to have some time daily
for handy workes, and such things as belong to their Habits, particularly [13r] certaine frize buttons, to button their Cloakes, and this all
in silence: thus employed upon Saint Athanasius his day,⁵¹ and praying
that these who should weare those buttons might never committ mortall
sinne: In this devotion and very attent, it occurred to her intellectually
that that state of Life was not what she was to honour God by, but an
other very much to Godes honnour, and the good of others, particularly

England.[52] According to her wonted and holy sinceare way, she made it known to her Superiour and Confessour both, though she was assured neither would be pleased with it, especially her Superiour who told her it was a temptation and illusion, and that as oft as it came to her mind, she should leave what soever she was about, and goe make a discipline, be it never so oft in the Day, which she faithfully observed from the first command to her going out, as also she did every particular Rule most exactly, in manner as if allwayes to [13v] remaine there, and as if noe other way for heaven then that.

This lasted neere a Yeare[53] in which time how great were her sufferances having all to oppose her, her Superiour and Confessour:[54] who though, he cou'd not disapprove what she did, would at least not approve it. It is to be imagined he did to comply with his Superiour his opinion, in fine all the World was against her, and the glorious Hosanna for her admirable and speedy ending the above said work, was turned to Crucifige: some said she was left of God, and woud dy in the Streets abandoned of all: others that pride and vanity had made her madd. But what was all this to that strong and magnanimos Soule? noe other then as if it had not beene; as their glorious acclamations had not put her up, neither did their despisings put her downe, referring to God[55] in the one, and relying on God in the other with unspeakable peace within and heavenly serenity without, so as her Superiour was in admiration, especially when her Ghostly Father, on[a] [14r] whom she relyed, had wholly left her, she still the same, woud put her hand on her head and aske how she did, adding, Is this the manner of your friends (naming the Order) to leave their Penitents in temptation and greatest need? to all which this blessed Servant of God would answer with a cheerefull countenance, I am very well.

a A repetition of on

---

51 2 May 1609.

52 Details given in AB 6. Mary's confessor was Roger Lee SJ, who was also her spiritual director from 1608 until his death in 1615. AB 6 note 24.

53 Cf. AB 6. Mary speaks of six months. When the Poor Clare community took possession of their new house at Gravelines on 15 September 1609 she remained in Saint-Omer.

54 Cf. Letter to the Nuncio Albergati; Mary Ward says that Fr Lee told her that she could be saved whether she stayed or left.

55 Cf. *Vision of the Just Soul* described in a letter from Mary Ward to Fr Roger Lee, 1 November 1615. AIM Letters 1. Copy in AIY.

4. New beginnings: a new way of religious life for women.

*Departure from Saint-Omer; vow of obedience to her confessor; pastoral
work in England (1609).*

When she was out of that house and in her secular habitt (which was
exactly modest, genteele and becoming) she tooke her selfe Lodgings in
the same Towne of Saint Omers, often visiting those she had left, loving
them as ever, most entirely dearly. She still keept[a] her former Confessour (a Man in himselfe truly holy and deserving) though she found a
speciall and Fatherly assistance from God, so as not the least discouraged, yet wanted she not sensibilityes, and apprehensions (doubtles to
her encrease of meritt) of the lonelynes and dangers of her now to be
taken in hand encounters, her so long loved and looked for solitude,
scarce [14v] possessed, but snatched from her, and she spoyled as it
were of all contents and assurances, but her Love to the will of God,
and dependance of his fatherly Providence: which togeather with the
mistrust of her selfe, knowing noe further what part she was to act, made
a vow of obedience[56] to her Ghostly Father, and to labour in England
in the good of her Neighbour, which latter guided by the former, she
with great speed and unexpressable fervour put in execution, and therein
passed a good space, still retaining an extreame beauty, went cloathed as
became her birth for matter and manner, and woare underneath a most
sharpe hairecloth, which by continuance did eate into her flesh, nor did
she omitt her daily disciplines, oft fastings and much watching. When
it was for the good of her Neighbour, what did she reserve to herselfe,
neither honnour, Life, nor Liberty: when it best suited with present
occasions, she put on Servants and meane [15r] Womens cloathes;[57]
noe prison did she dreade to visit, or daunger[b] to passe: so as in some
passages it was hard to say which vertue exceeded, her most innate
modesty (which some times she was wont smilingly to say gave her
trouble, she was so apt to blush) or courage had the upperhand: the one
retiring her from all conversation, the other making her uncapable of
feares and apprehensions, or memory of her tendernes and beauty, or
almost her Sex. It was visible in many occasions then, and multitudes
after, that God gave her an admirable power over wickednes in Man or
divell, and great protections in her selfe, and by her to hers.

a B: kept | b B: danger

---

[56] PL No. 16. Cf. Letter to the Nuncio Albergati, L 2; Mary Ward says that she also made
a vow of chastity at this time.
[57] PL No. 18.

Foundation in Saint-Omer (1610) and search for light; school for girls; opinion of the Bishop.

The prefixed time for England being expired, she returned to Saint Omers, and in her Company diverse Gentlewomen, desirous to make themselves happy by her direction, and in her imitation.[58] She bought a House[59] which she furnished, and ordered in manner so as to live in a regular observance, and their cloaths conformable, very [15v] grave and retyred, but not of the monasticall, the Example and fame of her Living drew many others, and those of the best sort. Though thus farre advanced, she remained nevertheles in great anxiety and anguish of mind, not knowing the precise will of God concerning the State of Live she was to settle in. But this did not hinder her from going as farre as she had Light, and conforme to what it ledd into, which in generall tearmes was her owne perfection, and good of her Neighbour, within the Limitts of her Sexe. To this end, for the first seaven Yeares,[60] she and hers eate but one Meale a Day, lay on Straw-bedds only, with diverse other austerityes, which she most prudently would tell hers, were not done as to be a settled observance, but as a meanes to obtayne Light etc.

Amongst other goods to her Neighbour a cheefe one was, to employ themselves in education of Youth, not onely those of our owne Nation (of which there were very many) but also those [16r] of the places where they lived, who were taught gratis, all that became good Christians and worthy Women. The english in regard of the distance, lived wholly under their care, tabled etc. and were taught qualityes to render them capable and fitt to doe God service in whatsoever State, Religious, or Seculars, and through Gods mercyes, the effects have very happily followed in all our English Monasteryes, and diverse in marryed state. But what must be the force of this magnanimous Servant of God, that with the burthen of an unsettled mind, and uncertainety of Gods will, cou'd attend to so many other occasions? which were performed with so devine an exactnes, that the blessed memory of Bishop Blasius their Bishop there, wou'd give noe other Rule to a Congregation of vertuous Ladyes that lived in that Towne under his immediate direction, but the Example of our dearest Mother and hers.

---

[58] PL No. 22. An early eighteenth century manuscript (AIM Doc. 1615–1720, No. 112) states that the first companions were Barbara Ward, Joanna Brown, Winifrida Wigmor, Susana Roockwood, and Catharina Smith. Barbara Babthorpe had entered the Benedictine Convent in Brussels, but an affliction of the throat caused her to leave and join Mary Ward in Saint-Omer. Mary Poyntz (1603/4–1667) was only six years old at the time; as an early companion and the third Chief Superior, the traditional inclusion of her in this Painted Life picture is probably a courtesy.

[59] At the corner of the Rue Grosse (now Rue Carnot) and the Rue des Bluets, close to the English Jesuit College. Peters p. 111.
[60] From 1609 to 1615.

In search of God's will; position of the confessor; God's revelation on the way of life.

But to returne to her suffrances in those Times [16v] which were so great that her selfe protested in the Congregation of Cardinalls appointed by the blessed memory of Pope Urbane the 8th 1629 to hear her reasons,[61] that all her Sicknesses, persecutions, and other Labours, were as nothing in comparison of what she passed and suffered for 10 Years,[62] to know the will of God, yet by her so borne as never perceaved by a dejected or troubled countenance, or doing any action in a devided manner; whole in her petitions, whole in her resignation, whole in her Labours, whole to her selfe, and whole to her Neighbour, great in her faith, and faithfull in her search to know all that God wou'd of and by her. He continued to confes her, to whom she had made her first and onely Vow of obedience, the singular graces he cou'd not but see, that God did continue to her and her correspondance, so as he had not what to contradict nor leave to see she was in a speciall manner guided by God Allmighty, [17r] which though a Priviledge so great, hath oft consequences of great sufferance, as heere happened to his dear Servant. She being tyed to the Confessour by vow, assured in effect God[a] cou'd not be against himselfe, made noe difficulty to obey, though wholly contrary to what she found interiourly God would with her, and though she know what he did was of force and contrary to his owne Light and judgment.[63] And this she did in so eminent manner, as that after she had a knowledge to her undoubted, what Institute[64] God would she should embrase and practise: Which grace God did her in the Yeare 1614,[65] being convalescent of a dangerous and mortall sicknes, of which to say truly she never recoverd; this grace of knowing Gods will, was so great as not to be expressed, but may be in part conjectured by the expression she made of the sufferance the want thereof had caused her. Yet did it not exempt her from great and sensible proofes, as above said, her Confessours contradiction in himselfe [17v] and of her; and that certaine Religious Men, by her dearely loved and respected, misliked, and to a straunge degree opposed what to her was so deare, as not to be chaunged or mingled to please or gaine thousands of worlds, nor could the neglect of it be a lesse crime in her then unfaithfull, and treacherous. The manner by which God Allmighty made knowe to her his blessed will concerning the Institute, and state of Life in which she was to serve and glorify him, was, retyred within her selfe, with extraordinary peace of mind, she understood intellectually but distinctly in precise words what Institute she was to take,[66] and this with such alacrity, consolation and vigour, that she remayned without power to will or will other, so as her usuall expression heereof was: All is as done with me, it onely remaines that I be faithfull.

a repeated in B

---

[61]   Cf. ff. 38r–39v below and L 3, Mary Ward's Petition to Pope Urban VIII and the Cardinals. Mary Ward spoke before this Particular Congregation of four Cardinals (appointed in 1629) in February or March 1630.

[62]   The biographer here includes the years spent by Mary Ward in the austere life of a Poor Clare.

[63]   Cf. Letter to the Nuncio Albergati L 2.

[64]   Institute (Institutum): See L 1, Letter to John Gerard SJ note 3 for an interpretation of this term.

[65]   The correct date for this revelation is 1611, as stated in Mary Ward's letter to the Nuncio Albergati, PL No. 24 inscription and Vita I. The error may be due to confusion between the serious illnesses suffered by Mary Ward in both 1611 and 1614.

[66]   For a full account of this revelation 'Take the same of the Society' see L 1 and 2: Mary Ward's letters to the Nuncio Albergati (1620/21) and to John Gerard SJ (1619). For safety, following the 1631 Suppression, no details were given in this biography, or in PL No. 24.

First Approbation (Bishop Blaes 1615); visit to England (1614–15); the 'Glory Vision' (1609).[67]

The holy Bishop Blasius[68] having pondred and well examined her proceedings, approved and [18r] priviledged her and hers as Religious (within his Diocesse) and their practise most necessary, and to the same[a] effect, wrott Letters to the Sacred Congregation of Regulars in the Time of Pope Paul the V. who ordained the Lord Cardinall Lanvellot[b] to write Letters of Approbation,[69] with promise of Confirmation in case they persevere, but our dearest Mother of happy memory could not dispose of her affaires in time, so as to goe to Rome in that Popes raigne, the afore said Infirmity happening in the meane time,[70] which had it begining by visiting two of her little ones who had the measells, and brought her to the last extreames, so as to receave the Holy Oyles, neither was her recovery held humane.[71] Inclination was conceaved with many probable signes of her present falling into a Consumption, and her weaknes judged incapable of other remedyes then her owne native ayre:[72] whereupon she went and by the many happy following effects it was not without a particular devine disposition. When [18v] once arrived there, her health was one of her last cares, occasions presented for the Service of God, and good of her Neighbour, she refused none neither cou'd any want what was in her power were it spirituall or corporall, neither did she dispute why this or that Person, or this or that place, her onely why and what was that Gods honnour were advanced, and

Soules gained to him, which was cause she assisted so many towards their being Religious, as her selfe did not so much as know the Persons, when by occasion of seeing her, they aknowledg'd the grace of being Religious to have come by her meanes. Loaden with those holy labours, so as to have scarce time to eate or sleep; once after her morning prayer combing of her head, she was surprised with something above her owne forces, and intellectually saw a glory[73] to redowne to God so great and so unexpressable, as the more she saw the lesse she found the End; it tooke away the sight of her corporall eyes, and in her [19r] Eares sounded nothing but glory glory glory; and this impression and sound in her Eares lasted for many Dayes. This happened to her in Lodgings in Saint Clements Church-yard in the Strand[74] in London.

a omitted in B | b B: Sanvellot; C: Lancellot

[67] Like the previous section, this section contains errors in the sequence of events and the years in which they occurred, possibly because the author was not present with Mary Ward during this time.

[68] Bishop Jacques Blaes of Saint-Omer (1540–1618), a firm friend and supporter of Mary Ward and her plans, published his open letter, *In Defence of the English Virgins*, on 19 March 1615. Later in the same year he sent a petition to Rome for papal confirmation of Mary Ward's Institute. Peters pp. 147–154 and 178ff.

[69] This important letter, 10 April 1616, from Cardinal Orazio Lancellotti to Bishop Blaes (quoted in Chambers I, p. 385) gave provisional approval of the Institute, and a hope of confirmation at a later date.

[70] This refers to Mary Ward's second serious illness in 1614. See notes 65 and 67 above.

[71] Human. Annual letter of St Omers College for 1614, quoted by Chambers I, p. 307.

[72] Mary Ward made two visits to England between December 1614 and September 1615. Peters p. 159.

[73] This revelation, known as the Glory Vision, certainly took place in London, but several years earlier, towards the end of 1609. PL No. 21; AB 6; Letter to the Nuncio Albergati; and Vita I.

[74] St Clement's Church stands in St Clement's Lane, off the Strand in London. There were many 'safe houses' for Catholics in that area.

5. Expansion. Liège foundations. Mission to England.

Foundation in Liège (1616); residence in England and apostolic work there (1617); reaction of the Protestant Bishops in England; noviceship house set up in Liège (1618).

Her occasions at home hastned her to returne to Saint Omers, and as well necessited, as opened a way to her begining at Liege, having till then but that one House at Saint Omers. In her passing by Bruxells, she receaved singular honnour and expression of affection from the Arch Dutches Isabella Clara Eugenia, as she formerly had, and did ever on all occassions. After she had settled this House at Liege, where she

did so dispose and order things in Schooles and Church as the Towne
acknowledged great obligation, and the Cleargy vouchsafed to say, they
learned to doe more exactly their functions and duty; thus settled as is
said, she went againe into England, finding it much to Gods service;
to have a Residence for Ours[75] there, which she did, [19v] her family
living so Religiously, as the perfecter sort avouched they found the same
as in their owne Colledges and homes in Catholicke Countryes; her
respect to Priests was such, as served the lesse perfect to enter into
consideration of the dignity of their caracter: noe doubt but her devotion was to some more then others: but her chiefe in all was that high
sate[76] of Priest-hood, and in consideration of that all were by her highly
esteemed, and she tooke it for an honnour to receave them in her House.
She kept constantly 2 in her House to the End her Family might not
want due assistance, and the other be free to helpe such as should neede
abroad, especially the poore to whome Priests could not get but with
great danger, and by Night, not having justifyable pretexts, as to those of
quality they have, their Houses being frequented by all sorts. To remedy
this want, our dearest Mother employed herselfe and hers, sometimes[a]
disguised[a], sometimes in her owne cloathes, using some times familiar
conversation, [20r] other times authority amongst the common and
poore sort, woud first put them in doubt of their owne errour, and then
lay the Light before them: when it tooke, they instructed them how to
make good Confessions, and so prepared them as the Priests had but
to heare theire Confessions, and so avoid the danger which a long stay
woud have brought them, and they also have more Time to employ in
such functions as alone belonged to their Caracter.

God so blessed these her endeauvours, as many and persons of note,
both for the quality of their birth and malice, and perversenes of their
Heresy were converted. Amongst the rest, a very notable one was as
followeth: A Ritch Yemon Man's wife,[77] extraordinary well qualified
for her[b] birth, and noe lesse maliciously grounded in her Heresy, so as
to put all that visited her out of hope of her Conversion, where of divers
were very vertuous and very learned Priests. One Day our deare Mother
went to visitt her in her wonted mild sweet manner [20v] shewed to her
the feeling she had of her Sickenes but more for her perversenes, putting
her hand upon her Head, said some few words to that effect, which
made so strange and unexpected a change in her Soule, as she cryed out
with great efficacy, but sereanely, I will be a Romane Catholicke, and
confess now now; which she did with so great exactnes and Light, with
so harty sorrow and feeling, as amazed the Confessour. Amongst others
that were reduced from badd Life, one was as famous for her bearth, as
enormious for her crime: this party woud say, she had as a bewitching
power to draw one from ones selfe, and put them where she wou'd, and
they ought to be: Diverse were with drawne from libertine Lives, others

put out of occasions, and many that desired to be Religious, and had not the meanes were holpen, and disposed so as they attayned the effects. The bountyfullnes and Largenes of her Hart, was so well tempered and conjoyned with her [21r] Religious[c] poverty, as a certaine very knowing and courious Person, after a long observance, and exact observation of the gouvernment of her House, made this expression: there was none wanted, nor anything wasted, no not so much as a peece of Bread, and that the comportment of hers to one an other, was like most deare, and discreete friends that had beene long absent, and did then meete. Though all this passed with what discretion possibly she cou'd, to the End she and hers might continue this good, and not be discover'd, yet was there information given to N N: then Bishop of Canterbury,[78] of the much evill (as they tearmed it) she and hers did, in so much as a particular search was appointed for her, and a precise description of her Person sett forth, and to make the better appeare the enormity of her crime the Bishop sayd she did more hurt then 6 Jesuits, which caused her Friends to importune her Leaving the Kingdome which yet it is probable she had not done, her Zeale and constancy in Gods Service considered, but that opportunity was [21v] offred of settling a Noviship at Liege;[79] which she as soone as arrived applyed herselfe unto, attending as if in perfect health to the particular exercises of the Novices.

a–a B sometimes in disguises (superscript) C: quelques fois deguisée | b missing in B | c A: repetition of Religious

---

[75] The chronology is again uncertain; see Peters Ch. X. Members of Mary Ward's Society worked in England from its beginnings, and a small mission community may have been established in London as early as 1612, operating from the Spitalfields. Anne Gage was appointed Superior in 1615, followed by Susannah Rookwood about three years later. The community moved frequently to various parts of London, including Knightsbridge and Hungerford House. There were many complaints about their presence and activities in the letters of the English secular clergy of the time; see note 93.

[76] State.

[77] PL No. 17 places this incident at Coldham Hall, the home of the Rookwood family.

[78] George Abbot, Archbishop of Canterbury 1611–1633.

[79] In the Rue Pierreuse, where Mary Ward purchased a large property, with land. The debts incurred by this purchase and the building operations to enlarge the house caused severe financial difficulties for Mary Ward's Society. Peters Chs XV and XVII.

Another stay in England (1618); trust in God during the dangers of persecution; reconcilation of a lapsed priest.

Which when well settled, and having still before her Eyes the profit was to come by the faithfull labours of ours in England, as also the necessity there was of Prudence, Zeale etc. in the carriage of businesses, wou'd herselfe be present, though with eminent danger of her

Life, which meerely in nature she esteemed a Slavery to be too much in
Love withall, as appeareth by the following passage. On a Time tyred
out with mentall employments, and other Labours, she was importuned
to take some recreation; at Length yealding thereunto, she found out a
very unexpected one, which was to give the Bishop of Canterbury his
wish of seeing her; and in effect, went to his House to Lambeth[80] with
noe small apprehension to her Companions, but to herselfe a reall recreation. God permitted he was not at home, but she left her Name, and
that she [22r] had beene there to see him written in the glasse Window
with a Diamond.[81] In these great dangers and particular searches as her
confidence and free relyance on God was great, so was his Fatherly
protection most miraculous, having beene taken twice in her passing the
Seas to and fro, and yet came of, though garded so strongly as notable
to be private in her owne Bed-Chamber, but that her presence had such
Authority, as seemed to command her owne freedome, and that their
power was noe more then to make apparant the Limitt God had given
them. One of these Times a Servant of hers forth of the faith she had,
all was safe that was about this Servant of God, gather'd togeather all
that she conceaved might be dangerous, and gave it her, but not with
so much advisednes but that the Guard saw it, and fearefull something
might passe that might argue their infidelity, desired to know what her
maide had given her, she answered it did not import them, but upon
condition they would promise [22v] to returne it her againe, they shou'd
see it, and taking out a fine christall Riliquary, shewed it them, which
they with great reverence and wonder beheld, and returned it her, and
this though a thing expresse against the Law. Having borrowed of a
speciall friend a Garden house neere London, which yet was private,
and secure for her, he being a Protestant, and powerful in regard of the
Office he held. To make a little digression, this man as[a] I said though
a Protestant[a] grew in great Light and understanding of the Catholicke
Faith, in the which he dyed, and so great an honnourer and admirer of
her vertues, and devine Qualities, as he would say with great feeling,
there never was such a Woman but the sacred Mother of God. In this
House for some speciall service to God she had much company, so as
information was given, and spyes sett, and finally the house besett, but
at distance, yet so as none cou'd passe in or out without note, which
was cause that all the Company, Ours in particular begged our dearest
Mother, to disguise herselfe and so slippe away. [23r] She answer'd, no,
because God's service required her staying. This was on the Saterday, all
passed quietly that Day and the next, the Munday morning her busines
ended, she gave order for her remouvall, which[b] others thought then noe
more needfull,[b] hearing noe more of the bruite, not willing to quitt the
place unless of necessity etc. but this humble and faithfull Servant of
God answered hitherto I have had my Master's warrant for my stay, his

busines requiring it, but that done I expect not a priviledge for my owne respects, and so immediately departed by the publicke doore in Coach, accompanyed with two other Coaches, besides horses, within halfe an hower the Officers came, brooke open the doores, searched and seazed upon all.

Amongst other blessings that God gave her Labours at her being this time in England, a very particular one was the reclayming of a Priest of a very good family, but who had so forgotten himselfe and his function, as he knew neither Masse nor Office, but what did [23v] she not lay at the stake for this gaine! even all that had not of God's displeasure, so had she the reward to heare he ended happily. This was the conclusion of that Times employment in England, which it may be supposed much displeas'd the divell, as he made appeare by the severall troubles and impediments he caused for the passing the Seas, the said Priest being in her Company, having beene some Time on the Sea, was turn'd backe into England and landed just in the Officers Hands, so as their was noe escaping, committed she was, and so farre from being frighted or daunted, that she aloud, with a couragious and heavenly voyce, said our blessed Lady her Litanyes, as she passed in Coach from the place of Judgment to the Prison, where arrived, she knelt downe, and kissed the tresshell of the gate, as a place sanctify'd by the cause for which she entred there, and this publickly before them all, which humanely was to incense their rage and fury against her, but contrary wise they seemed all [24r] her Slaves; whose honnour she advanced made her part.

a–a in B: though a Protestant as I said | b–b omitted in B; C: Les autres pensoient que cela n'étoit plus necessaire

---

[80] Lambeth Palace, on the south side of the river Thames, the seat of the Archbishops of Canterbury since 1188.

[81] Peters (p. 162) doubts the credibility of this incident, but it is in keeping with Mary Ward's fearlessness and high spirits.

Unrest in Liège caused by Sr Praxedis (1619); foundations in Cologne and Trier (1620/1621).

Her confidence in God was not so as to refuse humaine helps, which had a heavenly blessing, so as she passed happily the Seas, visited Ours at Saint Omers, and so on to Liege, where she found the disputes and differences Praxede her revelations had sett on foot;[82] but herselfe dead, having protested that if she dyed, all what she had seene or heard was false. This young Woman was daughter to a Countrey Man of Arden, innocent and vertuous, but had the ill Lucke to be deceaved and deceave. In these occurences much passed worthy eternall memory, and our dearest Mother her glory and meritts, which doubtles she now possesseth; but to other things, her designe now was for Rome, Pope Paul yet living, who had given Approbation above said,[83] with promise of a Confirmation, but occasion was offered of beginning a House at Collen[84] and Trevers[85] which tooke up all her Time till Saint Luke his Day 18 of October 1621.

---

[82] A young lay sister who claimed true enlightenment as to the form and spirit of the new Institute. Cf. L 1, Letter to John Gerard SJ, and Peters pp. 258ff, with references.

[83] See above, f. 18r.

[84] Cologne, in the Breite Strasse, near the Cathedral. Little else is known about the foundations in Cologne and Trier. Peters pp. 277–279.

[85] Trier, formerly known as Trèves.

6. Rome 1621–1626.

Journey to Rome October 21st to December 24th 1621. Audience with Pope Gregory XV.

At her taking [24v] Leave the Archdutches Isabella Clara Eugenia who had given so many proofes of her Love and esteme of her, intreated her not to goe to Rome in her owne Cloathes, for such was the malice borne her, as her Life wou'd be unsecure: the Servant of God cou'd not much apprehend this, but forth of her humility, to be thought as others needy of humane and ordinary helps, put on a Pilgrimmes habitt,[86] with 4 Companions,[87] a maide, a Priest, a Gentleman, and a serving Man, 2 horses, one to carry the bagage, and an other to ease who should be weary. In this manner on Saint Ursula her Day 21 of October she began this her journey in her Pilgrimmes attyre, and performed it without either Stoppe, or Stay but a Day at Nancy to writte Letters, when she wrotte to the Infanta telling her that God willing, on Christ Mass Eve, she wou'd be in Rome: one Day at Milan to performe her devotions to Saint Charles[88] a third at the holy House of Loreto, where with unspeakable devotion, faith and confidence in [25r] God she made her prayer, and tooke for her part and portion to labour and suffer for Christ,[89] having lively represented to her the much she was to suffer, which was cause that as soone as she beheld the Steeple of Saint Peeters Church 16 Miles off Rome, she knelt downe and profoundly enclined reverencing[a] those sacred Reliques of the Apostles, and rendred all submission to that holy Seat and Chayre of his Successours etc. according as she designed, she arrived on Christ-Mass Eve, and made the Church her first aboad, where she spent two howers in prayer. On Saint Steven his Day[90] had audience of his holynes Gregory the XV. (Pope Paul being passed to a better Life) who received her with all fatherly and benigne expressions, so farre as to say, God had in good Time provided for his Church, alluding to the profit was to come by her Labours: for though weake and ignorant Men, cannot bring themselves to be[b] believe, at Least confes, that much good can come by woemen, yet wise and holy Men ever [25v] have and still confes that truth, and in this sense his Holynes both speake and wrott to the Infanta as his severall Breves[91] extant doe shew.

a B: revencing; C: honora | b missing in B; C: ne peuvent se persuader

---

86   A portrait of Mary Ward wearing the pilgrim dress and hat is kept in the house of the Congregatio Jesu at Augsburg.

87   Mary Ward's companions on the journey to Rome are thought to have been Barbara Ward, Winefrid Wigmore, Margaret Horde and Susannah Rookwood, with the lay sister Anne Turner. The priest was Fr Henry Lee (real name Fines) nephew of Fr Roger Lee. The gentleman was Robert Wright, related to Mary Ward on her mother's side, known under the alias Lennard Morriss.

88   St Charles Borromeo (1538–1584) Cardinal and Bishop of Milan, an outstanding figure among Roman Catholic reformers after the Council of Trent.

89   Echoes of St Ignatius' experience at La Storta, where he knew himself to be placed with the Son, under the banner of the cross.

90   28 December 1621 was the correct date (Vita I). Mary Ward herself reported the audience with Pope Gregory XV in a letter to the Archduchess Isabella Clara Eugenia, dated 1 January 1622. Peters p. 321.

91   Letters. See Peters Ch. XIX for archival references on the correspondence between the Archduchess Isabella and Rome.

Audiences with the Pope and the Congregation of Cardinals in Rome (1622). Opening of a school.

Her ambition as well as her fidelity in her part of Labours, wou'd not permitt her to loose time, wherefore she immediately presented to his Holynes and the Congregation[92] he appoynted for her busines to be treated in, what her intentions were, and petitions of them; and this with all simplicity and integrity, which many Polititians condemn'd her for, pretending she might with more ease obtaine her ends, by onely making appeare what was more likely to be plausable, but she blessed herselfe at the name of Policy, or double dealing in the wayes and cause of God, not that she was ignorant what force humane wayes had, but disdayned it should be thought so devine a worke shou'd either need cloake or patches, or that other then the candid truth shou'd be treated betwixt her and his Holynes. It wou'd too farre passe the Limitts of this pretended Relation [26r] to particularise all her oppositions and opposers; some regardlesly publicke and in their owne colours,[93] others pretending friendship[94] had the larger field to gaine the effect of their designes, but God Allmighty gave his Servant charity enough to pardon the one, and the other, and prudence and courage so to carry the busines, as notwithstanding all their force, she obtained to doe in Rome as in other places; that was both in their owne personall practise, and assistance to others:

teaching gratis those of our Sexe both vertue and qualityes,[95] which produced such effects, as the wicked sayd if this went on, the Stewes in Rome wou'd fayle and poore Parents felt the pleasing benefitt of having their Children made fitt by qualityes to gaine their Livings honestly, and by vertue made capable to know it was their duty so to doe.

In fine so farre her heroicall vertue boare the sway, as to priviledge her selfe and hers to doe with applause of sanctity, what had beene thought inpossible, or criminall. Nor was this done [26v] without great search into her Life and actions, as may well appeare by what Cardinall Melino vicar then of Rome[96] himselfe told our dear Mother, that he kept not one or two, but 25 Spyes over her, in so much as there was not what passed in or out that he had not notice of.

---

[92]   The Congregation of Bishops and Regulars.

[93]   Early in 1622 the formal accusations of the English secular clergy were beginning to reach Rome. Peters pp. 337ff.

[94]   Mary Ward and her companions were unacquainted with the intricate diplomacy of the Roman Curia, and mistook the elaborate courtesy of the Pope and Cardinals for genuine support.

[95]   Permission was given in August 1622 for a day school for girls. This foundation was made near the English College, on the corner of Via Monserrato and Vicolo Montoro. No fees were charged. Peters pp. 332ff.

[96]   Cardinal Giovanni Millini (1572–1629), the Pope's Vicar General, was strongly opposed to Mary Ward's Institute.

Foundation of a house and school in Naples (May 1623).

Having had this Leave in Rome, after prayer and due considera-tion, she resolved to goe to Naples,[97] and try if her Labours wou'd ther take[a] effect and prove profitable. When her manner of going shall be well[b] considered, one must conclude there was litle, if any thing of the humane in it: naturally she loved to worke without note or noyse, but in these occasions there was added a necessity, for such was the Zeale of her adversaryes to hinder what good might be done by her or hers, that her greatest endeavours was to doe what she had to doe ere perceaved, which was cause she cou'd not, though she wou'd, have that assistance many worthy Cardinalls and Prelats wou'd have had content to have afforded [27r] her. Her Zeale of God's honnour and fidelity supplyed, so as on the 12 of May 1623 she began her journey from Rome on foote, with a small viaticum, with one Companion,[98] and a Lay Sister, a Priest and a Gentleman, who tooke it for an honnour to partake of her Labours, and were the same that came with her on foote to Rome, and had well experienced she had little need of any assistance they cou'd give her. She was so farre above the necessityes of sumptures,[99] carriages etc. as besides what each one carryed for themselves, one serving Man that she

had carried the rest, which did not over burthen him, for she knew well
how to joyne the heart of a Mother with the authority of a Mistress. In
this pompe she entred that stately Citty, unknowne to any body, tooke
up her Lodgings as other Strangers doe; where falling sicke a friend
procured her the loane of a House in good ayre, but nothing but bare
walls, where she lay on a Straw Bedd on the ground, till a Servant of
God moved to come and visit her, though [27v] he had never seene her,
finding her so, was so moved, as he made but a short Stay, hastening
to a Lady a Penitent of his, said, it is a shame to have so many Bedds
in your House, and God's servant to ly on the ground, upon which she
presently sent her a Bed. In briefe, she gained great reputation amongst
the best sort, and God so disposed as the Lord Nuntio[100] and the Archbishop[101] approved her designes, and soone appear'd not onely the profit,
but the necessity of such schooles, and her meere presence and going
in the Streete and Church was such as incited to piety and Religion, as
who found the effects avouched it publickely, with noe les wonder to
themselves then those that heard it.

a missing in B: | b A: repetition of well

---

97   Naples was outside the Papal States, under the jurisdiction of the King of Spain.
98   Winefrid Wigmore. The priest and the gentleman were Fr Henry Lee and Lennard
Morriss (alias Robert Wright). Peters p. 379.
99   Packhorses (sumpters).
100   Giovanni Pamphili (1574–1655) Nuncio in Naples 1621–1625. On the death of
Urban VIII in 1644 he was elected Pope, taking the name of Innocent X.
101   Decius Carafa, Cardinal Archbishop of Naples from 1613 till his death in 1626. It is
not entirely true that Mary Ward had full support for her designs; after initial hesitation,
the Jesuits supported her activities in Naples, but the Archbishop raised objections. Carafa
was succeeded by the more sympathetic Archbishop Francesco Boncompagni. See Peters
pp. 379–382 and 403–408.

Closure of the Roman School June 1625.

This[a] of teaching continued in Rome till the second yeare of Pope
Urban the VIII.[102] but in Naples and all other places till the Bull[103]
etc. when his holynes thought good to forbid it,[104] not without extream
moaning and complaint of the Childrens Parents, who contrary to their
wonted restraint, went in [28r] Troopes to the Cardinall Vicar his Palace,
Donna Costanza,[105] and where they might hope for reliefe. Meane time
the True Servant of Christ[b] having long since learned the value of Obedience, humbly submitted, and enjoyed as much peace as if the thing had
beene of her owne[c] procuring, and employ'd much Labour to make both
Mothers and Children contented. For contrary to the ordinary straine,
the youth that frequented our Schooles came to them as to a place of
satisfaction and content, not of rigour or force etc.

a C: Céte pratique d'instruire la ieunesse | b B: God; C: Jesus Christ | c missing in B

---

[102]   Urban VIII: Maffeo Barberini (1568–1644), elected Pope on 6 August 1623. The Roman school was closed in the summer of 1625, following a decree of the Congregation of Propaganda on 11 April 1625. In November 1625 the Cardinal Vicar, Giovanni Millini, ordered the closure of the house in Via Monserrato. Peters pp. 406–407.

[103]   The house in Naples remained open until 1628, protected by a more sympathetic Archbishop, and the support of the Jesuits. See Peters pp. 471–472 for the details of this confusing period.

[104]   This and what follows refers to the closure of the Roman school.

[105]   Donna Constanza, the Pope's sister-in-law.

Relationships with Church dignitaries. Esteem of several Cardinals. Pilgrimage for the cure of Cardinal Trescio (June 1624).

It is not of small consideration that of all her powerfull, great, and violent ennemyes, never any one had the courage to professe it to her face, or make other semblance then of friendship. The esteem she had was very great of all the Cardinalls and Prelats, but more singular of the Cardinalls Bandino,[106] Gimnasio,[107] Trescio,[108] etc. Zolleren,[109] the first of these was head of the Congregation wherein her busines was treated, and so had more meanes and occasion to treate with her [28v] and thereby came to know her great goods, and solid vertue, which gayned so high in his esteeme, that he was pleased to tell a Confident of his, such was the reverence he bore her, that did it not derogate from his caracter, he shoud have cast himselfe at her feete, and desired her blessing.[110] What particularly encreased Cardinall Trescio his devotion to this blessed Servant of God, was that she for the excessive payne she suffred of the stone, going to the Bathes of Saint Cassiano,[111] found the said Cardinall there, likewise for some Infirmity of his, which it seemes the waters aggreed not with they casting him into a violent feaver, so as after few fitts his Life was despaired of, which was a great affliction to our dearest Mother, not onely for the part she shou'd loose in him, but the common losse of so worthy a Prelate both for Learning and vertue. At 23 Yeares old he had the chaire in Salamanca, to passe the rest of his Life over: in Rome he lived with such Example [29r] as not onely himselfe, but his family had the note of Exemplar, his daily meditation, saying Masse and hearing on other, at which he would see all his Family present, at the shutting of the Day all his family must be in the House, at Bed time, all were assembled to Examine and Lytanyes which himselfe said. But to returne to what now imports, this Cardinall thus despaired of, she as I said considering him etc. resolved on a pilgrimage called our Blessed Lady of Monte Giovino, 16 Miles off Saint Cassiano in the way of Perugia, where as soone as arrived, which was about 2 of the Clocke in the after noone, she procured the Blessed Sacrament to be exposed, where she put herselfe to pray, and continued for 4 howers, which ended she turned herselfe to her Companions, and said I have noe more to aske, the Cardinall either is mended or dead, in fine ending her prayer, she went to her lodging to take some nouriture, being fasting [29v] till then. When the Servants had eaten, she shewed her desire to know how the Cardinall did, which was anough to the Man who then served her, who was a most faithfull servant,[112] to offer himselfe to go immediatly, as he did, going great part by Night, so as to arrive in the morning at the Bathes, where he found all ready for a journey, and the Cardinall upon immediate departure, which to him seemed a dreame, nor cou'd he believe his owne Eyes: but in effect so it was, at such an hower the evening before, his feaver left him, and all other paines which he had in great extreme, so as he was now able to make his journey to Caprarola, where he stayed all the heates.

---

106 Ottavio Bandini (1558–1629), head of the Congregation of Bishops and Regulars and vice prefect of the Congregation of Propaganda Fide, founded in 1622.

107 Domineco Ginnasio (1550–1639).

108 Gabriel Trejo y Paniagua (1562–1630). This Spanish Cardinal served on the Congregation of Bishops and Regulars and the Holy Office (Inquisition).

109 Friedrich von Hohenzollern (1582–1625), previously known to Mary Ward at Cologne, where he had spoken in favour of her foundation.

110 See note 94 above.

111 PL No. 36 records the pilgrimage to Our Lady of Monte Giovino and the cure of Cardinal Trescio in the summer of 1624.

112 Probably Robert Wright.

Foundation in Perugia (January 1624) at the request of the Bishop; esteem of the Bishop and Fr Dominicus a Jesu Maria for Mary Ward.

There was at this time Bishop of Perugia Mon Signor Comitoli Napolione, a Prelat of great fame, both for Learning, vertue and gouvernment, he hearing of our deare Mother her Person and proceedings, was so persuaded of her meritts, as with great instance he [30r] invited her to accept of a House he wou'd give her and though severall times putt off, woud receave noe denyall, so as not able to resist his Devotion, at Length, she went the Yeare 1624[113] and was receaved by the Bishop in his Pontificall attyre, with all his Cleargy singing the Te Deum, and made severall verses in her prayses, she cou'd never leave the place whilst he lived, his Body wrought miracles before putt into the ground. She woud say many times, God had regard to redresse her wants, by moving holy Servants of his to love her, but others concluded, that like loved their like. Father Dominicus of JESUS MARIA,[114] that great and noted Servant of God, a discalced Carmelitt, had her in high veneration, and wou'd often Times tell us, we must not be so ungratfull, as to lett her Life and Example passe without note, not onely for our owne, but others their profit. He woud also often tell us, how much she and hers must suffer and wou'd use those very words, that we must be trampled on, and have that dependance on God [30v] Allmighty, like as the litles Crowes left by the old ones, because not featherd like themselves, and for our comforts wou'd present us the Example of our Saviours flight into Egipt. Blessed be the hand from whence all comes. How true have we found both the one and the other.

---

[113] Mary arrived in Perugia to make the foundation in January 1624, and remained there for much of that year. Bishop Comitoli Napoleone died in August 1624, and the house closed in April 1625. Peters pp. 382ff.

[114] P. Dominicus a Jesu Maria (1559–1630) the internationally esteemed Spanish Carmelite, a friend and supporter of Mary Ward, spoke these words after a session of the Congregation of Propaganda Fide, which he had attended as an observer.

7. Departure from Rome and journey north (November 1626). New foundations in Munich, Vienna, and Pressburg.

Hospitality in Florence and Parma, and time spent in Milan with Cardinal Federico Borromeo. Christmas in Feldkirch.

She found there was not what needed her presence in Rome, and a necessity of it in the Low Countreyes and England, neither cou'd her magnanimous courage apprehend it hard, or any way unfactable to returne to Rome when God's service shou'd require it, thus resolved she began her journey[115] on the 10. of November 1626 by the way of Florence, where the Arch Dutchess Mary Magdalen of Austria[116] shewed her exceeding great Favours, even to the opening of the sacred picture of the Anunciation,[117] which is never done but with such Solemnity as too publike to neede a noting heere. At Parma likewise the Dutches Regent[118] receaved her with great expression and veneration, so as [31r] she wou'd needs oblige our Mother to give her blessing to the two Princes her Daughters, and Don Francesco her Sonne then young, and the late Cardinall of that Family.

Thence she passed on to Milan, there according to her custome, she resolved to seeke the blessing of the Arch Bishop of that place, then Cardinall Borromeus[119] of happy memory, Nephew to glorious Saint Charles, and inheritour of his Vertues, who by the common voyce was held some what seveare, so as some prudent Persons disswaded her much from going, especially for that it was his custome seldome to speake with Woemen, and never at all in his owne Palace, but in the Church, but she cou'd not be made unconstant[a] in her designes, which was good, and the losse but of her Labour; this was conforme to the humane, but in the devine somewhat more then ordinary as appeared by the successe. She went in her wonted even, humble manner, which made her too high to be hurt by any affront; arrived at the great [31v] Hall, the Cardinall his Gentleman, very civilly but for certaine assured her, their Cardinall wou'd see noe Woman kind whatsoever, noe not his owne Sister or Neece in other place then the Church, notwithstanding some one of the Gentlemen went to tell the Cardinall, but in such a manner as one might see he went and knew not why, but contrary to all expectation, the Cardinall came himselfe to fetch her in and ledd her into his Bed-Chamber, where he talked with her more then an hower, conferring with her businesses importing much, and particularly his foundations of Seminaryes, Monasteryes etc. telling her she must be content to stay 4 dayes, but that when she returned he wou'd not be content with so little, his Coach and one of his Canons shou'd be to attend her, and the last day she must eate at his Nunnes, where after dinner he wou'd come to her and speake more at large and take leave, as he did to the great wonder at his unwonted manner; for after he had [32r] spoken alone with her for some two howers he spent some time with each of her Companions alone, letting them see in very efficacious manner the obligation they had to God for their vocation and happines of being with her: in briefe such were the passages, as diverse yeares after certaine principall persons of Milan meeting our Dearest Mother on the high Way, perseaving it was she, say'd this is the Person whom our holy Cardinall and Archbishop so much loved and respected.

It was now December bitter cold snowes etc. yet she passed by the Lake Como,[120] and Grisons in equall danger to be killed by those wicked People, or by the Cold, neither of which daunted her. On Christmasse Eve in the afternoone she arrived at the first Catholike Towne belonging to the Archbishop of Insprugg, called Felkirch. She took some litle nourishment; between 8 and 9 went to Church,[121] where she remain'd till about 3 in the morning in as great Cold [32v] I thinke as ever was felt, but what was more sensible to her, as she of her goodnes was pleased to impart to us, was an unexpressable affliction of mind, which dured till 9 at high Masse at the Cappucins Church[122] (where she passed the Night was the Parish Church) particulars she wou'd never tell, but in generall tearmes that it concern'd the Conversion of England: It was admirable to see the Love and respect she had from all Persons of Quality, Religious and all, and how the one wou'd call the other to goe and see her, each finding what suited and agreed with them; yet she allwayes the same, without the least apparance of faining or force to comply with any, her greatest inclination being to see none (unles a certaine duty and obligation) in regard of spirituall respects as also for the great necessity, her great infirmity and weake Body had of rest.

a B: inconstant

115　Mary's companions on this journey were Mary Poyntz, Elizabeth Cotton, an unnamed lay sister (probably Anne Turner), Fr Henry Lee and Robert Wright. See Peters pp. 429ff. for details of this and the next sections.

116　Maria Magdalena, Grand Duchess of Tuscany, sister of the Emperor Ferdinand II of Austria and wife of Cosimo II de Medici (d.1621).

117　A treasured painting in the Church of the Annunciation in Florence.

118　The Duchess Margareta, widow of Duke Farnese (d.1622) acted as Regent for her young son Francesco, who later became a Cardinal, and her daughters Maria and Victoria.

119　Federico Borromeo (1564–1631), nephew of St Charles Borromeo, Cardinal Archbishop of Milan 1595–1631.

120　The route from Milan: Como, Riva, Chiavenna, the Spluga Pass, the Canton of the Grisons (Protestant and hostile), Via Mala, Chur, and along the Rhine to Feldkirch. This was one of Mary Ward's most challenging journeys, made even more difficult by her preference for travelling in winter.

121　The parish church, where Mary Ward spent Christmas Eve. See PL No. 43, one of the most attractive panels of the Painted Life.

122　PL No. 44. The inscription says that Mary's prayer concerned the conversion of the King of England, the ill-fated Charles I.

On through Innsbruck to Munich (Monaco). Foundation with a school (1627) at the request of the Elector and Electress, Maximilian I and Elisabeth.

At Insprugg the Arch Duke and Dutches[123] entertayned her in a very singular manner, [33r] giving great testymonies of the esteeme they had of her, sent her in Coach[124] to Hall where she was to embarke, there those devout Ladyes[125] invited her and wou'd have had her made some stay, but it must have beene some great matter indeed, that must have hindred her journey once begun. The last dayes journey betwixt that and Monaco after her wonted prayer, she told those with her, that she feared her intended journey for Flaunders wou'd be stopped, and after a little she sayd, what will you say if we have a House heere? In effect so it was, her Highnes wou'd not lett her passe, noe not so much as upon condition to returne and bring others to settle there, the Dutches said, she had long designed and expected what God had now sent her, and it shoud not easily escape her.[126] It was generally believed that there had beene correspondance betwixt her Highnes and our dearest Mother, if there had it was devine, for humane there had beene none. A House was sought out, Men and Money sent to Collen[127] to fetch more of ours; meane time the newes went [33v] abroad, and the constant Friends and Lovers of our heavenly gayne, cou'd not brooke us such possessions on earth, and for that end wrott to the Duke, that he knew not what nor who he entertayned, and that they had great debts, and more tending to disparagement,[128] but so as it was playne through God's mercy to see,

he had much to doe to picke out what to furnish his designe with, which
God gave the Duke light to see, in so much as that he said, this is the
divell; and that whereas he had beene slow to resolve on the rents to be
settled on that house he wou'd doe it ere he stired thence, and in effect
did so, when he had done, sent our dear Mother the letter by his owne
Confessour, who wou'd not give her the letter, but read it to her, saying,
it was from a Prelate of great note, but noe sooner heard she it read,
but she named the party to his great astonishment. But what is all this
world worth, or favour of Princes, when a Prince thus pious, and thus
perswaded even above the humaine cou'd be induced to consent that this
[34r] Servant of God shoud be imprisoned as an Heretike in his owne
City,[129] but of that more in it due place, and now as it passed.

---

123   Leopold V, brother of the Emperor Ferdinand II, who had married Claudia di Medici,
the sister-in-law of Maria Magdalena of Tuscany.
124   PL No. 45 shows a coach nearing Munich, carrying Mary Ward and her three
companions with Fr Henry Lee and Robert Wright on horseback. The landscape is imagi-
nary and shows no snow, although this is early January.
125   An unenclosed religious community living under Jesuit direction, founded by the
three daughters of the Emperor Ferdinand I.
126   The Electress Elisabeth became a firm friend of Mary Ward. She and Maximilian
had long wished to provide for girls the same kind of education, academic and religious,
as the Jesuits were offering to boys.
127   Cologne. On 16 February 1627 Mary wrote to Barbara Babthorpe to ask for members
from the northern houses to be sent to Munich. AIM Letters No. 37; copy in AIY.
128   Maximilian ignored the warnings which were sent to him, the majority probably from
Rome, but others from English Jesuits. The Jesuit General, Muzio Vitellesci, dealt with
these severely. Peters pp. 438–440.
129   In 1631 the Elector did not feel able to oppose the decision of the Holy Office to
imprison Mary Ward on a charge of heresy, but he allowed the members to continue to
live in the Paradeiserhaus. Wetter pp. 167–169.

Gratitude of the Elector and Electress. Foundations in Vienna (1627) and Pressburg – now Bratislava (1628).

When the House[130] was delivered into her possession, well furnished
and rented, she went to his Highnes to thanke him, his answer was, that
Christ had assured him, the workeman was worthy of his hire, and that
he thancked her for the acceptance; the English had beene the first to
teach them their Faith,[131] they were now to teach them the manner of
Christian Living. Soone after wrott such Letters to the Emperour then
Ferdinand the Second[132] that his Majesty thought it unworthy him, not
to doe as much in Viena, as his Brother in Law the Duke had done in
Monaco, and for this end bidd our dearest Mother take her choyce of
all the houses in Vienna,[133] for which she wou'd shou'd be hers, which
when chosen, being inhabited by 8 severall familyes, there was not that
hast made his sacred Majesty wou'd the Court being upon removall for

Prague[134] [34v] he protested as he was Emperour, he wou'd not depart till she was in possession, which with other passages expressed him the holy Prince he was and the devotion he bore to her meritts.

God through his mercyes gave such blessings to the Labours of ours in both places, as made them desired in Prague and Presburg. The latter being neere hand, and Cardinall Pasmanus[135] then Arch Bishop of that place, extreamly carryed for it, was presently gone on with, but found great difficulty,[136] because the Heretikes had great power (halfe the Counsell being such) and sayd, it wou'd be the greatest hurt cou'd come to them, if not a totall destruction, the gouvernment of the familyes depending on women, who bred up Catholikes wou'd doe the like to their Children, in the End the Cardinall, to his unexpressable consolation, gayned the victory, with great profitt to the youth of that place.[137]

---

[130]   The Paradeiserhaus in the Stiftsgasse (now the Weinstrasse) which the Elector had fitted out and placed at their disposal in April 1627, together with an annual income. The community numbered about ten English members, who were soon joined by new members of various nationalities. This house was to become the cradle of Mary Ward's Congregation. Peters pp. 436ff.

[131]   St Boniface, eighth century English missionary to Germany and to Holland, where he was martyred.

[132]   A copy of this letter, dated 19 June 1627, is kept in the Munich State archives. The Habsburg Emperor Ferdinand II's aim was to restore the Catholic faith in central Europe. Mary Ward made the foundation in Vienna at his invitation, but without the necessary ecclesiastical permission. Peters pp. 443ff.

[133]   The choice was the Stoss am Himmel, opposite the church of Maria am Gestade. The Emperor also arranged for an annual income.

[134]   The Emperor's dominions included Prague (Bohemia) and Imperial Hungary.

[135]   In March 1628 Mary Ward travelled from Vienna to Pressburg (Bratislava) at the invitation of Cardinal Peter Pázmány (1573–1637), Archbishop of Gran, a man of great determination and one of the major figures of the Counter Reformation. He attached much importance to the education of girls.

[136]   Peters pp. 448ff.

[137]   A house for the community and a school was eventually made available near the Cathedral, in the benefice of St Andreas. Barbara Babthorpe was appointed Superior of the small community.

Unsuccessful attempt to make a foundation in Prague (1628).

The beginning of Prague[138] through God's permission[a] [35r] found violent oppositions from Cardinall of Haroke,[139] then Archbishop of that place, and this by the instigation of the good Father Valerio Magno Capucin,[140] whose Zeale in this particular did not onely hinder this beginning, but made it seeme necessary the Servant of God shoud returne to Rome.

In her passing betweene Viena and Prague, going and coming, she was earnestly invited by the Lady of Neyhause,[141] which she accepted

more in regard that she was a great and holy Servant of God, then for
her other qualityes which were great, and the greatest of that Kingdome of Bohemia, and accordingly esteemed of all, even the Emperour
himselfe called her his Mother, but she had learned that excellent art
to make that which in it selfe temporall to her eternall, for very many
Yeares she never slept but upon straw, and that for few howers, and
eate but one meale a Day, built herselfe a little house distant from
the Castle with a Convent for [35v] Religious Men to say the devine
office at which she was present without omission or intermission nor
wou'd she omitt any one of her wonted holy customs to comply with
the Emperour himselfe but when our dear Mother was to passe, she
wou'd not let her lodge in her Little House, but gave order she shoud be
entertayned in the Castle whither she went to receave her, and mett her
at the Coach side, and coud not be content to depart from her, layd all
devotions a side and wonted exercises, to the admiration of all that ever
had knowne her, which was such as she herselfe coud not but perceave
it, and gave this answer to their wonder, pray she cou'd allwayes, but not
have such company, which she tooke to be one of the greatest happynes
God did ever doe her, and calling upon her onely Child the Lady Lucy
Slavato,[142] with teaers in her Eyes wou'd say, Lucy my Child Lucy, if
thou either hast Love or duty to me expresse it by thy Love and service
to this servant of God and hers wheresoever thou findest [36r] them,
and turning to the rest there present added, it is for my sinnes, and the
Sinnes of this Kingdome that she hath not a House in Prague.

Returning a second time to Presburg she was invited by the Lady
Palvy[143] who was by birth a Countesse Fuggerin of Swabenland. She
lived upon the confines of the Turkes Dominion, that is in the Siben
Bergs, where she had yearely occasion to expresse her great charity and
magnanimity making her Castle the refuge of all the poore when the
Turke made his yearely incursions, where she both fedd and defended
them[b] for diverse Monthes. This Lady as said, so importunely invited
our dear Mother as she coud not refuse her and being there, did as she
had for many yeares before communicate every day, which a young
Priest a Curate seemed to carpe at, the Lady with great seriousnes and
noe les devotion said, you may censure as you please, this Servant of
God, but I am sure my Child that had as you all know the feaver for 2
Yeares [36v] in the instant that she entred my House recouvered, and is
well as you all see.

a B: permissio | b repeated in B

---

138 The failure in Prague is said to have been the turning point which finally led to the
total suppression of Mary Ward's Institute in 1631. For details of this attempted foundation, and the resulting complexities, see Peters pp. 452–460.
139 Ernst Adelbert von Harrach (1598–1667), of Vienna, appointed Archbishop of

Prague at the age of twenty-five and Cardinal at twenty-eight. He seems to have been much influenced by his Capuchin advisor, Fr Valeriano. See L 3, Petition to Pope Urban VIII and the Cardinals.

140   Maximilian Magni, b. Milan 1586; entered the Capuchin order in 1602, taking the name Valerio. Passionately opposed to the Jesuits and to Mary Ward's Institute, he handed on the matter of the foundation to the Nuncio Giovanni Pallotto, who brought about Mary's return to Rome.

141   Katharina, widow of Count Adam von Neuhaus.

142   Lucia, widow of Count Wilhelm von Slavata.

143   Countess Maria Pálffy, née Fugger. She supported the community at Pressburg financially and in other ways. Peters p. 468.

8. Second journey to Rome (1629). Audience with Pope Urban VIII and a hearing before a special Commission of Cardinals.

Second journey to Rome (1629).

Being returned to Monaco to goe for Rome,[144] she fell into a violent Sicknes, with certaine paynes which made her unable to goe but with her breast even downe to her knees, she cast all she eate, never slept but when rocked as in a cradle, thus she continued above a Month and still with intention to goe on her journey, which in effect she did on the 2[d] of January 1629[145] in such state of health as the Physitians affirmed most assuredly, that according to the humane she cou'd not live to goe out of the gates of the Citty, neither cou'd they find by what naturall cause she lived: the colds were extreame, and snowes excessive, yet did this Servant of God begin this journey with as great tranquillity, joy, and magnamiting as if in perfect health, and had what might ease and please nature, whereas the onely provision was a little bagg of oatemeale grawts to make watergruell with, which alone was her foode all [37r] the journey long; and it without other seasoning then a litle Salt, and thine so as to drinke, which she neither kept past halfe an hower, then cast it unchanged as she tooke it. When she was asked whither she thought she shou'd live to the end of that journey, she answered there was more apparance she should not then shou'd, neither did it import her, where or when she dyed, in her Bed, or under a hedge, so it were in her fidelity to God, that she had made severall generall Confessions and lately one for her last, her daily Communions had beene for many yeares for her last, for the rest, she was sure lived she, or dyed she, she served a good Master. Thus disposed in mind and body, she began, and through God's goodnes ended her journey with Life, but with paynes of many deathes, so as many times she consulted in her owne thoughts whiter best yea or no to aske the holy Oyles: conforme to her owne satisfaction she had done it, but apprehended what sensibilityes it might put her Companions into who saw not other [37v] Signes of such a danger or change in her, for she went still on her journey, and did her devotions at the holy House of Loreto, but as soone as at her owne home at Rome she went to Bed, where she lay 3 Weekes, nor was there any reason why she ever rose, but that God wou'd have it so for his service etc.

144   The Nuncio Giovanni Pallotto, covertly hostile to Mary Ward and wishing to remove her from the area of Vienna and Bavaria, persuaded her make this journey to Rome to submit a further request for the approval of her Institute. Peters pp. 480ff with archival references.
145   Mary's companions were Winefrid Wigmore, Elizabeth Cotton, and Anne Turner. Fr Henry Lee and Robert Wright probably travelled with them. Peters p. 502.

Audience with the Pope (May 1629). Appointment of a special Commission of Cardinals (late 1629) at which Mary Ward presented in person the case for her Institute (February or March 1630).

Those 3 Weekes that she lay in Bed she dictated a relation of her proceedings,[146] and those of hers from their first Living in Community, which when presented to his Holynes and the Cardinalls of the Congregation was both admired and praysed in so much as some of them sayd, it must have beene dictated by the Holy Ghost. Though the number and violence of her opposers were great, yet the innocency and Justice of her cause with the Prudence of her carriage had so much power with his Holynes (whose excellent parts and Qualityes befitting his devine call and place were ever inclining him to doe [38r] each one right) as to take her busines out of the Congregation wherein it was because the Number to be treated with being many, it was harder to bring businesses to an End, treated there, and therefore had it committed to Cardinall Melino his Vicar, and to the Generall of an Order,[147] whom his Holynes was persuaded was mightily a friend, but in effect was wholly the contrary, and she insinuated so much to his Holines, who persuaded her of the contrary, when she had done her part, she rested satisfyed, and treated with them as holding the place, not conforme to their private opinions. In this occasion her opposers had the greatest power imaginable to quite overthrow her busines, yet prevayled not but so as to leave her so much grace and good opinion with his Holines, as he was pleased to appoint an other Congregation of 4 Cardinalls[148] to witt Cardinall Borgia who was the head of the Congregation, Cardinal St Onophrio, Cardinall [38v] San Sixto, and Cardinal Scalia, in which Congregation herselfe was to be present, and to declare what she desired and her reasons. She presently conforme to her wonted candour, made be coppyed an abridgment of the Institute, and gave it to every one of them, so as they had time to ponder it before the appointed Day, which when come, and she appointed to be there, God permitted that she had so sore[a] a cough, that she rested neither Day nor Night, yet there she appeared with her wonted cheerefullnes, and modest confidence, all being satisfyed with her, and she with them. Cardinall Borgia as head aforesayd, made her signe to speake, which she did for the space of three quarters of an hower without being interrupted with her owne infirmity, or any present finding what to contradict or oppose, then Cardinall St Onofrio had some few words to say, which she then answered with a bow onely, going on with her speech by which she made it appeare the Institute was not onely lawfull, but laudable and necessary, and[b] [39r] that there was nothing in it, nor practised by her or hers, which had not beene practised by Holy Woman, and approved by the Holy Church in particular Persons, but never practised by a community, nor did she wonder the Holy Church made difficulty in a thing that was new, contrary-wise she did profoundly reverence that vigilancy of theires, but for her owne part, she did there protest before them, that the much it had cost her in 10 Yeares of Labours and sufferance to know God's will,[149] was such, as that once knowne all her infirmityes and other suffrances seemed toyes, nor cou'd she frame to herselfe what cou'd be difficult, or had she other ambition, but at her Death to be found to have beene faithfull, so as to desist if his Holynes and their Emminencyes thought good she cou'd, but alter or take other she cou'd not: She was there, they might dispose of her as they wou'd, as the cause of God the busines was more theirs then hers. None there were unsatisfyed. Cardinall Borgia[150] referred what had passed to his Holynes, adding [39v] he held it to be of God, and that he neither cou'd or durst be against it, nor was his power enough to assist it, such and so powerfull were her Ennemyes, therefore he humbly intreated his holynes he might deale no more in it.

a A: soon corrected to sore in a different hand; B: soone corrected to sore by Laurence
Toole | b repeated in A

---

[146] This important petition to the Pope, written in Italian and dated 25 March 1629, conveys a vivid picture of Mary's determination to complete what she saw as her life's task, and to fulfil what she saw as the will of God. The text is included in this book, Selected Letters and Documents L 3.

[147] Unknown, possibly the General of the Jesuits. Cardinal Millini died on 1 October 1629. This may have been the reason for the appointment of a new Commission of four Cardinals.

[148] Cardinals Gaspare Borgia (1584–1645), St Onofrio (Antonio Barberini (1569–1646), the Pope's brother), Laudivio Zacchia (d.1637), and Desiderio Scaglia (d.1639).

[149] Cf. ff. 15v and 16v with notes 61 and 62.

[150] On 13 April 1628 Cardinal Borgia had been a member of a special Commission of Cardinals where it had been decided that Mary Ward's Institute should be suppressed, as not in accordance with canon law. Grisar *MW* p. 292.

Decision to return to Germany.

The busines standing thus, our dear Mother went to Donna Constanza Barberina, the Popes Sister in Law, a most vertuous Lady and her great and deare friend, telling her, how it went, and that there was nothing for her to doe but to expect God Allmighty his devine disposition, therefore she wou'd returne into Germany. At the same time wrott to who had care of our House in Monaco[151] that she was beginning her journey towards her, though she had but 200 crownes in all the World for her journey; when she told those about her, every one not having all her faith, had some apprehension what might or wou'd happen, which she perceaving, merrily answered, I have found out a good way to make our monyes hold out, to be sure to [40r] deny noe poore body an almes, which she punctually observed, and had it effect, but not without intollerable toyle to her feeble body, making the greatest part *

---

151   Mary Poyntz.

[* *Editor's note.* There is a lacuna of about three pages in both the English manuscripts A and B at this point. In manuscript A this omission is made good by three additional pages of an older date, in two separate hands. These pages, incomplete and considerably damaged at the margins, have been bound in at the end of the book. Dr Haigh, whose nineteenth century transcript (manuscript F) is a copy of the Hammersmith/Manchester manuscript B (manuscript A being unknown at the time), completed his work with a retranslation from the French manuscript C, which had been lent to him.

In this edition, the lacuna is printed synoptically, using versions A (the additional pages), Dr Haigh's retranslation, and the French manuscript C, so that the stages in the tradition can be traced.]

9. Return to Germany. Arrest and imprisonment of Mary Ward on a charge of heresy and rebellion against the Church.

Return to Germany (April 1630).

Additional pages in A	F: Dr Haigh's retranslation	C. French version
[1r] deny noe poore body an almes, which she punctually observed, and had it effect, but not without intollerable toyle to her feeble body, making the greatest part of the iournay on foot, having but one horse to ease the most wearyed by turnes, nor but one payre of shoues fitt for travelling, which must serve severall persons of very unequall feete: in all these sufferances, in respect of the contagion, which then was very h[eavy] in her direct rode, she was forced to goe about by Ven[ice] where the most curious sowing silkes are to be had, she d[id] not forget, they would be very beneficiall to our house i[n] Germany, nor consider the want she might have of th[e] money being so slenderly provided.	deny no poor body an alms". Which she punctually observed and had its effect but not without intolerable toil to her feeble body, for having but one horse to relieve by turns the most weary she herself made the greater part of the journey on foot, and with the inconvenience of having but one pair of shoes for the journey which did not fit her. The plague raging furiously at this time in the places which were on the way to Bavaria our mother was compelled to take the route of Venice where they make the most beautiful silks. Amongst all her troubles she remembered that these silks would be very useful to our house in Germany and without considering the need she might have of money of which she had so little, did not fail to make provision for them.	ne refuser l'aumône à aucun qui nous la demandera, ce qu'elle observa exactement, et la chose arriva comme elle avoit dit; mais sa foiblesse et sa debilité, en éprouva les intollerables fatigues, car n'ayant qu'un cheval pour soulager tour à tour les plus incommodées, elle-méme fit la plus grand part du chemin à pied, et avec l'incommodité qu'on peut s'imaginer, n'y ayant qu'une paire de souliers propres à faire voyage, qui devoit servir à des personnes de taille, fort disproportionée. La peste ravageant furieusement en ce temps là les lieux qui étoient sur le chemin de Baviere, nôtre Mere fut contrainte de prendre la route de Venise, qui est le pays où se font les plus belles soyes. Parmy tant de souffrances elle s'avisa que ces soyes seroient fort utiles à nôtre maison en Allemagne, et sans s'arrêter à considerer le besoin qu'elle pourroit avoir de l'argent, dont elle avoit si peu, ne manqua pas d'en faire provision pour elles.

Arrival in Munich. Visitor (Winefrid Wigmore) sent to Flanders. Mary Ward to Vienna.

Additional pages in A	F. Dr Haigh's retranslation	C. French version
Arrived that she [was] in Monaco, and fore-see-ing what the * voilence of [her] ennemys might arrive to, to doe all that mig[ht] quitt her of her fidelity before God and her own, [sent] one whom she knew faithfull and had seen her carri[age] in bussi-ness, [152] into Lower Garmaney and Flanders [some] of the Superiours of those houses having proceeded other way than became them (I hope not with ma[lice] but it shou'd seem, not without remorse because they us'd juggling and inderect wayes, for good [and] noe bad.	Being arrived at Munich and foreseeing how far the violence of her enemies might go, so as to omit nothing on her part to acquit herself of her fidelity of God and ours some Superioresses of our houses in Flanders having behaved themselves otherwise than they ought perhaps without malice (it is at least to be believed that it was not without remorse of conscience) having used finesse and indirect ways whereas good has no need of evil our mother sent one whom she knew to be entirely faithful and who had seen her way of acting and her conduct in business.	Etant arrivée a Munic, et prevoyant iusqu'ou pourroit aller la violence de ses ennemys, afin de ne rien ômettre de ce qui la pourroit acquitter de sa fidelité devant Dieu, et envers les Nôtres, quelques unes des Superieures de nos maisons en Flandres s'etant comportées autrement qu'elles ne devoient, peut-être sans malice, mais il est à croire que ce ne fut pas sans remords de conscience, ayant usé de finesses et voyes indirectes, au lieu que le bien n'a pas besoin de mal, nôtre Mere y en envoya une qu'elle reconnôissoit tres fidelle, et qui avoit veu sa facon d'agir et sa conduite dans les affaires.

* Change of handwriting at this point.

Additional pages in A	F. Dr Haigh's retranslation	C. French version
In the Duke of Baviers his Court is noe immedi[ate] nuncius but if ought occures the nuntius of Lucer[ne][153] hath the charge, which was cause togeither wi[th] the high esteem she had of Cardinall Palatto hi[s] meritts that she went to Viena to attend what [...] The manuscript is damaged here and line(s) are missing. [2v] [in]tended journey for Flanders and England, taking a [...] all to hart her due reference to the Pope and [to] holy church.	She abandoned also altogether the design which she had had of passing into Flanders and England having at heart above all things the deference and submission which she owed to His Holiness and to Holy Church. She went therefore to Vienna to wait the good pleasure of His Holiness because that at the Court of Bavaria there was no Nuntius but if any matter of importance occurred it was remitted to the Nuntius at Lucerno, and because of the high esteem she had conceived for Cardinal Pallota.	Ainsi elle remit tout à fait le dessein qu'elle avoit eu de passer iusques en Flandres et en Angleterre, ayant à coeur au dessus de toutes choses la defference et sôumission qu'elle devoit au Pape et à la Sainte Eglise. Elle s'en alla donc à Vienne y attendre le bon plaisir de Sa Sainteté, tant à cause que dans la cour de Baviere il n'y a point de Nonce resident, mais s'il s'agit de quelque chose d'importance l'on s'en remet au Nonce de Lucerne, comme aussi à raison de la haute estime qu'elle faisoit des merites du Cardinal Pallott.

Return from Vienna to Munich.

Additional pages in A	*F. Dr Haigh's retranslation*	*C. French version*
It was found nott fitt nor possible to put in execution in the Emperrors Court, the orders for our dear Mother her imprisonment, she left that place and returned to Monaco where she fell in to a voilent and dangerous feveur, not with apprehension of what she was to pass, for the [dis]curse of it serv'd her for a divertisment and [...] to those a bout her it seem'd horrid, she [ha]d a devine way to make it seem easie, just, [and] holy, at least to who wou'd use it so as [s]he did, but all had not that grace to beare [...] so; yet was his mercye and fatherly goodness [s]uch that it pass'd without sinn or scandall.[154]	But seeing that they judged it neither suitable nor possible to put in execution in the court of the Emperor the command for her imprisonment she left Vienna and returned to Munich where she fell sick of a violent and dangerous fever not for fear of that which they plotted against her for she spoke of it familiarly, pleasantly and by way of passing time, and seeing that it seemed horrible to her companions she represented in a way all therein as very sweet very good and very holy for those who would use it aright. But the grace was not given to all. It passed nevertheless without scandal by the goodness and mercy of God.	mais voyant que l'on ne iugeoit ny convenable ny possible de mettre en execution dans la Cour de l'Empereur le mandement pour son emprisonemment, elle quitta Vienne et s'en retourna à Münic, òu elle tomba malade d'une fievre violente et dangereuse non pas par l'apprehension de ce qui se conspiroit contre elle, car elle en discouroit familierement et aggreablement par divertissement, et voyant que cela paroissoit horrible et épeuvantable à ses compagnes avec une maniere toute divine elle le representoit comme fort doux, juste et saint, pour le moins à qui s'en vouloit servir comme tel, mais cette grace là ne fut pas donnée à toutes ; tant-y a par la misericorde et bonté de Dieu il ne s'y passa ny peche ny scandale.

Memorial sent to a prelate in Rome to give to the Pope (November 1630).

Additional pages in A	C: Dr Haigh's retranslation	F: French version
All virtues in her had that heavenly harmony without […] As one could not tell which was the loudest or [w]hich was the sweetest. Her zeale to suffer for her [fi]delity, nor her content to suffer in her innocency [did] not make her forgit what startlings and amaz[m]ents such proceedings might seem to cause, and noe less hard for those who live at home to apprehend the qualities of rimote countrys and the […] who was carry'd by pasion had to consider [w]hat might foler which was cause she did writ [to] a certain Prelate[155] (in himselfe of great meritey [by] his passed employments in a degree interes'd by [w]ay of justice), that wheare as she hear'd it [was] treated in the present Congregation of the holly *[…] The manuscript is damaged here and line(s) are missing.* [3r] horror in the eyes of the world, her imprisonment for an heretick was to fore goe it,	All virtues met together in her with such heavenly harmony, and were balanced with such equality that none could say which shone with the greatest brightness. The ardent zeal which she had on this occasion of suffering for her fidelity and the sweet content to suffer innocently did not make her forget the surprizes which this proceeding might cause, the pain also which she had for those who have never gone from home to experience the qualities of distant countries, considering moreover the little reflection which those who might let themselves give way to passion might make of the consequences of this affair she wrote to a prelate of great merit (and who by his past employs was in some sort engaged by way of justice) that at the place that she heard that in a private congregation of the H. Office it was being treated of the suppression of our manner of life, and that to the end this should be done with more horror in the sight of the world they treated of previously imprisoning her as a heretic.	Toutes sortes de vertus, se rencontroient en elle avec une si celeste harmonie, et se rapportoient avec une si iuste égalité, que l'on ne pouvoit dire laquelle de ses rares vertus brilloit avec plus d'éclat, laquelle retentissoit d'un son plus haut ou laquelle attiroit d'une plus aymable douceur. Dans cette occasion l'ardent zele qu'elle avoit de souffrir pour sa fidelité et le doux contentement que ce luy étoit de souffrir innocemment ne luy firent pas oublier les étonnemens que ce procedé pourroit causer la peine aussi qu'il y a pour ceux qui ne sont iamais sortis de chez eux de concevoir les qualités des pays éloignés; de plus considerant le peu de reflexion que ceux qui se laissoient ainsi emporter à la passion, faisoient sur les consequences de cét affaire, elle écrivit à un certain Prelat (Personnage de grand merite, et par ses employs passés, en quelque sorte engagé par voye de iustice) qu'au lieu quelle entendoit que dans la Congregation privée du St Office il s'agissoit de la depression de nôtre maniere de vie, et qu'afin que cela se fit avec plus d'horreur à la veue du monde l'on traitoit de faire preceder son emprisonnement en qualité d'Heretique,

Additional pages in A

Yf his holynes judg'd it fitt a desisting shou'd be; there needed but the least insinuation of this his will, it shou'd be done with intire submission and satisfaction to his Holyness without injurie to any and to this same effect incloss'd a memoriall to his Holyness,[156] adding her humble petition to the said Prelate, that in case he cou'd not nor thought not fitt to present it his Holynes, to let her know so much, and she wou'd find some other way, esteeming it as a burthen of conscience not to doe all in her power in that perticuler, which she had done, had she not been sure these letters we[re] deliver'd, and therby her duty discharg'd. All must be left to that abiss etc.

The Dean of our Blessed Lady her church in monaco was the man to whom the orders [from] the Congregation of Rome were derected for imprisonment, the Duke intreated to allow of it and in case she resisted to lend his secular power. But alas how little was this needed! For whereas the Duke who though through tenderness of conscience wou'd not protect her, thought it unfit and inhumane to

F: Dr Haigh's retranslation

If His Holiness judged it proper for her to desist he had but to give the least insinuation of his will she would obey, making the greatest part submission and satisfaction to His Holiness, adding her humble petition to the said prelate without injury to any and to the same effect enclosed a memorial to His Holiness that in case he could not, or that not fit to present it to let her know so much she would find some other way, esteeming it as a burthen of conscience not to do all in her power in that particular. Which she had done had she not been sure these letters were delivered and thereby her duty discharged. All must be left to that abyss of the inscrutable judgments of God.

The Dean of our Blessed Lady her Church in Munich was the man to whom the orders from the Congregation of Rome were directed for her imprisonment, the Duke entreated to allow of it and in case she resisted to lend his secular power! For whereas the Duke who, though through tenderness of conscience would not protect her, thought it unfit and inhuman and

C. French version

Que si sa Sainteté iugeoit à propos qu'elle desistât elle [sic] n'avoit qu'à donner la moindre insinuation de sa volonté, elle y obeiroit avec une entiere soûmission et pleine satisfaction de sa Sainteté, sans faire iniure à personne. Elle enferma dans la lettre au Prelat un memoire à sa Sainteté à ce même effet, suppliant de plus le dit Prelat qu'en cas qu'il ne trouvât pas bon de presenter lui-même le memoire à sa Sainteté qu'il luy fit scavoir; elle trouveroit quelque autre moyen, estimant que ce seroit trop charger sa conscience que d'ômettre aucune chose de son pouvoir et en effet elle l'eut éprouvé par d'autres voyes, si elle n'eût été assurée que lesdites lettres avoient été données au Prelat, et elle par là quitte de son obligation. Il faut se remettre de tout aux abismes inscrutables des iugemens de Dieu.

Le Doyen de l'Eglise de Nôtre Dame à Münic fut celuy à qui fut envoyé de la part de la Congregation dans Rome le mandement d'emprisonner nôtre Mere, le Duc fut supplié de permettre qu'il sexecutât, et en cas que nôtre Mere fit resistance, de prêter main forte; mais helas que cette precaution fut peu necessaire! Le Duc quoyque d'une part, par tendresse de conscience il ne voulut point luy donner sa protection, d'ailleurs neantmoins il l'estimoit chose indigne et inhumaine

152 Winefrid Wigmore was appointed as Visitor to Liège, Cologne and Trier. Her conflict with the Nuncio Pierluigi Carafa severely aggravated the situation. See introduction to Letters and Documents L4. with the references to Wetter contained therein.

153 Nuncio Ciriaco Rocci.

154 See Peters pp. 568ff. and Wetter pp. 73ff.

155 The identity of this Cardinal is not known.

156 For the text of this letter see Letters and Documents L4. It was written by Mary Ward in Italian, dated 28 November 1630 and addressed to Pope Urban VIII. It seems to have reached its destination, but no answer to it was received.

[*Editor's note.* The text of the English manuscripts A and B resumes from this point.]

Memorial sent to a prelate in Rome to give to the Pope.

[…] submission and satisfaction to his Holynes ᵃadding her humble petition to the said prelateᵃ without injury to any, and to this same effect, enclosed a Memoriall to his Holynes¹⁵⁷ ᵇthat in case he could not or that nott fitt to present itᵇ letᶜ her know so much, she would find some other way, esteeming it as a burthen of Conscience not to doe all in her power in that particular which she had done, had she not beene sure these Letters were delivered, and thereby her duty discharged. All must be left to that abisse etc.

a–a added superscript in A. B: included in main text | b–b added superscript in A. B: included in the main text | c B: to let

157 See note 156 above.

Mary Ward's arrest.

*The Deane¹⁵⁸ of our Blessed Lady her Church in Monaco, was the Man to whom the orders from the Congregation of Rome were directed for her emprisonment, the Duke¹⁵⁹ intreated to allow of it, and in case she resisted to lend his secular power, but alas how little was this needed! For whereas the Duke who though through tendernes of conscience wou'd not protect her, thought it unfit, and inhumane to [41v] emprison one, he was most sure was not as accused and in a present infirmity having kept her Bedd 3 Weekes before, which she never did but upon greatest extreames, to ly in Bedd being to her Infirmity alone. How this came into her thoughts God alone knowes, but on Saint Sebastian his Day in the morning she sayd to us, I hinder my Friends their designe, I will goe abroad that they may see I am not afrayd, nor unwilling they doe their pleasure, and did so, and it had the effect, for on the 7 of February (then a Fryday) about 4 of the clocke in the afternoone, came to our house the fore-named Deane with 2 Canons of the same Church,

reading a Letter directed to himselfe to this tenour. Take Mary Ward for an Hereticke, Schismatike and Rebell to the Holy Church.

She blessed her selfe with horrour to heare that named, which she had as much aversion from as hell it [42r] selfe, and more if Hell cou'd be without Losse of God. She was most undauntedly cheerefull, which indeed the good Priest was not, for the Deane trembled both in voyce and hands; the other 2 Priests had teares in their Eyes: when they named secular power she smiled and told them they shoud not need that trouble, she wou'd goe with them to what soever prison they would, adding sufferance without sinne was not a burthen, they said it shou'd be in the night, when it might not be knowne. She said by noe meanes, the more knowne the better, and that it wou'd be a wrong to her Innocency to seeke darkenes. She ever loved Light, and to doe her workes in and by Light. There were 40 of ours in Family at that time,[160] yet none but her owne Companion, and she that had care of the house knew any thing till she was gone, our dearest Mother wou'd not take Leave[161] to avoyd unquietnes which might have happened.

[* The page numbering in A now follows on consecutively from [40r].]

---

[158] Dean Jakob Golla (1568–1648), Dean of the Frauenkirche in Munich. Peters p. 569.

[159] The Elector Maximilian I.

[160] Five weeks later, in a letter dated 14 March 1631, thirty-three members of the Para-deiserhaus community declared their obedience to the Pope. The seven members who did not sign this declaration were probably lay sisters. Wetter pp. 78ff.

[161] Mary Poyntz (Rectrice) and Elizabeth Cotton (Mary's secretary) were witnesses to the arrest. In a letter dated 13 February 1631 to Elizabeth Keyes in Rome, Elizabeth Cotton says that Mary Ward was not permitted to take leave of the community. ACDF. St. St. O-3g, f. 159rv. See Peters pp. 568–569.

10. Mary Ward's imprisonment in the Anger Convent of Poor Clares.

Description of the Anger Convent. The first night.

I must not omitt how that morning she asked seriously in [42v] what part of the Towne the Monastery of Saint Clare was, which was the place of her emprisonment, and where of the Fryers were Superiours and in that quality were present to see her enter. She had one of her owne who formerly had that happy charge to tend her,[162] her owne Bed, and we were to dresse and send her her Meate which was a most singular satisfaction to us for all respects, and God so thereby[a] disposed[a] that we had meanes to receave and write Letters,[163] for all that passed in her owne name or ours came out of that blessed head and hart of hers, excepting what we wrote to the Duke when she had the holy Oyles, nor was the art God knowes great of our conveyance, yet they searched her very meate, God that knew both our need and our innocency did use that mercy with us.

All that coud be said or done to make her seeme horridd or criminall to the Religious was done, her Prison the Roome that had beene used for all desperate and infectious diseases, [43r] the seeling one might reach with ones hand, two litle Windowes which looked upon the Graves and yet those borded up saving the space of ones hand to give a little light through the glasse, her doore with double Lockes, and chain'd, so many to watch by turnes, and others allotted to come into her, and none but such, none at all to speake to her.

The Abesse[164] commanded under payne of excomunication to let none of hers converse with her by word or Letters, the Religious all in horrour and amazement, exspecting to receave according to the cypher was given this monstruous Heretike, found themselves in a strange surprise of reverence and devotion, beholding they knew not what of Devine in her presence which they found so humble, meeke, peacefull and couragious, which made some of them, one in particular goe to their prayers, she was an auncient Religious, and of noted sanctity, who returning to the Mother Abbesse sayd, how are we misinformed, [43v] this is a holy Servant of God, and our House happy in receaving her; let me have the happynes at the Doore to see her though I speake not, which at her extreame importunity the Mother graunted, and was noe small admiration to our deare Mother to see that dumbe shew, a venerable Religious Women in the Doore on her knees with her hands up, not knowing what it meaned; but this and much more we had from the Religious themselves, as also the precise following words God forbid Christian eares shoud heare what was ordayned them to doe with her.

But to returne to our blessed prisoner, the dispotion[b] of her mind which she so candidly and sereanly recounted herselfe, thus locke up and cheaned etc. there was noe appearance than Death, not onely in regard of the condition of her health and the quality of the place, but also that it seemed impossible that men that had witt shou'd proceed so farre, and let her ever [44r] againe appeare abroad. She knew full well the persons and actours of the busines making an act of resignation, and oblation of herselfe to God, finding an unspeakable content peace and joy of mind in the hope she had that now was come that long wished for Time, wherein she might have nothing to doe but to thinke of God, love him and depend upon him, with confidence he wou'd have care of hers. In this disposition she went to her Bed, hoping to rest very quietly, all Labours being now taken out of her hands, but in all these her contents, she found as it were a suspension of the graunt from above and rather something that had of the checke that she shou'd thinke it enough to suffer and not labour, she did not murmurre, but had a little inclination to dispute, but resolved to doe neither then but sleepe, and this notwithstanding the condition of her mind, and the extreame smell the Bedsteed [44v] and Walls had of spitt, and such like as contagious and dying People doe ordinarily leave. The exteriour she soone overcame, but in her mind grew a strong force and threate if she did not resolve to labour in the defence of her owne and hers their innocency, and consequently her owne delivery, which at Length she promised to doe and so fell a sleep which till this resolution made, she by noe meenes cou'd doe, so slept well according to her slepes.

a–a B: disposed thereby | b B: disposition

---

162   Anne Turner. Peters p. 571.
163   Mary Ward used the wrapping paper to write letters in lemon juice to Mary Poyntz and Elizabeth Cotton. Twenty-three of these letters survive, with transcripts of sixteen further letters in Elizabeth Cotton's handwriting. AIM Letters 56, and 57–78. The other side of the lemon juice correspondence has not survived. Peters pp. 570ff and Wetter pp. 73 ff.
164   Katharina Bernardine Gräffin. Peters p. 572.

Unceasing prayer at the Paradeiserhaus. Petition to the Pope. Death of two adversaries and severe illness of a third. Permission for Mary Ward to attend Mass daily.

But what or who can expresse the sensibility hers were left in, considering the state of her health. The power and violence of her Ennemyes seemed to shut up all recourse but to God, to whom they betooke themselves day and night without ceasing. The next morning after her being carried away from us, came 2 Fryers, those that had beene present at her going into the Monastery.[165] I confes my wickednes, it was [45r] growne a horrour to me, to see Priest or Fryer but at the Altar, and in the Confession Seate, which that blessed Servant of God did sharpely reprehend, seeking to imprint in us all, that treasure which she herselfe possessed in an unexpressable degree of loving Ennemyes. But these good Fryers came with mutch charity to comfort us, and related the assured innocency that the tranquility of her mind, her alacrity and courage did testify, and that seeing a tendernes in them so farre as to weepe, she used persuasive words of consolation, and that for her part there was noe need, she found herselfe too much honnour'd, being a Sinner to be treated in the manner of Saints, that sufferance without sinne cou'd be noe burthen.

Three Dayes after we receaved a note from her of what we were to doe, and the Memoriall to be presented his Holines in our names the contents of the which were, a briefe [45v] Relation of what had beene done with most humble petition his Holynes wou'd call her to Rome, and let her be judged under his owns Eyes, freed or condemned,[166] which Memoriall found beyond expectation grace and acceptance in the fatherly hart of his Holines, in so much as he made it be treated in his owne presence, and order sent for her immediate freedome,[167] without any ty[a] to appeare in Rome or other whatsoever, and this was sent to our owne hands, not to the Deane who had emprisoned her.

In this interim which was from Friday 7th of February till Fryday 15th of April, two of her greatest Ennemyes dyed suddenly,[168] to the publike note of all the Towne, the third[169] in a strange and sudden accident was despaired of by the best Physitians, which this true Servant of Christ our dearest Mother hearing, put herselfe in prayer, with protestation not to rise till his Life was graunted, her prayer lasted long and he recovered, we may believe at her [46r] Instance, both for the proofes we have of their efficacy, and that few if any prayed for him.

We perceaving that our dear Mother was not permitted neither to heare Masse, nor goe to the Sacraments, argued the matter with the said Deane, and laid it to his charge to answer as his owne action; the good Man of himselfe was sufficiently enclined and enough assured of her Innocency and holines, but durst doe nothing but by order of some in Towne, who did and had made use of him in that busines all along. What with this and the endeavours we used to lay before the Duke the unbecoming the Piety of his Highness to let such things passe, order was given the Abbesse she shou'd heare Mass daily, which made not onely greatly to her owne comfort, but common Consolation to all the Religious, who were come to a high esteeme of her eminent vertue, and seemed as if their Soules profited by the onely sight of her.

a missing in B; C: sans l'obliger de parêtre à Rome.

---

165 The Superiors of the Anger Convent. See f. 42v.

166 Wetter pp. 77ff. These official letters, written by Elizabeth Cotton on 13 February 1631, are in the archives of the Holy Office. Mary Ward's lemon juice letters directing Elizabeth Cotton are in the Congregatio Jesu archives in Munich. See Note 163.

167 Mary Ward and her companions were unware of the true situation in Rome. The documents in the archives of the Holy Office (to which there was no access till 1998) show that every decision, including the Decree for Mary's imprisonment and the summons for her to appear in Rome (ACDF Decreta S.O. 1630, ff.196v–197r) was either ordered or approved by Pope Urban VIII. Wetter Ch. V and VI.

168 These were Jesuits: Johannes Ludovico SJ and Jakob Keller SJ, who died on 19 January and 23 February respectively. AIM Letters 56/9.

169 Adam Contzen SJ, who in the early months of 1631 suffered from very severe attacks of the stone. AIM Letters 56/11.

Dangerous illness with violent fever. Declaration of unfailing loyalty to the Church. Reception of the Sacraments and last rites.

About the 18th of March she fell into a violent Feaver, so as the Physi-tians [46v] assured there was eminent danger, and no hopes of Life if she remained in that place, upon which we made a petition to the Duke he wou'd use his Authority in behalfe of her Innocency and the justnes of the request, and cause that she might come into our owne House[a], that we might serve her as her need and our duty required on which condition we yealded our House to be the Prison, and our selves all Prisoners with her and His Highnes might putt what guards he pleased. At first the Duke thought it very reasonable but tendernes of Conscience enclined him to consult it and it was concluded a thing out of his power etc. so as the busines still lay in God's hands alone. When it was ordayned she shou'd have her Viaticum, the good Deane his Leave was to be procured,[170] who pleased to take the courage to deny her the Sacraments of Confession and Communion, unles first she signed a Paper of his presenting of these contents, that if she had ever sayd or done any thing contrary [47r] to Faith or holy Church, she repented her and was sorry for it. She lying as it were in agony, her lower parts already cold tooke the paper and read it, and after some small pawsing with great serenety, and as much resolution sayd God forbid I shou'd to cancell veniall sinnes which through God's mercyes are all I have to accuse my selfe of, I shou'd comitt a mortall, and cast so great a blott upon so many innocent and deserving Persons. My if[b] with what already[c] is[c] acted by my adversaryes, woud give just cause to the World to believe I suffer justly. No I will cast my selfe on the mercyes of Christ[d], and rather dy without Sacraments. Her adversaryes thought heare had beene a notable proofe of her obstinacy and perversenes, which some weake headed People enclined to interpret so, but wise and prudent People knew[e] the obligation there is for each to stand upon their owne right, especially in that abominablest of crimes. She called for Penn and Incke, and wrott, that she [47v] never had, nor to gayne millions of lives, wou'd doe, thinke or say the least that might be contrary to the Catholike Church; but contrary-wise from youngest yeares she had employed her Life and Labours in service of holy Church etc.[171] This Paper she caused us to present to the Deane, and lett him know that other for certaine she wou'd not signe, and if he let her dy without the Sacraments, it shou'd be his charge to answer etc. He had not a word of dispute or contradiction, so as she had the Sacraments[172] and last rights of holy Church, with as much expression of Love and esteeme from all the Religious, the Confessour himselfe had teares in his Eyes when he gave her the Holy Oyles.

---

a B: house to be the; C: qu'elle s'en retournât chez elle | b in A: *if* crossed out and replaced by *doing so*, seemingly in another hand; C: En disant, Si i'ay fait ou dit quelque chose contre la Sainte Eglise etc | c–c B: is already | d B: God; C Jesus-Christ | e B: knew well; C: scavoient bien

170 Peters pp. 179ff. and Wetter pp. 81ff.
171 Copy of this letter in Elizabeth Cotton's handwriting dated 27 March 1631 in AIM
Letters 82. The original was sent by Dean Golla to the Holy Office in Rome.
172 Mary Ward received the sacraments and last rites on 28 March 1631. Peters p. 580.

Farewell to the Companions. Unexpected recovery.

This hapened on the first of Aprill 1631 all about her expecting
when she wou'd give up her last breath, she looking made signes to
her Companion that served her, to give her her cloaths, insinuating
she wou'd [48r] rise, which she, as also the Mother Abbesse tooke for
proposterous, nay said she I know what I doe, I must take leave of
my deare ones, Mother Abbesse will not deny me the grace to see and
speake to them at the grate (for she knew we were in the Church) sayd
she, you will doe me the Charity to carry me, as they did with such
amazement, as they had not other word to say but, oh what love, o what
Love! She bid us take courage, and confide in God, who wou'd not let
her dy then if not so most for his glory, bid us be sure lived she or dyed
she, we shou'd have noe bitternes against the actours of it, but pardon
them intirely and pray for them hartily, which done she returned to her
Bed in the same Agony as before, which continued till about 9 of the
cloake at Night, when she fell into a short but sweet and naturall sleepe,
and when awaked sayd I know not what our Lord will doe with me, me
thinkes I am better. The Physitian [48v] coming the next morning found
a remarkable change to the better to his unspeakable admiration and
past his skill to find out the why or by what meanes. And with this his
admiration hastned to tell the Dutches,[173] whose venerable and tender
affection he knew to be so great to this Servant of God, and told her
Highnes to recover in any place had beene miracle playne enough, but
to recover in that place which was sufficient to have killed her when in
best health, was that God wou'd make it more then playne to be seene
to the confusion and reprehension of her Ennemyes.

173 The doctor attending Mary Ward was the personal physician to the Electoral family.
AIM Letters 56/10.

Release (April 14th 1631).

On the 15th of Aprill[174] came the order for her freedome, which ours
with unexplicable[a] joy hastned to carry her to the Monastery hoping
to have brought her out with them. But she noe more joyed to come
out, then daunted to enter in, after complying with their expressions,
desired them to have [49r] Patience till Munday (this was Fryday) for
she had devotion to passe her Palme-Sunday with those good Religious,
it being a Day whereunto she bore great devotion, having on it made

her first vow of Chastity.[175] As she said she did, and on the Munday she returned home, notwithstanding much tendernes in the Religious, but to the generall joy, and with the congratulation of all abroad, even the Citizens and Townes Folkes as she passed in Coach the Streets.

a B: inexplicable

---

[174] Once again there are discrepancies over the dates. The Friday before Palm Sunday was 11 April. Dean Golla must have spoken to Mary Ward on that date, but he released her on the evening of 14 April. He wrote to Rome on 15 April to say that he had done so and had given her instructions for her journey to Rome. Permission from the Pope and the Holy Office came later, in a letter dated 10 May. See Wetter pp. 84 ff.

[175] Palm Sunday 1609. See AB 6, note 29.

11. Journey to Rome and audience with Pope Urban VIII. Continuing surveillance by the Inquisition. Continuing illness; visit to San Casciano dei Bagni. Community life allowed, but as lay persons.

Journey to Rome. Audience with Pope Urban VIII (March 1632).

Now[176] had her adversaryes a new game to play, by the petition formerly mentioned appeared her desire to be in Rome, which wou'd wholly crosse a designe they had by having reported, that were she in Rome, she wou'd have beene burnt alive in Campo Fiore, and for this End pretended orders from Rome the was not to stirre, meane while negotiated in Rome to the same End alleadging, she was old and decrepit. But they much missed of their marke, ayming to bring her to their wayes, by her [49v] beliefe of their simple and silly propositions who without seeing orders from Rome[177] wou'd not move the least and what came thence submitted to at what somever price, without disputing if[a] God by direct or indirect wayes[a] laying her Life and honour before the very shadow of what had report to the Churches Authority, nor did Allmighty God leave unrequited in some degree this Liberality of hers to his sacred Spouse the Church; for what aymed at ignominy as was her change of cloathes[178] before all the rest, the Bull etc. God turned to her glory, as appeared particularly by the singular and extraordinary favours done her by all the Princes along in her way to Rome, where when arrived found a wonted or more benignity from their Eminencyes the Cardinalls, and lastly when she had the happynes to be at his Holynes his feete,[179] what more coud there be of benignity expressed? When she said holy [50r] Father, I neither am nor ever have beene Heretike, his Holynes interrupting woud not let her goe on, said we believe it, we believe it, we neede noe other proofe, we and the Cardinalls all, are not onely satisfyed but edifyed at your proceedings, neither must you thinke

much to have beene proved as you have beene, for such have beene the
proceedings of other Popes with other Servants of God.

a–a C: si les voyes dont on y avoit procedé étoient directes ou indirectes

---

176   This period was complicated by cross-currents and different interests in Rome, and
by the anxiety and suspicions of Elizabeth Cotton. Orders had been given by the Holy
Office for Mary Ward's journey to Rome, with stringent conditions under which she was
to travel. See Wetter Ch. VI, which draws on the correspondence kept in the archives of
the Holy Office in Rome.

177   Mary set out for Rome on 24 October 1631. After a difficult journey, impeded by
the plague in Italy at this time and the requirement to present herself to Inquisitors in the
cities through which she travelled, she reached Rome on 4 March 1632, or shortly before.
Wetter pp. 97–99.

178   Mary Ward and her companions had been ordered to live as lay people and to wear
secular dress. Wetter pp. 88–89.

179   The audience with Pope Urban VIII took place soon after Mary's arrival in Rome.
On 26 May 1632 the Cardinals of the Inquisition, at a sitting in S Maria Sopra Minerva,
decreed that Mary Ward and her companions had been found to be innocent of any offence
against the faith. Wetter pp. 99–103.

Permission to travel to San Casciano dei Bagni.

When the yeare after diverse of our Gentlewomen going to Rome,
some Prelats by instigation of our wonted good Friends spake to the
Pope, as if nott fitt they shoud live together with our dearest Mother
alleadging, it wou'd be a disannulling of the Bull etc. his Holines with
earnestnes answered where shou'd they live, or where can they live so
well?[180] But o the infatigability of her Ennemyes, when their malice was
blunted in one place, sharpened it in an other, forgetting God who was
present in all places, had an[d] hath still the Protection of the Innocent
in his owne hands. Things standing thus in Rome, they spred [50v] in
England and the low Countryes, that she was confined for her life in
Rome, and to make this good they found much to doe, but thought noe
Labour too great, and effected so much, that our dear Mother vehemently oppressed with the stone (which was one of her daily infirmities,
and had beene of many yeares, both in kidney and blader) was going
to the Bathes of Cassiano, a remedy by her experienced, his Holynes
sent to her a Prelate of note, to let her know it was his will, for some
respects and reasons of state, she shou'd not goe out of Rome,[181] to
which she replyed with her wonted sweet und undaunted manner, I am
then a Prisoner am I? The Prelate againe, no on noe termes, you are
free, most free, neither is there any thing in you doubtfull, nay I can be
witnes how tender and fatherly a love his Holynes doth beare you, but
there are some respects for the which he wou'd you shou'd not stirre.
Heere her Ennemyes had two great bootyes [51r] in hand, the confirmation of the report made, as also hopes that the want of this remedy

wou'd soone end her Life. This blessed and magnanimous Servant of
God replyed, hard case my life and honour lyes heer at the stake. I know
how farre my obligation by^a me^a, but tell his Holynes I lay the both at
his feete not onely willingly but with devotion: at which wordes and the
maner with which they were spoken, the Prelate was so touched, as the
teares trickled doune his cheekes, which when he gave account of to his
Holynes, who was the perfection of Noblenes and good nature, wou'd
heare of noe more respects but she shoud goe whither she wou'd and^b as
she wou'd. Which message when brought our dear Mother who satt fully
contented in what the devine disposition shou'd part to her, prepared for
her journey, and went.

a–a A: the reading is uncertain; *lies* seems to have been altered to *by me*; B: by me; C: ie
scay bien iusqu'où le devoir m'oblige | b B: or; C: où et comme

180   Winefrid Wigmore and Catherine Smith, travelling from Liège, arrived in Rome in
December 1632. In 1633 they were joined by others, including some of the young English
members who had entered in 1630. It seems that common life, lived as lay people, was
eventually tolerated in Rome, Munich and a few other places. Wetter Ch. XI.
181   Mgr Alessandro Boccabella, a prelate of the Pope's household and consultor of the
Holy Office. The documents in the archives of the Holy Office show that the situation was
not as simple as the author of the *English Vita* makes out. Mary Ward's original request
(February 1634) was for travel to her native England, to recover her health. When this
was refused, she asked permission to take the waters at San Casciano dei Bagni, and to
stay there for the summer. Permission was given, provided that she was kept under the
surveillance of an Inquisitor. Wetter pp. 174–176.

Time spent in San Casciano (1634). The watchfulness of the Inquisition.

When arrived at the Bathes[182] (which is a place mightely frequented
by all sorts for the great vertue of those waters) the second day being
at the Fountayne she told her Companion such a Religious Man there
present shewing her him, is put to be my [51v] Spy, and perseaving
her to be somewhat daunted there at, sayd doe not doubt God will help
us, we will so pray to his good Angel, as he shall not be able to say
aught in prejudice of God's honour or our Innocency, and so went on
with all alacrity. Two dayes after the father sickened, and in 8 Dayes
dyed. This past she tooke on her waters, but not in that quantity her
infirmity required, her forces not permitting her which made the Physitians conclude she must drinke them again in the Autumne, and passe
those heates in some good ayre,[183] and for that purpuse Piano Castagnano (a most delicious solitude of the Marques de Monte) was judg'd
the most convenient qualifyed so as to contribute to her health, and
please her mind, which allwayes delighted in solitude. The Marques
with all imaginable civility gave her the full power of that place, with
such exactnes as the Governour thereof wou'd not so much as lodge

the Capucins without her Leave, though she used but few roomes [52r] and the house consisted of 300 nor woud admitt of the Spanish Embassadour, he requiring to refresh himselfe for some few howers, being hunting there about, without our Mother her Leave. As soone as arrived there, she informed herselfe what Priests or Religious there were, that she might choose her a Confessour, and concluded to take one of the mitigated of Saint Francis called there, Gaudentes, (there being but that and the Parish Church) a Man of singular Learning and exemplar Life which was what she had regard unto; but God had therein his speciall Providence, as by what followed, appear'd.

Two miles off, lived a vertuous but afflicted Gentlewomen, who for 2 Yeares had had a languishing desire to speake with our dear Mother and thought this a most convenient occasion, and for that End invited her to her House, for herselfe cou'd not stirre abroad, the request all circumstances considered was so reasonable as not to be deny'd, whereupon the Day was [52v] appointed, but the very night before she was seazed with a violent feaver, and Recipula[a] in her Face and Head, both the suddenes and violence amazed each one, herselfe in her wonted even manner sayd, there is some thing in this more then we know, we will not goe this Time, but keepe in the ordinary way. The evill went away as it came without any remedy which confirmed the former supposition, and was cause she deny'd an other invitation which a Cardinall made her, desiring to make acquaintance betweene her, and a vertuous Sister of his.[184]

When the Time fitt for drinking the waters came, she returned to the Bathes directly, where she was loved and honoured of all, for she had a most devine art in making this Life happy and so as to gayne heaven, for her very presence carryed with it a curbe to vice, and vertue did as its due, clayme and take the first place. It was straunge; but so it was the most iealous Italien, esteemed her company a sufficient [53r] Guard for their Wives, and with her they might go abroade, and recreate, and such were her civilityes and compleatnes, as it was ordinary to say her Presence made each place a court. She had indeed as one may say joyned and made agree in one the excellencyes of Nature and grace. 5 Dayes after her above said returne to the Bathes, a Religious Man wholly a stranger to her, came to her saying he had a secret to discover, which he had many motions to doe, and as many motives to forbeare, and those greatly importing his owne interest, or he shou'd be undone, if it came to be knowne, but finally he found remorse of conscience in willing to conceale it, and that the example she gave assured him. She was highly wronged, and charity did forbid to see Innocency suffer when one coud help it. In fine he up and told her, how that such a Religious Man of his owne order had beene appointed to be her spy (who was the same hereselfe had told us of and then dead). [53v] For as soone as she departed

Rome, information was given, that she had God knowes what designes, meaned to goe for England, and that it was of exceeding great consequence that she were prevented whereupon order[b] was[b] given to all the Inquisitours to stoppe her, and namely Perugia, Citta della Pieva, Siena, Ratiofani and Piano Castagnano where she had passed the heates, and without knowing had the Inquisitor for her Confessour, who by occasion of seeing her admirable Life and conversation, wrott such an Information as they said was not onely sufficient for a Justification, but even a Canonization. So many orders given out, coud not long be conceald, so as, not onely this good Religious Man, but Seculars there at the Bathes came to know it, to their noe small feeling that a Person so qualifyed shoud be so wronged, and persuaded her not to venture her Life and honour where force might carry it. She was bound to help herselfe, their Persons [54r] and Moneys were at her Service, they were Toscans and free from the Ecclesiasticall Estate. She was gratefull for their civilityes, but had too strong a Faith, for feare to produce other effect in her then a smile, saying, she woud end her waters and then for Rome. But first made her wonted visitt to our Blessed Lady of Monte Giovino,[185] to the noe small I may say mortal apprehensions of her Companions, being to passe Citta della Pieva, where one of the orders lay. In her returne from our blessed Laydes[c], they counting the Stepps and moments till she was out of the Popes Estate, saw her stand to speake to a poore Priest that asked for an Almes, thought they had all right on their side to wonder she woud doe aught, might hazard her Person, and she with much earnestnes replyed I had rather perish in doing my duty, then by the neglect escape.

a C: une grande inflammation au visage | b–b B: orders were; C: des mandemens furent envoyées | c | B: Ladyes

---

[182] Mary, with two companions, travelled to San Casciano in May 1634. Wetter Ch. XII.

[183] July and August.

[184] Aware that she was being watched, Mary was careful to keep within the Papal States. She returned to Rome in November 1634.

[185] Mary Ward had a particular devotion to this shrine of Our Lady. See above, f. 29r, and PL No. 36.

Audience and appeal to the Pope.

After her returne to Rome, visiting divers Cardinalls of the Congregation, found the wonted [54v] and also more civility which did not so lull her a Sleep as to make her forget the right she had to her honnour, and the cause she had to bemoane herselfe for the carriage of business. Having the grace to have audience[186] of his holynes which was most willingly and gratiously granted her, she said as followeth. Holy Father

what more remaineth whereby poore Mary Ward may give testimony of
her fidelity and Loyalty to your Holynes and the Catholike Church, but
that thus my life my honnour and my Liberty must be put into the hands
of men too too easy to be subordned and corrupted? Though his Holynes
forth of his great benignity gave her Leave to end her speech, his eyes
and countenance did seeme fatherly to interrupt her, and finally sayd, be
satisfyed it shalle be so noe more; none shall be able to wrong you with
us, which his holynes did not onely performe in effects, but by many
singular expressions, as the augmentation of her pension, the^a ordaining^a
a Coach [55r] out of the Palace Stables to be ever at her service, tooke
care what Wine she drunke, appointing her to have the same himselfe
drunke of, saying, that kind of wine woud best^b suite with her stomake.
In a Sickenes which she had, he called Donna Constanza, his Sister in
Law to him, bid her see our dear Mother wonted^c for nothing, that his
Physitian shoud visit her, and have all cordialls or other from his owne
Apothecary. His Holynes never denyed her private audience.

a–a B: the ordinary ordaining | b missing in B | c C: qu'elle ne manquât de rien

[186] The documents of the Holy Office record this audience as having taken place on 16
November 1634, but not the content. Wetter p. 181.

12. Following a grave illness (1636/1637) Mary proposed a journey to Spa, near Liège, to take the waters. The Pope consented to her request.

Severe illness (1636/1637). Plans to travel to Spa. Papal approval.

December the Yeare 1636 she fell into a great Infirmity and paynes of
the Stone, of the which there was litle or noe mitigation. From the 2 of
January 1637 till the 13th of March she never went forth of her Chamber
which was as much as to say her Bed, then the Physitians concluded the
Sea ayre might doe her good, whereupon she was carryed to Neptuno,[187]
where her infirmityes had some relaxation so as she cou'd goe to Masse,
(which for the [55v] first time was on our blessed Lady her Annoncia-
tion) and some times walke in the woods: His Holynes unasked gave
order to the Gouvernour to shew her all the civilityes that place cou'd
afford. For some litle Time after her returne to Rome she was more at
ease, but on the 22 of July, she fell into a most violent feaver, so as
in all humane opinion it was her last. On the 30th of the same Month
she had her Viaticum and holy Oyles as also his Holynes his blessing,
which Cardinall Saint Onophrio delivered with great feeling and to us a
condolence of our Losse, but recalling himselfe said, we were to blesse
God for having left her us so many yeares, and till such time as she
by her words and example had left who to governe us in her absence.

Thus she continued with litle or noe change, onely she did live cou'd hardly breath, sleeping or waking, noe longer then fanned. On^a the 10th of August having paste the night in great paine, ^a she told the party that watched with her (which was her owne Companion) that she woud go to the Spaw,[188] who wholly [56r] amazed knew not what to conclude, but greatly feared the Feaver was more violent in her head then wonted, which she perceaved, and answering her thoughts sayd, No I am not out of my selfe, but I will goe to the Spaw. I doe not my selfe know what God will doe by it, but in the humaine be it as it will, heere I must dy, there I may recover: the other replyd, but where is there where^b withal? God sayd she will provide.

When this was once knowne abroad one might perceave an unquiet, and dislike in some that durst not expresse why nor whereatt, but force cannot long be conceald. They durst noe more endeavour her injury with occasion of evill, therefore now it was insinuated to his holynes as an action worthy himselfe to stay her going, so to preserve her Life. The greatnes of his Holynes his charity, and goodnes of his nature was sufficient to make him have those apprehensions, but the opinion he had of her sanctity swayed all, as his words to those of hers that were to take leave and his Holynes his blessing in her behalf (she [56v] not being able herselfe to goe or stand) did make appeare, and were these. It is certaine that humanely speaking the journey must needs kill her, without a possibility to escape but she is Gods Servant, he will guide her to doe what is best, and we know not what God will doe by her, all our Nuntios[189] where she passeth, shall receave her, where she may stay and rest herselfe by the way, when and as long as she will, for we doe esteem her a Women of great Prudence, of great courage and spirit, and what is most for a holy and great Servant of God. And you that goe with her obey and serve her, and so long you will doe well. Neither may I omitt (though not in its due place) an other expression or testimony of his Holines his singular esteeme of her. Many English and Persons of note being in those Times in Rome, as well Heretikes as Catholikes, one told his Holynes (in what sense God and himselfe knowes) that there was [57r] great resort of those English to our House, to which his Holynes answered, we are glad, for none but good will haunt that place, or will gett good by it.

a–a A: inserted superscript, followed by the words *and disaster* crossed out | b missing in B; C: mais où y a-t-il de quoy?

---

187   Nettuno, a small town on the coast, south of Rome.
188   Spa, near Liège, where Mary Ward had gone to take the waters in 1616. Peters p. 186. The Pope's permission was given on 13 August 1637, followed by permission on 20 August 1637 for two or three companions to accompany her. Wetter p. 185 (the ACDF references are given in the German original).

13. Departure from Rome (1637). Journey to Liège via Siena, Florence, Bologna, Milan, Turin, the Mont Cenis Pass, Lyons and Paris, where she stayed for five months, reaching Liège in late May 1638.

From Rome to Paris. Meetings with friends and hospitality received throughout the journey.

But now to the passage in hand. The appointed Day to begin that journey and in effect was the 10th of September 1637.[190] The raines not being yet fallen in any quantity, divers judged it temerity, her answer still was, God will dispose, and in effect we found it, it beginning to rayne excessively an hower or two before Sunne sett, continued till about 2 of the cloake next morning, so as all occasion or rash judgment was taken away, and this blessed Servant of God began her journey taken aut of her Bed by force of armes, and layd into the Litter. This was the beginning of her last carreere, of her great if not greatest sufferance. Every passage and action carryd with it I know not what of note and weight as if a full point or conclusion to all the fore-passed.

She went on till Siena, where she fell ill of a great Feaver and Plurisy so as fayne [57v] to lett bloud, as a desperate cure her weakenes considered. She was entertained by a Gentleman of that place, that had long wished such an occasion to expresse his owne and Wives devotion. He was Signor Girolamo Mann, and she[a] Isabella Guelfi, and none of the Nobility did faile to visitt her, and particularly those of the Pucolhuomini, with some of which she had very speciall friendship. Neither did the Arch Bishop of that place leave to expresse himselfe by his letters to his Brother the Generall Pucolhuomini, that famous Warrier. In 10 Dayes she was able to be layd in Litter and so on to Florence, where she rested 12 Dayes in the Duke of Northumberland her ancient acquaintance his House, partly to gaine her owne forces and partly to give satisfaction to Friends. In Bologna she was lovingly, longingly, and reverently expected by her intimate dear Friend that great [58r] Servant of God, Signor Cesare Bianchetti of the most noble by Birth and more by vertue. He was so covetous of occasions to expresse his esteem as to be envious of the honnour Servants had, and when he cou'd did displace them, leading her sometimes carrying a stoole or chayre, seeing that there wanted not wood for her fire, yea and that her very Servants had what he thought fitt for them. From thence she went on to Milan where she did her wonted devotions to Saint Charles though ill as she was. Heere was great difficulty to goe on in regard of the Wares betweene Spayne and Savoy, so as she left Litter and went in Coach, and passed where of two Yeares none ever had, and not onely safely but without appearance of danger never seeing what might frighten or terrify, arriving at the River side of Vercelli the Captaine of the Guard came in boate to fetch her Passe to the Gouvernour, who imediately sent his Coach to fetch her in, making extraordinary demonstration of the honnour he boare her, and amongst others gave her the freedome of a Prisoner an English Souldier. [58v] As soone as Monsignore Nuntio (then Monsignor Cappelli[b]) at Turino, had notice of our dear Mother arrivall there, he sent his cheefe Gentleman to invite her to his Pallace, there to repose her selfe till at least the hart of winter were past, but she refused, not intending to make any stay. But this worthy Prelate wou'd take noe denyall so as she was forced to yeald and accept of his curtesyes, which indeed were great above expression, and he was pleased to say, his Holynes his comands included so much, as depriv'd him of the happynes to serve her in any thing as his owne act. Her Altezza Reale (though then in the height of her mourning, the Duke being newly dead) sent the Master of Ceremonyes with a most gracious message, and twelve staffiers loaden with most curious[191] sweet-meates, wine, and choycest fowle, gave her Audience, though all others were excluded, offering her any pleasure or favour she cou'd doe her.

[59r] On the 3[d] of November she parted Turin in the Nuntio his Coach to the Foote of the Mountaine which she passed in chaire upon Saint Martin his Day in a most terrible Snow and wind, so as fouer passengers perished, as had all but by God's singular mercyes, not onely by the cold, but on the topp of the hill, the Guides so blinded by the snow, lost their way, and had noe other humane Guidance[c] but the instinct of a little dogg, which served through God's providence to bring us safe. She made noe stay till Lyons,[192] where she was forced to rest herselfe one whole day, thence to Paris, where she made full account to have found her bills of exchange, and so to have passed on without stay, but they fayled her and some proved unkind who had great obligation to her. But God that permitted the one, provided an other unexpected to supply.[193]

a B: the | b C: Caffarelli | c missing in B

---

190 Mary Ward was accompanied by Mary Poyntz, Winefrid Wigmore, and four servants, one of whom would have been Anne Turner. See Peters pp. 600–604 for the details of this journey and the friends who assisted on the way.

191 'elaborate'.

192 Vita I says that from Tours to Lyons Mary Ward rode on horseback. From Lyons to Paris she had to take a litter.

193 The English Benedictine monastery of St Edmund in Paris assisted with a generous loan, which was later repaid. Peters p. 601 and Douai Abbey, England, Council Book 17 December 1637.

From Paris to Liège during the unrest and dangers caused by the Thirty Years War.

But meane time Winter over-tooke her, and her paynes of the stone extremly encreased, so as till about the 20th of May she cou'd not stirre, and then [59v] were such desperate times for Souldiers and robbing, as all that spoake humanely assured her she woud not passe one dayes journey with the cloathes on her backe, with such she held noe dispute, but with those that understood the wayes and Language of God Allmighty his Servants, she wou'd say, she found noe warrant but where her busines lay, and there she cou'd not feare, her busines was to the Spaw, what God wou'd with her, she confessed she cou'd not tell, whither her cure or what. But thither she must goe as she did, and passed without any one danger, so that who robbed others in her sight, passed by her with hatt in hand.

And whereas upon the river[194] betweene Charleville and Dinant fifteene Souldiers at once bourded her boate with barbarous and horridd aspects, no sooner had they beheld her, but one might visibly see a dread and feare to seaze upon them which made them thinke long till out of the boate againe, and petitioned it as a grace. She had hyred the [60r] Boate for herselfe and her owne Company, and gave 3 poore Passengers, 2 Men, and one Women their place. The Men seeing the power of her words and being to passe yet greater dangers, begged the grace, that she wou'd owne them as belonging to her, which she did, when the Officiers at Charlemont came to make their search, (which is allwayes done with great rigour) the poore Women seeing the good successe of the others and herselfe deprived of it, gave into one of her Companions hands all the litle stocke of money she had. When some 10 dayes after, in which Time she had suffred much she found us out at Leege, she cou'd not satisfy herselfe with expressing, and admiring the miraculous things she had seene, knowing by experience what it was to passe that way, for her husband being an Ingenier[195] in France, and she and her Family being in Liege, went oft too and froe though with hazard of her Life to fetch of his gaynes for their livelyhood. In fine she desired noe other protection [60v] then a passeport in her hand which our dear Mother smiled at, calling it great simplicity and folly, but cou'd not satisfy her importunity without something, so she wrott[a] to her Kinsman Father Thomas Conyers[196] then[b] living at Dinant. But it was not this poor Woman alone that admired this her passage, but all that heard it, and knew the present state of things in particular the sayed Father Thomas Conyers[a.b] sayd it was evidently miraculous. And that most Venerable Religious Father Bernard Berrington[197] answering her Letter which gave him notice of her safe arrivall in Liege, said she ought to esteeme the happy successe of that journey amongst the principall graces God ever had done her.

a–a C: luy donna une lettre à porter au Pere Thomas Conyers son parent qui demeuroit pour lors à Dinant. Mais cette pauvre femme ne fut pas la seule qui admiroit cét heureux passage, car tous ceux qui en eurent cônéssance, et qui s'entendoient au present état des choses, demeurent dans l' extreme étonnement d'une chose si nouvelle et inouye, nommément le dit Pere | b–b missing in B

---

194   The journey between Charleville, Dinant and Liège was usually made by boat along the Meuse.
195   Engineer
196   Thomas Conyers SJ (1562–1639), related to Mallorys, Middletons, Wards etc, had founded a Jesuit house in Dinant. Foley III, pp. 210–214.
197   Bernard Berrington OSB resided at St Edmund's Priory, Paris, for many years. Appointed Vicar for part of France in 1620 until his death in 1639. Allanson, *English Benedictines*, 1842, ed. Cramer 1999.

14. A year spent in Liège and Spa, from May 1638 to May 1639. Business in Cologne and Bonn. Arrival in England.

Care for a woman suffering from cancer in Liège and Spa. Time spent in the Abbey of Stavelot.

The season not serving as yet for the Spaw she continued in Liege, in which interim a certaine Lady of greate note and fame in eminent danger of her Life with a Cancer in her breast, had beene informed that our dearest Mother [61r] had many fine receipts, and done great cures. So as she sent a very compleate and submissive message entreating she wou'd comme and see her, and for that end sent her coach, this blessed Servant of God had too much charity to deny any the comfort or assistance she cou'd give them, and this with laying a side all that had of the proper, after once or twice seeing the soare, she told her opinion, and desired the Lady shou'd not rest upon her skill, but the Lady as if careles of all but to have her visit, wou'd heare of nothing but of seeing her as oft as she cou'd. And for this end when the time of Spaw came, made hereselfe be carryed thither, and lodged in the same house. Nor did she alone receave the satisfaction, her husband protested, that where as he had beene as a Man halfe distracted, both for the great and merited affection he boare his Lady, as also well knowing the consequence her Life was to his Estate and family, the moment [61v] she came into his house, he seemed to see as an Angell from Heaven sent to take all weight and anxiety from his hart. Which happynes never left him as he acknowledged in word and deed, not onely to her owne Person, but to others at their intreaty. But to returne to the Lady her paynes encreased, which had noe sweetning neither day nor night but by the presence of our dearest Mother whose charity ever felt more the paynes of others then her owne, putt her Life by this occasion in eminent danger, having so great necessity of the Waters, and taking them with so unproportionable circumstances. The Lady coming neere her End, none but this true and disinterested friend durst propose her preparing for that last passage, which was putt of with a strange and unexpected unwillingnes, not enclining to confesse or communicate though but of devotion. And whereas all her delight was to see her [62r] she now grew awfull, which did not serve to lessen the fidelity of this Friend and Servant of God, who by her importune, and opportune means gained her to receave the Sacraments with much satisfaction, and at last dyed with great peace and quiet to the unexpressable satisfaction of all the whole Family.

The paynes she tooke and incomodity she suffred in and by this occasion, was cause that the Spaw Waters had little effect, and when we murmured at it she wou'd smile and say, So I doe what my Master sent me for, what imports it whither I recover? Which God Allmighty was pleased to make her ratify in a mortall sickenes, which tooke her at Stavelot,[198] a place exceeding remote and solitary, which she loved so much as she thought it capable to restore her health, which we cannot say did not, at least God did cure her in it, for in despayre according to the humane of Life, recover'd without humane helpes, to the great admiration of the Religious [62v] of that great Abbay, as was the alacrity and peace of mind where with she did suffer it.

---

[198] The royal Benedictine Abbey at Stavelot, two miles from Liège, where the Prince Bishop Ferdinand of Liège was titular Abbot. Chambers II, p. 451.

Business in Cologne, Bonn and Liège. Arrival in England on 20 May 1639. Audience with Queen Henrietta Maria, letters of recommendation having been written by Cardinal Francesco Barberini, the Pope's nephew, in the previous September.

One may say that her Life was but a subsistance so fare as to suffer. Now that Winter was come on, and she but convalescent, and after her drinking of the Waters was forced to goe to Collen,[199] thence to Bone to speake with the Prince Elector about busines not to be put off, returned to Liege in November, and in December began her journey for England, fell sicke at Antwerp[200] where after having layed a while, with noe small incomodity was fayne to returne to Liege, both in regard that winter and her Infirmity made her going on difficult but also a busines much importing God Allmighty his Service which she had left in a very good and secure way as she thought, but in her absence there was found who employed themselves to putt all backe.[201] It was generally observed by ours, that the divell carryed himselfe very cowardly in his attempts against her by himselfe or others, still expecting her absence. [63r] Till about the Month of May she cou'd not get free to begin for the 2d Time her journey for England, which through God's goodnes she passed happily.[202] She arrived there the 20th of May 1639.[203] Her presence made many motions in all sorts, some suspecting, some admiring, and true Friends rejoycing and praysing God for his mercyfull fidelity to his dear Friend, whose Ennemyes had beene so bold as to make it passe for an undoubted truth that she was a condemned prisoner for her Life in the Inquisition, and nothing but her presence cou'd have cleared this thruth. As much had beene told her in Flanders, and the reporter of it named to her, and he was a Priest[204] and a Religious Man. Her ayme being a speedy returne for Rome, she employed herselfe immediately for the dispatch of her busines, in which she found the great Benignity of our Queene as to her naturall, and her Piety willing to make appeare her answer to his Holynes his commendations of our dear Mother.[205] There was at the same [63v] Time for Nuncio Signor Conte Rossetti,[206] soone after Cardinall of the holy Church who was pleased to speake very feelingly of the commands he had had from his holynese Cardinall Barberino, and Donna Constanza to serve her in all he cou'd, and that he longed to see her of whom he had heard so much, and seeing her was satisfyed. The qualityes of this most deserving Prelate were such as the onely want was of capacity in our miserable Countrey to deserve him.

---

[199] It appears that Mary Ward saw some new possibility in Liège, perhaps the founding of a small house for educational work, similar to what had been allowed in Munich. The purpose of Mary's journeys to Cologne and Bonn would have been to consult her friend the Prince Bishop, Ferdinand von Wittlesbach, brother of Maximilan I. See Peters p. 603 and Chambers II, pp. 453–455 for further detail.

[200] The journey to England was being made via Antwerp, where Mary would have seen her sister Frances, who was professed as a Carmelite in 1611 and had been Sub-Prioress since 1619.

[201] It is not known which of Mary Ward's many enemies in Liège frustrated her designs. Mary Poyntz went again to Cologne and Bonn to see the Prince Bishop, but the plan came to nothing. AIM Letters 129.

[202] This time Mary Ward travelled by Saint-Omer and Calais. PL No. 49 and 50.

[203] For the correspondence 1638–1640 between Mary Ward and Cardinal Francesco Barberini (1597–1679) and Mary's letters to Pope Urban VIII, see Peters pp. 605–607 with the archival references. It was clear that Rome knew about the extension of Mary's journey beyond Liège, and did not disapprove of it.

[204] The name of this opponent is unknown.

[205] Letter of recommendation from Cardinal Francesco Barberini to Queen Henrietta Maria, dated 28 August 1638. Copy in BayHStA. Kl. Lit. 432/1, f. 27. Mary Ward's audience with the Queen took place some time during the summer of 1639. Peters p. 606.

[206] Count Carlo Rossetti acted as agent or envoy accredited to the Queen, rather than as Nuncio, as there were no diplomatic relations between England and Rome at that date. In September 1639 he had succeeded the Scottish priest, George Con, in this office. Mary maintained contact with Cardinal Francesco Barberini and with the Pope through the services of Con and Rossetti. Her final letters to the Pope and to Cardinal Barberini were written on 14 February 1640.

15. Dangers of the period leading to the outbreak of the Civil War 1642. Children entrusted to Mary Ward's care. Journey north, to Hutton Rudby in Yorkshire.

Difficulties of residence in London 1639–1642. Departure from London (1642) and journey north.

At last so violently began our miseryes as all negotiation was fayne to be layed a side, and her returne made impossible but none dreamed of what did follow. When the malice was come to such a height, as to treate in Parlament the making lawfull to kill a Catholike where soever he was found,[207] this blessed Woman was not afrayd to have her Lodgings frequented by Priests who usually goe disguised, but by the Pope his Nuntio[208] who was knowne to be so, to which confidence of hers the devine Providence gave such efficacious effects as that the Officiers belived undoubtedly she had some [64r] powerfull protection, otherwise wou'd not have dared to have done so as she did, and so durst not attempt what their authority gave them power to doe, seeing she was to make some stay in England, diverse and those very considerable both for their titulary quality and that of Friendship, importuned her to make some young Gentlewomen happy by partaking of her excellent education.[209] Others her owne charity moved her to take, because not onely needy of that happynes, but uncapable to have it, but where there was like charity. So as notwithstanding the great danger of those times, she kept a great Family and a Chappell standing till the searches were so dayly, as noe time was secure, some times foure times in one Day. And what was most admirable her Chamber was still as[a] a Sanctuary and exempted, for either they entred it not at all, or entring their cheefest care was to hasten out, with an humble craving pardon that they had entred [64v] and this not once but allwayes, and as well Souldiers as Pursuivants, and Pursuivants as Souldiers, so as I confes in admiration I consider it, what this grace might be, and it occurres it was the reward of her strong and constant faith, and her profound submission to God Allmighty his holy, just, and secret judgments without disputing or wrangling: Nor did she looke upon herselfe as exempted from the necessity of needing humane helpes, which was cause that after due consideration, she resolved to goe for the North,[210] a place in apparance of more security, the parlament then not having there much hold. But this removall cou'd not be without great hazard and danger; but with her wonted Protection of confidence in God she passed through all safely. She had a Priest in her Company with Church-stuffe, and all convenient to say Masse by the way. Her Company consisted of 3 Coachfulls,[211] and 4 horsemen,[212] in one word it was esteemed miraculous. [65r] Her first aboade in Yorke-shire was in Cleveland at Hewton-Rudby,[213] as most obscure and solitary place, formerly belonging to the Carthusians of that most famous place of Mountgrace,[214] arrived there at the Exaltation of the holy Crose, 1642,[215] her first care was to find a convenient place for a Chappell where the blessed Sacrament was kept continually with a Light burning, and the Altar so adorned as moved all to reverence and devotion that beheld it, and was in fine an exceeding consolation to all the poore Catholikes about.

a missing in B

---

[207] Parliament had demanded the strict enforcement of the earlier laws against recusants.

[208] For the good relationship Mary Ward enjoyed with Count Rossetti, see Mary's letter to the Roman community. AIM Letters 130. Copy in AIY.

[209] This accords with Mary Ward's desire to found a school in London. AIM Letters 130. Helena Catesby, foundress of the house at Burghausen in 1682, was one of the children entrusted to Mary's care, at the age of nine. Chambers II, p. 463.

[210] Letter from Mary Ward to Elizabeth Keyes in Rome, written the day before departure from London, late April 1642. AIM Letters 131. Copy in AIY.

[211] Mary's companions were Winefrid Wigmore, Mary Poyntz, and probably Anne Turner, Catherine Smith and Frances Bedingfield.

[212] One of the horsemen would have been the priest. Another would probably have been Robert Wright.

[213] Hutton Rudby, an isolated village in Cleveland, near Mount Grace, where a house was leased to Mary Ward through her Ingleby relations. Aveling, *Northern Catholics*, pp. 267–268.

[214] The Charterhouse at Mount Grace, near Osmotherley, had been suppressed in 1539. The little chapel on the hill above, though then a ruin and forbidden by the recusant laws, remained a place of pilgrimage for Catholics, and was restored in the twentieth century. A. J. Storey, *Mount Grace Lady Chapel*, Beverley 2001.

[215] 14 September. It is probable that Mary and her party had stopped at various Catholic mansions on the way, many of their owners being related to her.

Time spent in Hutton Rudby, about six months.

About the middle of October she fell very sicke as her Life was held in great danger, and her recovery attributed to a pilgrimage made for her to the above sayd Mountgrace[216] a place to this day of great devotion and where many graces are graunted, though so destroyed and defaced, as onely the bare 4 walls remaine without roofe or cover, and in regard of the great height of the Mountayne on which it [65v] stands exposed to very great winds. Yet shall you find Catholickes praying there howers togeather, and this Pilgrimage herselfe made, when recoverd of the above sayd sicknes.

The parlament grew to have the stronger part in this countrey, so as all Catholikes Houses were searched and plunderd, but ours which was oft attempted, but as oft diverted by unexpected occasions, coming with that designe and with in a mile or two of the House, faine to turne backe. At length 40 of the most barbarous Dragoners they cou'd picke out with a Captaine were sent for this exploit expressly which made not onely Catholikes, but morall Protestants very sensibly lament our ease. At two of the clocke in the afternoone upon the Saterday they came to a litle Village hard by us: When notice was given, I am sure all but that blessed Servant of God were in a great terrour. She called us all togeather to our prayers, when done expected [66r] every moment when they wou'd come, but heard nothing of them till 8 of the clocke at Night, and then came one Souldier alone to aske in very civill tearmes for oates for their horses adding we shou'd not be afraid but goe to our Beds, they wou'd not come to us that Night. This excesse of curtesy where we expected all the contrary put us into greater jealousy, so as none went to Bed but our deare Mother, who was exceeding ill. Till morning we heard noe more, then came 2 Souldiers desiring we wou'd give them something to drinke for they wou'd be gone and not trouble us. A good harty playne Gentlewomen in the House undertooke to goe with them to the Offi-ciers, esteeming those 2 not to be trusted: The Captaine told her, they had beene informed of trunkes of gold we had buryed, Armour and what not, so he woud come and search. She bidd him come in God's name. When come, our dear Mother sent downe to him, and he was mett [66v] at the Hall doore, where all the discourse passed, he was told in few plaine and sinceare words, that this Information proceeded of ill-will. He answered there were some indeed that did malice us, but generally we were well beloved, carryed himself very civilly and indeed awfully, like one not onely not willing, but not daring to offend. He had 20 Shil-lings given him, and he parted very kindly without any search, saying he believed what we told him, and as he was scarcely gone a stones cast but he returned asking for the Gentlewomen he had spoken with to whom he rendred the summe he had taken, saying, if what we had told him was true, it was pitty to take it from us, it might doe us good, and the Souldiers not much who wou'd spend it in drinke and smiling added besides you give it not willingly, to what was answered, in regard of his civility, most willingly. At parting he sayd most seriously, God forbid I or any belonging [67r] to me shou'd doe you any wrong and not onely he but the very Souldiers made such expression of respect and submis-sion, as if the power had not beare theirs but ours as in effect it was by the meritts of that blessed Servant of God, in whome was verifyed that verse of the Psalme: Voluntatem timentium se faciet Deus.[217] And it was a heavenly sight her manner in those occasions, her confidence and cheerfulnes was so humble, peacefull and communicative to others.

---

[216] Note 214.
[217] 'God grants the desire of those who fear him.' Ps. 145:19.

**16. Move to Heworth, near York (early 1643) and then into
the City of York (April 1644) which was under siege by the
Parliamentarians. Return to Heworth soon after the surrender of
the city on 16 July 1644.**

Disadvantages of Hutton Rudby. Move to Heworth.

She called all her Family togeather the 18th of January, and the Gentlewomen that lived in the other end of the House, telling her designe
that all shou'd come together etc. honnour the 9 Quires of Angells with
one Pater and 10 Ave Maryes each Quire, at the end the Angells and
Saints Litanyes which were never omitted but continued till the last, and
imitated by others, who confessed to have found helpe and comfort in
and by this devotion. This place being something inconvenient for the
difficulty of sending and receaving Letters,[218] it being [67v] so remote
and out of all rhoades, she was forced, which yet cannot be truly said,
because her Love to her best Masters will made all passe without force,
evenly and sweetly, and in this quality she left solitude which she loved,
to goe to Hewarth,[219] where she must suffer conversation and visits
which she lov'd not, it being but halfe a mile off Yorke, which then
was full of the Nobility and Gentry, not onely of the North part, but
most part of England. Yet she continued the manner of her Chapell and
devotions, kept two Priests and wellcom'd any that passed that way,
some time 3, 4, and 5 at a Time: and well she knew how to distinguish
her particular devotions and the gererall honour due to the caracter of
Priesthood, which in her was so great, and with such Light and feeling
as of power to encrease where it was, and to correct where it wanted,
yea and to make Priests themselves consider it, nor must whatsomever
imperfection serve for excuse of want of duty in this particular.

[68r] In those times of danger which daily encreased and her infirmity
and weakenes very great, she cou'd not excuse the importunity of many
visits, some for Love and Friendship, others confessing the need they
had and profit they reaped of and by her presence, and others for novelty,
and curiosity, which by sight and speaking grew to reall Friendship as
severall themselves have confessed. One was wont to say (a Person of
judgment) that our dear Mother her presence had the same effect for
the correcting of impertinent Tongues, that Princes their appearing in
publike had to quiet tumults.

When Yorke came to be besieged,[220] and great appearrance it cou'd
not resist seeing the apprehensions and feares of those about her, she
said feare not, we will have our recourse to God and his Angells and
Saints, they will helpe us, we will place Saint Michael at one end of the
Village, and Saint Joseph at the other, and put the power of the great
Canons and Peeces on the sacred name of JESUS which will keepe them
from hurting. The effects [68v] of these her devotions were apparent by

the protection of herselfe, and hers with all belonging to them as also in^a
that with the shott of 500 Canons bullets that were found, besides those
that were lost in the water and other hidden places, and 30 granades
onely two Men were killed.

a C: en ce qu'il n'y eut dans le Bourg que deux homes de tués, quoyque les ennemis y
eussent ietté trente grenades et tiré un si grand nombre de coups de canon, que l'on y
trouva cinq cens boulets sans ceux qui furent perdus

---

218 Mary was anxious about her companions in London and on the continent, and Hutton
Rudby was too isolated for communications to reach her. Peters p. 609.
219 Heworth, north-east of York, about a mile from the city centre. The house was the
property of Sir George Thwing, who had married Sir Thomas Gascoigne's sister Anne, a
relative of Mary Ward. The companions remained there till 1650. Kirkus p. 2.
220 April 1644. For the Civil War references in this and the next section, see P. Wenham,
The Siege of York 1644, Sessions Book Trust York 1970.

The Siege of York (1644); refuge within the walls. Return to Heworth after the capture of the city.

Her inclination was farre more to have remained at Heworth then to
goe into Yorke, and did not stirre till the Ennemy was camped before the
Towne,²²¹ when the perswasion of Friends was so strong as she not to
seeme particular or temerarious left her selfe and followed the common
opinion. When being to remove must passe the Ennemyes Scowtes and
Troopes, who pillaged all they layed hands on. While they were robbing
of others, and searching them to the very skinne, her Servants passed
by with Pots, and bedds on their Backes and heads, (for Men or horses
durst not venture) without a word or whatsoever least interruption. The
like blessing she found during her stay in the Towne [69r] and in her
returne backe to Hewarth when Yorke was taken by the Parlamentarys;
one may conceave part of her sufferance in that seege, when but briefly
is considered her so great infirmity, as to be either in Bed, on bed, or
in a little chayre rocked so to get some litle rest and ease of the great
paynes of the stone that she suffred, deprived of all kind of fresh or free
ayre which of the humaine was her chiefest Livelyhood. Yet she as it
were so much Lady and Mistrisse of herselfe and sufferance as to give
Life and courage not onely to her owne Family but to all sorts of Persons
that came to visitt her. Many wou'd say they came to her as dead and
lost with her revived, and went away with courage. Nor did she this in
a severe saintly way, but with such a humane manner, as made each one
not onely capable to doe it, but ashamed to doe other.

When the Towne was allready rendred,²²² and all that cou'd as this
greatest happines prepared and [69v] hastned to goe with the King his
Army to their Garrisons (which was one of the conditions aggread upon
at the yealding up of the Towne) our dearest Mother not onely for her

Infirmity which she suffered was made uncapable to doe the same; but forth of a great feeling that she had that so was the best, and therefore perswaded other Friends to doe the same. Which was so farre from humane conceipt, as none cou'd believe it, but to their cost afterwards proved, and by word and Letter expressed with sadd repentance. When one of her owne said, what will become of us now? well I warrant you said she, I am assured God will helpe me and mine, where ever we are. and in an other occasion saying we must be content, she replyed. Nay, we will be content. Notwithstanding all these feelings of her owne, and her great desire to returne to Hewarth, did so farre condescent to others as to informe herselfe of all the Garrisons[223] what convenience and security there was for her selfe and family butt found there [70r] was none, and that her first inclination carryed to what was best, and so returned to her former habitation of Hewarth which was in an ill condition to receave her, all the Leadd off the House, all the Iron from the Windowes and Doores, full of stinck and vermine, 400 Soldiers beseides the sicke having lodged therein. But what was very remarquable, was that God shou'd please to put as it were, a defence so powerfull, that the Roomes that had beene employed for the Chappell and our dear Mother her Chamber were both left neate and cleane, not so much as the matts on the floore hurt. In the garden they had buryed divers of their Soldiers, the whole ayre so infected as in the whole Village there were not three well, all that was delightfull taken away, the lovely trees cutt downe, the Garden unpaled and wholly ruinated. In this manner the blessed Servant of God returned joyfull, content, and satisfyed as if all senses had found their satisfaction, nay more, because her satisfaction [70v] was above all sense, and certainly that devine satisfaction of her mind did contribute to the prolonging of her Life, and the supporting of so many paynes which daily encreased, as did her charity endeavouring to prolong her Life for the good and comfort of others, though to herselfe teadious, as once with a litle smile herselfe expressed, saying, I have much to doe not to begg our Lord to take me.

---

221 Between 20 April and 3 May 1644 Mary and her companions took refuge within the walls of York city, passing though the Parliamentarian army which had occupied the approaches between Heworth and the city, and then though one of the gates which had remained open.

222 The city of York finally surrendered on 16 July 1644.

223 None of the King's garrisons were safe, and the decision to stay at Heworth proved to be the best.

17. Final illness and death of Mary Ward 30 January 1645.

Account of Mary Ward's last illness, Christmas 1644.

From Saint Ann her day[224] till all Saints[225] there was noe possibility to gett a Priest which was an unexpressable sufferance, neither any meanes to gett a Letter out of the South, where much busines lay of consequence, which was cause that at last she was faine to resolve, and in effect to send one[226] of her two Companions on foote disguised with a Woman Servant onely, in snow and ill weather through both Armyes, but when she saw me anxious wou'd say, doe not feare, she will come safe. And certainly God gave her that satisfaction to see what passed she [71r] telling me from time to time, now she is heere, now she is there, and such a Day she will be at home, as proved and that she wou'd come to helpe to bury her. She returned indeed just 8 Dayes before she dyed.[227]

Towards Christmas her forces diminished exceedingly, her paynes encreased: all that cou'd helpe nature or conduce to the prolonging of her Life, grew not onely unpleasant as of many Yeares they had beene, but very painefull to her. Yet having a Priest for the holy Days, (for now was noe possibility to keepe one in the House such was the watch and ward kept, and continuall searching) she satt up Christmas Night, and heard all 3 Masses with singular satisfaction to see all the poore Catholike Neighbours have that comfort by her means, though with her great danger. On Saint Thomas of Canterbury his Day[228] at Night a deadly cold and payne all over seazed upon her, and she said this is something more then ordinary. [71v] I will goe offer my selfe to our dear Lord in the Chappell (where the blessed Sacrament was then kept for a sicke body) where she stayed some halfe howre, and thence tooke her bed: the second Day of the new Yeare the Priest being to goe away, she importuned him to give her the holy Oyles, but he cou'd not be brought to apprehend her in such danger, which when she perceaved, very quietly and resignedly said, Patience I must not have that happines, nor will there be meanes heereafter. On an occasion speaking to me she said, but with great peace and serenity, that nothing may be wanting to my sufferance, I doe not onely want my daily Communions but also want the satisfaction to feele, I[a] feele the want of that great benefitt, as if I did not esteeme it as I have done. When one Night perceaving she was in great payne and more then ordinary, which was not by any moaning of herselfe, or gestures of impatience [72r] but rather want of her accustomed sweetnes (concealing her owne paynes not to afflict others) and asked where her paines were, she answered from the sole of my Foot, till the crowne of my Head. I have noe part free, but in my Eyes excessive torment. The tendernes she had for our sufferance was such as made her forbeare to tell us her apprehension of her so neare approaching hower of Death, and consequently her necessity of the Sacraments, which when she had done raysing up herselfe cheerefully sought to sweeten our griefes with comfortable and devine speeches of God's goodnes, and Providence, his favours to us, and causes to confide. And seeing still signes of sadnes, she said fy fy looke sad on it, come, let us sing, and actually sung herselfe, truly like the Swanne dying within les then 24 howers after it.

a in A: repetition of I

---

224 26 July.
225 1 November.
226 Winefrid Wigmore. Letter from Mary Poyntz to Barbara Babthorpe L 6.
227 Winefrid returned from London on 23 January 1645 (new style), bringing letters with news that all was well with the companions in Rome and elsewhere. Vita I f. 47.
228 29 December.

Death of Mary Ward.[229]

On the Munday morning 20th of January /style veteri[230] 1645[a] bitwixt 5 and 6 in the morning, having passed a paynefull night, but without [72v] disturbance to any, she called for all ours, and when told that all were there, she with a very feeling manner tooke up the word, sayd, I wou'd all were heere, and then went on with these few words I comend unto you the practise of your vocation that it be constant, efficacious, and affectionate which last word came with a particular accent, after which embracing each spake noe more but once or twice to be raysed in her Bed, and when asked to take some nourriture answer'd nothing but a litle cold water. At about a quarter before eleeven the same morning gave up her blessed Soule to its Creatour having lived 60 Yeares and 8 Dayes: From thirteene Yeares without dispute resolved to[b] serve[b] God in a consecrated state. At 16 vowed Chastity, at 20 left England,[231] at 21 laboured in the beginning of the poore Claires, at 25 began our Course of Life. From 26 never had perfect health, at 36 went on foot from Trevers to Rome in the hart of Winter. From 40 Yeares never lay downe in her Bedd.

a A and B: 1641 corrected to 1645 | b–b repeated in B

---

229 Cf letter from Mary Poyntz to Barbara Babthorpe L 6.
230 Old style. According to the new calendar 30 January.
231 Cf. Mary Ward's Autobiographical Fragments for a different chronology. According to these, Mary was about fifteen at the time of her vocation to religious life, and twenty-one when she left England; she writes that she made her vow of chastity on Palm Sunday in 1609, before leaving the Poor Clares. AB 6, note 29.

18. Burial at Osbaldwick. Description of Mary Ward's appearance and personality.

Burial.

[73r] Times of persecution were such, and the malice and hatred of Heretikes at such a height as they wou'd not permitt Catholickes to have Christian buriall in place or forme, yea and digged up severall Catholike Bodyes out of the Earth, which gave ours intollerable sufferance and apprehensions, not onely for that they cou'd not give that blessed Corps the honnour due for birth and meritts, but how to find wayes to obscure it. Which was cause we found out a little Church-yard[232] where the Minister[233] was honest enough to be bribed, and the Church yard, not the Church, because lesse profane, and might make our recourse to her Grave[a]. As the custome is, the Neighbours were invited, and came willingly, for they boare her great respect which they were very desirous to expresse, and it was heard like an Eccho amongst them these words, there was never seene such a Woman no never. One onely Man there was, that wou'd not come [73v] to the buriall, whom when the rest mett coming from the field togeather as their custome is, challenged him of it as on unworthy action to which he replyed the divell shou'd carry her for him, it had beene fitter to have throwne her into a ditch then to have shewed her any honnour, she was not content to be wicked alone, but she drew many others with her into Idolatry: at which all tooke so great dislike at him, as they with great satisfaction recounting the busines tould how at that instant cholikes and paynes all over tooke him, that he roared as one possessed, which held him so long and sharpely that he came to our House for remedy, and grew so farre, to acknowledge his fault poore ignorant creature, as to say there was noe Religion but his or ours, to the which all the rest in the end wou'd submit after which he was freed of his payne, and became able to doe as before.

a C: comme moins prophane, et où nous pouvions avec plus de liberté avoir recours

---

232 The churchyard of St Thomas' Church, Osbaldwick, a village near Heworth. It is not possible to locate the actual place of burial, as the gravestone was moved several times. This has now been placed within the Church, and can be visited.
233 Samuel Hollins, ordained in 1626 after studies at Cambridge, described as poor in the York Visitation Records 1638.

Appearance after death.

[74r] It was forgot in it due place, what seemes very worthy note. Her last infirmity was accompanyed with a generall swelling all over, and it lasted the first day and night after her decease, but[a] next morning it was wholly fallen, yet noe skinne broken, nor the least moisture perceaved in

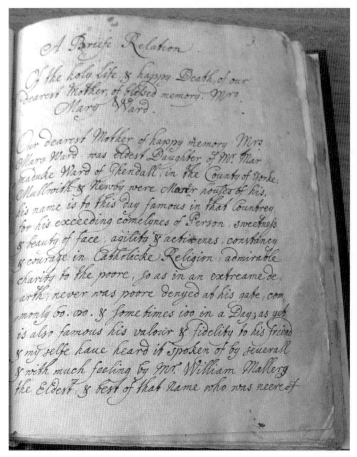

A Briefe Relation.

Of the holy Life & happy Death, of our
dearest Mother, of blessed memory. Mrs
Mary Ward.

Our dearest Mother of happy memory Mrs
Mary Ward was eldest Daughter of Mr. Mar
maduke Ward of Ghendall in the County of Yorke.
Mullwith & Newby were Mannèr houses of his,
his name is to this day famous in that Countrey
for his exceeding comelynes of Person, sweetnes
& beauty of face, agility & activenes, constancy
& courage in Catholicke Religion, admirable
charity to the poore, So as in an extreame de
arth, never was poore denyed at his gate, com
monly 60. 80. & some times 100 in a Day; as yet
is also famous his valour & fidelity to his friend
& my selfe haue heard it spoken of by seuerall
& with much feeling by Mr. William Mallery
the Eldest & best of that name who was neereof

1. The first page of the *English Vita*, known also as the *Briefe Relation*. From the earliest manuscript copy (1716) kept in the CJ archives at the Bar Covent, York.

2. (a) Mary Poyntz. Seventeenth century painted portrait, at the Bar Convent, York.

2. (b) Winefrid Wigmore. Seventeenth century painted portrait at the CJ house in Augsburg. Copy at the Bar Convent, York.

3. Mary Ward's First Word. Panel 1 of the seventeenth century Painted Life. The inscription reads 'The first word that Mary uttered was Jesus, after which she did not speak again for several months'. Vita E, f. 1v.

4. Mary's Vocation to the Religious Life. Panel 9 of the seventeenth century Painted Life. This took place as she listened to Margaret Garrett in the Babthorpe household c.1600. See Mary's account in her Autobiographical Fragments 3 and 4.

5. The Spilling of the Chalice. Pl. No. 14. This happened in 1606 in Baldwin Gardens, London, where there was a hidden chapel. See Vita E, f. 8v and note 33. Mary counted this as one of the greatest graces in her life, because after Fr Holtby's change of heart, her father consented to her going abroad to try her vocation.

6. The First Companions and the Departure for Saint-Omer. PL No. 22. See Vita E, f. 15r and note 58. In the left hand panel Mary (right) is seen with five of the young women who were attracted to her mission. The second panel shows the embarkation for Saint-Omer, Flanders, in 1609 or early 1610.

Maria, als sie † 1620 bei ander mabl nauer Mü-
nchen gereist, hat auß der vernunnfft so ihr Got eingeben
erfahren dauon von den dieberg herm mugetham wegflugt
habt sie Curfür: Dur. zuan in Mr seiner Reisten, hat ein
bequema wohnung und Häße verschäffung geben werdt
welliche sich nach ihrer aufkunfft mit grossr ehrlic machen z

7. Near Munich, January 1627. PL No. 45. See Vita E, f. 33r. Mary Ward, as was her usual custom, had made most of this journey on foot, but she had been lent a coach (shown here with a magnificent team of horses) for herself and her companions on the last part of the journey. Fr Henry Lee and Robert Wright are shown riding as escorts.

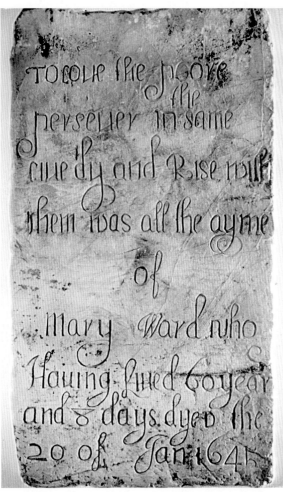

To followe the poore
the
perseuer in same
cue dy and Rise with
them was all the ayme
of
Mary Ward who
Hauing lived 60 year
and 8 days. dyed the
20 of Jan 1645

8. (a) Mary Ward's gravestone, in the Church of St Thomas, Osbaldwick. See Letter 6, from Mary Poyntz to Barbara Babthorpe. Like this letter, the inscription on the gravestone is written in coded terms. For the date see Vita E, note 230.

8. (b) Mary's signature, at the end of one of her letters.

any thing about her, her veynes a perfect and lively azure, her Lipps a lovely but fading redd as when in Life, the dy of her skinne as when in Life not as a sicke or dead body without the least offence rather gratefull and inviting, all these did continue with encrease to the last moment that her coffin was shut up which was as is sayd above from Munday morning till Wednesday evening.

a repeated in A

Mary Ward's personality; physical appearance and manner; two paintings.

What remaines is her stature which was of the compleate rather of the tall, most perfectly shaped, her complexion delicately beautyfull, her countenance and aspect most pleasing and aggreable, with I know not what of excellent mixture that noe Painter (though very excellent in his art) cou'd expresse or describe the two [74v] Times that she yealded to the exceeding importunity of most deserving friends.[234] Her presence and conversation was most attractive, her action generally becoming. It was a generall saying she became what somever she woare or did, her[a] voyce in speaking very gratefull and in song melodious: her constitution delicate but perfect, the composition and posture of her Body had of the Angelicall modesty and courtly freedome without the least affectation, all togeather carryed great Maiesty with it, such as made Princes find great satisfaction yea profit in her Conversation, for so some have beene pleased to say, and such a meekenes and humility as gave confidence to the poorest and most miserable. There was nothing she did seeme to have more horrour of then that there shou'd be any thing in herselfe or hers, that might put a barre to the free accesse of who should be needy of ought in their power.

a repeated in A

---

[234] The two paintings of Mary Ward from life are kept in the CJ houses at Augsburg and Altötting, Germany. The portrait at Augsburg (School of Rubens, the court painter to the Infanta Isabella) is traditionally considered to be the most authentic likeness.

19. Portrait of Mary Ward: qualities of mind and heart, illustrated by examples from her life.

In general: Mary Ward's virtues in balance, centred on her love of God.

The will to say somewhat of the heroicall vertues [75r] of this blessed Woman brings the same difficulty with it, that abundane of delights doe the will to enjoy all takes of from each particular. The conformity and straight union which her vertues had, make them seeme lesse easy to describe a part. Her Humility and mistrust of herselfe was full of

Magnanimity and confidence in God, the tender care she had of her
owne Salvation, did not lessen the ardent Zeal of her Neighbours salvation, neither her Love to solitude and retyrement hinder any enterprise
shou'd cause her to quitt the same, and what rendred her most admirable
was the Freedome and integrity of every action, sweetnes and facility
with which she did them. So as I thinke it may be concluded her Love
to God seasoned them all. Her owne words as also her Workes assure
us, the Spirituall conflict[235] was her first Master, and she so faithfull a
Disciple, as to the last Yeare of her Life, she had not onely the substance,
but almost the particulars verbatim.

---

[235]   See f. 6r and note 22 above.

Diffidence; mistrust of herself and confidence in God; peace of soul.

[75v] Doubtles the mistrust of herselfe was what made her have such
recourse to God by Prayer, and the facility to heare the opinion of others,
and that was her generall practise when any thing was to be done or
taken in hand, first to pray and then to impart it to her Companions and
those of hers about her, and she was wont to say, there was noe Bodyes
opinion but she found profit by it more or lesse in one thing or other.
This mistrust of herselfe was without doubt the cause that she with such
an entirenes did put herselfe for mater of her vocation into her Confessour his hands, to such a degree as in it due place hath beene sayd.[236]
And for what she did in matter of the Institute, she was wont to say, any
poore Servant for 40 shillings a Yeare wou'd doe as much as ever she had
done, and that God Allmighty had begun his worke, by one so unable
to the end none might diffide, and if by such a one what then by those
endued with vertues [76r] accordingly. From this diffidence in herselfe
proceeded an admirable confidence in God, which tooke from her all
difficulty of undertaking whatsoever occurred for God's greater service,
letting noe impossibilityes appeare where[a] God wou'd aught in herselfe
or out of herselfe, her owne or externes, and brought a great facility of
resolving, and avoiding delayes. Her actions all along carryed great testimony of this truth, and that her constant operation was, In Spe, contra
Spem.[237] Nor cou'd she have undertaken the toyles and troubles of so
many journeyes wherein she oft wearyed out her very Servants, with a
body so extenuated, as when she was but 26 was judged by the course
of Nature cou'd not last above 5 yeares. But much more did argue her
confidence in God, the perseverant alacrity wherewith she endeavoured
to advance God Allmighty his worke notwithstanding the innumerable
oppositions, and in the humaine [76v] all impossilityes, and chiefly
the infidelity and ingratitude of her owne to God and herselfe: From
this doubtles proceeded her devine peace of mind which she possessed

in all times and upon all occasions, her emprisonnements in England, when to others her Life was in eminent danger, her greatest care was to pacify and consulate others. Her emprisonment in the Monastery, which carryed so many and the most sensible circumstances immaginable, she enjoyed so great a peace of mind as it made part to her Body; for her presence and countenance, as the Religious them selves said, did compose and pacify, and the litle notes she was wonte to write us thence were dated as followeth, from my Palace, not Prison, for truly, so I find it. Nor was there ever seene a diminishing of this Peace, when by the Bull she saw not onely as it were a Periode to her further Labours in what was dearer to her then her life, but such a ruine [77r] of her passed Labours, the losse of so many houses put into a being, by her so great Labours and paynes, so many that tooke this occasion to turne their backes on God Allmighty. To all which she wou'd answer with a sereane countenance, If it be not my fault, they will be still Houses to me[b].

a repeated in B | b C: Si ce n'est ma faute, toutes ces maisons me seront toûiours des maisons, et le desir que i'ay eu d'avancer les autres dans la perfection ne sera pas vaine ny inutile pour moy.

---

[236] See above, ff. 16v–17r.
[237] Romans 4:18. 'In hope [Abraham believed] against hope.'

Humility.

Her humility was such as became or might be exacted of the meanest subject, yet tooke away nothing of what was fitt for the most decerning Superior. It appeared in her workes, as it was described in her words, for she was wont to say, humility was truth, and so great a grace the possession of it, as noe Labour too great to obtaine, nor enough for it must be asked of God and that daily and instantly. In fine her Humility was not a Humility of vile expressions of ones selfe, or certaine exteriour signes, but grounded in that opinion of truth as was the same in all times and occasions, without needing to seeke but [77v] what was at hand, to her owne great profit, and edification of others. On a certaine occasion wherein God his blessings and concurrance were both eminent and evident, a Priest and Religious Man, so farre forgott himselfe as to tell her to her face, that she was as proude as Lucyfer, and that in his conscience there was noe cure for her Pride, but that God shoud permitt her to fall into carnall sinne, and so humble her. To which she quietly said God blesse me from such a cure. But what argues the grace of God and guift in this particular was, in her very young yeares she had so faithfull a practise of this vertue of humility, that soone after God had touched her soul with the Love of Perfection, she so tooke to hart the practise of this devine vertue, that living in a Kinsman's house of hers, she wou'd take occasion to be thought a Servant trussing up her sleeves, taking a broome in her hand, or a bowle of water and so passe [78r] through the Hall where the Strangers were.[238] Nor cou'd it be a low degree of Humility cou'd make her content to take the degree of a Lay Sister in the french poore Clares, knowing she possessed in her selfe the qualityes togeather with a portion fitt to make her wellcome in what soever Monastery.[239] These two later passages the divell made use of, where he found sufficient malice and ignorance togeather, hoping so to have obscured what was truly illustrious in her both for vertue and Birth. That of the poore Clares happen'd in her owne dayes, which when she heard, smilingly she said. Nay for that you must begg of Allmighty God grace for me to be gratefull, and not to attribute to my selfe what was so farre out of my power, there can nothing be found in that to my disgrace, but my want of correspondance towards God. The effects proceeding of Humility in her later Dayes, gave assurance [78v] it was as well the consumation as foundation of all vertues, as hath beene said her whole Life did shine with it, but me thinkes with this differance, the first playing the Mistris to her selfe, the latter an entire possession without any more discourse. The occasions embraced not onely peacefully but joyfully, there was noe deiection, but yet an entire Separation from all those priviledges which generosity of birth and mind may chalenge without vice. And thise one might see her exercise in occasions towards the poorest yea wickedest of the Parlament Soldiers and officiers.[240] A giving to God his due and soveraigne Power to chastise by whom and what he wou'd, which was not unrequited by that devine Liberality, giving her as hath beene said such a protection and indeed power etc.

---

238 See above, ff. 6v–7r.
239 1606. See above, f. 9r, and AB 6.
240 During the Civil War in Yorkshire, 1642–1644.

Obedience.

Her obedience did not want occasions of Exercise, nor meanes to make appeare how [79r] dearely it was loved by her. In her Youth being given much to scrupulosity, so as to shut her selfe up in a Roome farre from company to say her prayers that she might heare herselfe, specially when it was her Pennance; when her Confessor forbad her without regard to her owne satisfaction she presently obeyed. In the poore Clares, both French and English are many rare Examples of her obedience, not onely to her Superior but the Lay-Sister to whom she was Companion abroad in begging, and it was done with such a sweetenes, that herselfe recounting some passages of that kind did seeme to savour it, and one might see an addition of sweetnes in her very countenance. The vow

of obedience which she made to her Confessour[241] at her coming out
of the English poore Clares, was so inviolably and reverently kept by
her, that she submitted whatsoever supernaturall Light or grace, [79v]
and this without dispute, when first she had declared sincearely how
she understood the matter. She well knew God cou'd not be against
himselfe and that it was noe abuse to his grace, which she receaved
but to use for his service, to leave for his will and in many of these
occasions she saw full-well her Confessors commands came with force,
and contrary to his owne judgment oft times,[242] she made not therefore
any difference. After so many yeares of pennance and anxiety to know
Gods will, when knowne with such assurance and clarity as never more
to doubt in herselfe, in such manner as she wou'd oft tell us, and even
to her last Dayes, that all was to her as done[243] and that as oft as she
open'd her Eyes, she did as it were visibly see it. Notwithstanding all
this, her Confessor comanding her to lay a side both, her thoughts and
her Institute, which she did without delay, and obeying was victorios
for all ended as she wou'd. When Infirmity [80r] did necessitate her
a relaxation of[a] labour and seriousnes her pleasantest recreation[a] and
discourse was of the pleasantnes of Living under obedience and her
hopes to enjoy it: Her Love to this vertue without doubt did contribute
to her so peacefull and contentfull obeying the Bull, and all the orders
of the holy Congregation, notwithstanding the circumstances which she
did not overlooke, nor let passe without profound consideration.

a–a A: superscript

---

241 Roger Lee SJ. 1609. PL No. 16.
242 Cf. Mary Ward's letter to the Nuncio Antonio Albergati, L 2.
243 This refers to the definitive revelation given to Mary Ward in 1611. See above f. 17v
and notes 65–66.

Chastity.

Her love to Chastity was such as to have place with two other causes
for the which she desired to give her Life, to witt her Faith, the honnour
of our Blessed Lady, and her Chastity. The meane opinion she had of
herselfe, and the eminency she conceaved of that vertue put her into a
necessity to aske it daily and importunely of God almighty.[244] She had
also a great guift in perswading others to doe the same. Her flying the
occasions was most exact and in the manner she was wont to teach[a]
others not creeping and fearefully, which hath of the inviting, at least
dispute[a]. God allmighty [80v] gave her an admirable guift in that her
presence had with it a great correction of vice, and invitation to Chastity, as severall in their youth, never before having any such thought,
by her sole presence have resolved upon a chast Life. Severall of our

knowledge in themselves deboist by her Conversation and presence have protested, they have beene imperceptibly or unewares drawne to hate vice, which till then they loved, and to love vertue which before they never knew. Once unknowing she happened to be lodged in a place haunted with ill Compagny, so that in the Night late at her prayers (as ordinarily she was) heard a very great noyse in the low roomes, such as gave her to suspect what the place was, so as severall apprensions seazed her, horrour of the place, her owne and those with her their safetyes, and the impatience to be under a roofe where God was offended. Which latter so boare the sway, as she resolved [81r] to goe downe and speake to them as in effect she did, notwithstanding all the diswasions of her Companions. Noe sooner had she open'd the doore of the roome wherein they were, but they all amazed startled as frightned, stood up, and heard with reverence what she said, and as she bidd them departed peacefully, and quietly. The preventions which she putt in all our Houses even England it selfe, were admirable for the efficaciousnes of them and yet without certaine restraints which have of the formall and affected. In fine a manner to put one in mind of our owne weakenes and necessityes, and that God's will brings a force to doe it if we receave it, as we ought. Of exteriour cautions one was that ours shou'd never be alone for any space of time[b], though the Men were Religious and spirituall, in our owne Houses or abroade. The serving Men be they of what quality or desert soever, must not onely respect her owne persone, but all [81v] ours, yea the meanest Lay Sisters, for she wou'd say familiarity was the beginning of further evill.

a–a C: qu'elle l'enseignoit aux autres, librement et absolument ; non pas craintifvement ou lâchement, ce qui ressentoit disoit elle l'invitation, ou du moins la dispute ou deliberation | b C: temps avec des hommes

---

244 'I saw suddainly and very clearly that the gift of Chastity ... was allways a peculer gift of God.' 12 October 1619. AIM Various Papers I. 18/23.

Poverty.

Poverty was to her in her Hart a treasure; in her cloathes an ornament. Severall that visited her, have said when they beheld her, it was with admiration of what she was adorned withall, and viewing more precisely each particular, found it was meane of valew, old and patched. Poverty it seemes wou'd requite the veneration she bare it, with honnour and ornament. She had in fine a rare Quality of uniting Religious Housewifery and magnificent Liberality.[245] Her exercise of Poverty commanded the respect due to it, ever from those that knew not the value of it. In the same manner was her contempt of wealth and superfluityes, making appeare the meannes, and unworthynes of it. She wou'd often tell us, she cou'd not be afray'd of Poverty, but great by apprehended the hurts

[82r] of Riches, but that God willing during her Life she wou'd take an order. To conclude her words, yea Lookes and accents when she spoake of ritches, had efficacy and force to put a horrour into any resonably well disposed Soule: She cou'd not endure to heare Religious Persons speake feelingly of their commodityes; she wou'd take time and make it her recreation to tell us how to have our Houses apt for health, and free from superfluity and for feare least the minds of ours might grow earthly and from houseweifery to secularity and covetousnes, she was an Ennemy to keeping of Cowes, Barnes etc. no not so much as hennes but at a distanc, and not to be but for a necessity, and consequently more a Shame then a glory, and more a grudge then a possession. It was so wonderfull to see the much she did with litle, as that it is very pardonable the not believing in those that saw it not, and as impardonable in any others, to be so bastardly and meane harted [82v] Children of so noble a Mother as to be needy of such trash, as hath noe valew but when and as contemn'd.

---

245   See above, f. 21r.

Love of God.

Charity as it was her particular and immediate Love to God, one might say was the onely vertue she had, it being the beginning and ending of all, not onely in the degree that none can be out of Charity: but as it were with an immediate practise of it, and without other reflexion, which certainely was what gave all her actions such force and sweetnes.
Once in the time of her Inquisition emprisonment, a sufferance certainely with all imaginable circumstances of displeasure, one of Ours ready to burst with feeling, lett slip in her presence the following words, I cou'd almost take it unkindly at God Allmighty. She tooke up very sharpely the word saying. If you thought so, it were impossible to love you and beware to lett such a thought come into your mind. On an [83r] other occasion one saying that our sufferances were dry suffrances, she replyed: O no they are pleasant and fruitfull. And this said with so heavenly sweetnes and smile, as if she tast'd it. This love did doubtles summe up all ambitions in that one of being found faithfull to the Last; there was noe place for choice of matter and manner.

Charity: Mary Ward's love of her companions, and of her neighbour.

One might conclude without seeing there must needs follow great Love to her Neighbour; but we did see and heare what never can be expressed. First to her owne, who found in her the tendernes of whatsoever naturall Mother, with as much advantage, as is betweene humane and devine. Nor cou'd any of their faults or ingratitudes breake this

band, and what her exercise in this particular was, God onely and
herselfe can tell. But in the height of all she wou'd say, and with much
sweetnes who but I shou'd beare and excuse their faults. In Sicknes what
was spared for the gaining of health, nay but the prolonging of Life. No
charge [83v] was too great, of which she gave a rare example in the
Person of Mistress Jane Browne, who after a long sicknes, and all imaginable remedyes at Naples, for a meere supposition that change of ayre
might prolong her Life some time, made her be brought from Naples to
Monaco in Litter,[246] with Man and Maide to attend her. When there had
her 2 Chambers to herselfe, and one free from all other employments to
serve her alone. When this was alleadged as a superfluity, this blessed
Servant of God wou'd reply, what will you that we save cost on her, who
when time was spared not herselfe for Christ. Her words and actions
made it seeme intolerable any apparance of want of this charity towards
one the other, in either word or worke, taking it as done to herselfe, but
with much more ressentment. When one of our had the Plague in Viena,
and the rest disswading and begging her of all loves not to goe to her,
she broake away seeming rather to [84r] fly than goe. But her Charity
had not its Limitt heere. What was her tendernes over her men Servants, submitting her owne intrest to their profit and consolation, how
great her care they shou'd heare Masse daily, and all profitable for their
Souls good. When once an English Man reconciled in her Service trans-
ported with a strange impetuosity to returne to his home, which cou'd
not be without eminent danger of the Losse of his Soule, which had
so deepe a ressentment in her hart, as all else was layed a side though
at that present there was at hand what highly imported her. To prevent
this evill; he had some litle knowledge in painting, of which she wou'd
seeme to neede, and while he wrought made good Bookes, and such as
she thought most for his purpose be readd, and so at Length gayned the
effect of her devine and sweet will. Her proposition to her Servants was,
to doe the part of Servants, which doing they shou'd [84v] find from her
the tendernes of a Mother.

---

[246] Jane Browne, one of the first companions, Mother Minister in Naples before being
brought to Munich c.1628. With the other members of the Paradeiserhaus community, she
signed the letter of submission to the Pope on 14 March 1631. The exact date of her death
is unknown, but it probably took place soon after Mary Ward's release from prison.

Generosity.

In fine her Charity found noe distinction of Persons, or Nation,
Quality or Condition, and what she had was more hers to give then
possessed. There was a Marchant in Naples like to breake up, owing her
aª 1000 Crownes. A Priest and Religious Man to whose order the sayd
Marchant owed a lesser summe by farre perswaded her as a Chief credi-

tour to clappe him up, which done all the rest had power to sett upon him. She reply'd it will be his undoing and consequently his Family, he replyed it was against Prudence and she wou'd loose all, to which she answer'd and against charity to undoe a poore Family, and she did pray to God to blesse her from that Prudence which did prejudice charity. And this she sayed with a horrour, as not conceaving how one cou'd[b] thinke to[b] be saved by other way, and God gave her the consolation to see good effects of her charitable [85r] Patience. She gave it as for a Rule to us, that Charity shou'd still preceade, and Prudence follow, for humane Prudence and Charity cou'd hardly goe together, and that the greatest number of Men did very much abuse themselves in doing as for curtesy what was highest duty that we were bound to give our Lives for our Neighbours Soules, and our goods for their Lives, and not our superfluityes, but what may touch us.

a missing in B | b–b missing in B; C: ne pouvant pas s'imaginer comment l'on pouvoit esperer de se sauver en faisant autrement

Love of enemies.

What may yet more make her appeare quite beyond the sense of flesh and bloud, and truly Christian, was her unexpressable Love to her Ennemyes,[247] which was so observed in her by hers, as one tooke the confidence on a time to tell her, she thought it was more advantagious to her, to be her Ennemy then her friend, the truth is, that if it were possible to make an addition it was to her Ennemyes. When she had receaved any iniury, it was her speciall care first to frame in her selfe an entire [85v] pardon, grounded and harty, not formall and verball, then to pray for them and seeke out occasions to render them service, and this with efficacy, but not without Prudence knowing and avoyding the effect of their ill will and malice, as also to discerne what in them was good, and what badd. Alas well may we put downe a few words, but never come neere to expresse the efficacy of the actions, which were with a perfect sight and knowledge, freedome and integrity. When the Person cheefe actour in that unchristian and inhumane action of her emprison-ment[248] (I call it so, because he knew assuredy she was most innocent) lay languishing despayred of by all, the notice thereof coming to her, she put herselfe in Prayer, protesting to allmighty God not to rise till his devine Majesty pleased to graunt her petition which was his Life. Which the Physitians accouched[a] to be absolutely miraculous, [86r] voyding a stone in the perfect forme of a crosse. When she heard that any of them was dead, she left whatsomever then in hand, to say Pater and Ave for their Soules. Which doing one a time for one that had in great measure wronged her in what was dearer to her then her Life, the worke of God in her, and this with misusing of Light and grace given him by God, as also her particular confidence in him, praying as hath beene said for him, she found her prayer to have a straunge and unwonted repulse, but did not therefore leave off, rather endeavouring to add efficacy said, I doe pardon what he did against me, which argueth a kind of right to challenge your pardon Lord. To which she had this answer intellectually, It was not against thee, but against me, which tooke from her all capacity to pray further, and left her in such an amazement as her countenance discovered, and was cause she resolved, that since after Death the busines was taken out of her hands [86v] during their Life she wou'd be more diligent, and from that Day forewards while she lived, offered every weeke one Day her Communion and all she did for her Ennemys.

a C: avouerent

247 PL No. 41.
248 Probably Adam Contzen SJ. See above, f. 45v and note 169.

Charity; service of the poor.

One cou'd not see a thing more pleasantly profitable then her expressions of Love to the poore, were it by her conversing with them her serving them or speaking of them. All which was done with greatest affection, esteeme, and satisfaction. She wou'd never deny any thing asked her, if in her power, and she wou'd be sure it was not in her power, or effect it, not thinking much to borrow or begg for that end, and give what she had when she had not what they asked. When they were to be served, she wou'd reprehend us very heighnous if two severall things were putt togeather or the dishes not as cleane, as if to serve who was the best. She esteem'd it as unsufferable that one shou'd give them harsh or uncivill words. She conversed with them in manner as if to her an honnour. In fine [87r] her reverence to the Poore was such as gently forced in others to a degree the like effect.

Fidelity to the Will of God.

By what hath beene sayd, all doubt may be taken away of her want of Conformity to the will of God but the rare Examples she gave, and the occasions of her proofes in this particular were such, as meritt the best penns to putt them downe. She began thise practise while yet young upon the death of her Eldest Brother,[249] who was killed in duell (but so as to have the Sacraments, and dyed Christian like) and was to her the dearest of all her Brothers and Sisters, and most like and simpathising with her. Yet had not this accident the least power as to make a breach

in this union of her will with God's, or chaunge the serenity of her
mind or countenance. Hearing[a] that her younger Brother[250] shou'd say,
he hoped to live to revenge his Brothers Death, though as a sleepe to the
former, found efficacy so to labour and without cease till she brought
him [87v] over[a], where he might by applyed to his Studyes, and learne
to make use of his courage. A great testimony heere of she gave at the
Death of her Sister Barbara[251] in whom (as she was wont to say herselfe)
was summed up all that cou'd be desired, in a Sister, in a friend, and
in a Subject. All which the will of God had power to dispossese her
of, not onely without murmuration, but without displeasant looke, had
courage enough to dresse her when dead, and finally helpe to lay her
in her Grave, as if some pleasing service to a Friend, as doubtles it was
to the friend of Friends, to see her part for his will, and because his
will not onely with a portion of her hart, but her Soule, and in maner
as if glorious to her to have the occasion. In her owne Person, with
what a perfect integrity was it equall to her to dy at home or abroade,
in House or under a hedge, yea with the Sacraments or not, supposing
not by her fault. Nor was this in [88r] Speculation, for how oft hath
Allmighty God beene pleased to dispose that she had occasion to make
him these offers, and gave all the signes of entire effect. What but the
devine conformity cou'd have made her see, and passe over without the
least disturbance, sadnes, or least unquiet, the totall destruction of 30 or
more years Labours,[252] in the spirituall as well as temporall (that is out
of herselfe) excepting some very few prevented and kept by her great
charity and speciall care. And what may one thinke was wanting to this
ruine, when Confessours them selves made it their worke to contribute
to this ruine. When in her last journey passing Liege and Cullen,[253] in
the first place she had left 2 houses, in the other one, well furnished
and settled, capable for Ours to serve God in conforme to our vocation,
and now found neither house nor so much as a bedd for herselfe or
Companions to ly on, besides many other circumstances [88v] capable
to move a hart of stone. Yet as hath beene said, was there not seene in
her a sigh or sad looking backe, no nor an unpeacefull looke or word, or
least condemnation of the Actours. It suffised her all was sign'd by the
will or permission of God, and therefore noe further to be questioned.
And of this she gave not few nor small proofes in her latter yeares in
England, in so many horridd occasions, and not the least the being so
many Monthes without hearing any word of, or from ours in Rome,[254]
which with all the rest was confirmed and consumated by her Death,
without inclination as one may say to any will but God's, which made
appeare in her an apparent sweetnes. One did not find any thing gone
that was wont to be of amiable in her, but some thing more was seene of
addition, and of a higher nature as well surprising, as inviting, and gave
to understand in every action, that there [89r] was an absolute adew,

and separation from all things of this world. It was a greater strength then to languish, for she was present to every action compleately, but it enclined that way. In fine she seemed to have a most sweet, devine and secure possession, which yet did not exempt her from the sense of her most sharpe paynes.

a–a C: entendent par après que son cadet avoit dit, qu'il esperoit vivre pour venger la mort de son frere, elle qui sembloit insensible au premier, fit pour lors parêtre combien elle étoit active à travailler par empêcher que Dieu ne fut offencé, se rendant infatigable iusqu'a ce qu'enfin elle le fit passer la mer

---

249 David Ward, b. c.1587. Neither the date nor the circumstances of the duel are known.
250 George Ward b. 1595. Ripon Parish Register 1, p. 16. Entered the Society of Jesus in 1619, and died in 1654.
251 Barbara Ward b. 1592. Ripon Parish Register p. 11. She joined Mary at Saint-Omer, travelled with her to Rome in 1621, and died in Rome in November 1623. Peters p. 313.
252 The thirty years are counted from Mary's call to religious life at the age of fifteen, to the suppression of the Institute in 1631.
253 Final journey to Liège and Cologne 1638–1639. See above, ff. 60v–62v.
254 See above, f. 70v and notes 226 and 227.

Patience, fortitude, steadfastness. Inner freedom; qualities in balance.

The above sayd conformity did greatly conduce to her unlimited Longanimity, which freed her from all irkesomones, and conforme to what she tould the Cardinalls in Rome, what was not done in one yeare might be done in an other, she had noe hast, she cou'd attend God-Allmighty his time and Leasure. And when probabilityes and hopes had fayled, wholy quiet and sereane, if not by one meanes then by an other still prosecuted what she conceaved her fidelity to God and on occasions wou'd say, we must follow not goe before God Allmighty; the force [89v] and vigour of her mind did not onely carry her along to so many encounters with that weake body of hers, but made it effect above all humane expectation. She measured not her Labours by her forces, but drew her forces to the necessityes of her Labours were they spirituall or corporall, at home or in journeyes, and had her spent body in such oblivion as made such as were her Companions recreation some times. The Cart wherin she and her Company were, being once overthrowne in a great snow and bitter weather whereas every one doubted she had beene hurt, she was the first on foot, and seeking to lift up the cart with her Shoulders, as if the best able indeed all were litle enough being almost nummed with cold. In like manner on severall occasions where a necessity was presented, her mind made her believe none more able. In a journey once after having gone 35 Miles in one Day [90r] neere being benighted, and in danger to find the gates shutt, wou'd have undertaken to have hastnied her pace and to have gone before, to have kept the Gates open. Many and many more Examples might be brought in proofe of what hath beene sayd, and made appeare that she might truly say. Omnia possum in eo qui me confortat.[255] Who had the happines to be able to sett downe the great stability, firmnes and strength of this Servant of God, would make our age and Nation see them selves happy, solving that great difficulty Mulierem fortem etc.[256]

So many excesses at least surpassings, and each their due and orderly limitt. A hart so soft yet never melted, a nature so pleasing, and willing to please, wholy employed in pleasuring, fancy had not aught to doe, reason and discourse, faith and profound submission ruled her. Sweetnes was turned into severity where but an inkling of God's [90v] displeasure, how did this strength appeare when the Institute was treated, what applause might she have procured and have beene admiration to the world, and gayned a number of Friends (but they worldly ones) woud she but have relented soe little in points of the Institute! But with her herselfe was layed aside without regard to what pleased or displeased fidelity to God being her sole ambition, and to such a degree as for the performance of it, she had found facility (but not without sensibility) to loose friends, gaine[a] Ennemyes, despise honnours, embrace contempts, neglect ritches and cherish poverty. In this quality of Mulieris fortis, whatsoever seemed great in this world, whither in point of honnour, fame, Ritches, or pleasure, was meane and of noe value with her, as they did not please, so neither did their oppositts displease: her tempered calme freed her from their ebbs, and flowes. This appeared admirably when she left the English [91r] Poore Claires, by which she seemed at once to be deprived of all most pleasing and satisfying in this World, and greatly promising for the next, and yet done without repine or murmurre towards God, losse of courage or Confusion before Men, ever sereane peacefull, and judiciously present to herselfe in all occasions. Which she persevered in, all her 10 Yeares of serious Labour, rigorous pennance, and humble prayer to know Gods will touching her State of life etc:[257] Which when knowne and seemingly disapproved by her Confessour[258] (to whom she had vowed obedience) felt noe difficulty to obey him, and as little doubted of Gods assistance when the said Confessour in a threatning way wou'd pretend to free her of her vow, and leave her to herselfe.

a B: and gaine

---

255   'I can do all things in him who strengthens me.' Phil. 4:13.
256   'Who shall find a valiant woman?' Proverbs 31:10.
257   See above, ff. 15v–16v.
258   Roger Lee SJ.

Independence of mind and judgement.

When Cardinall Bandino (who for his owne excellent parts and particular respects expressed to her had duely the power of a meriting friend)
perswading her to admitt of the enclosure of Torre di Speechio[259] (which[a]
in effect is lesse then in all our Houses was to be[a] [91v] observed[260]) on
which condition she shou'd have freedome to sett up as many Houses all
over the World as she wou'd. Which he thought was noe litle offer, since
those noble Ladyes have never beene able to procure the begining of one
more nothwithstanding there being amongst them so many Sisters and
Allyes to Popes and Cardinalls. But to this faire offer our dearest Mother
gave for answer, that to obtayne the foresaid grace of propagating etc.
she wou'd not admitt of two stakes putt in crosse in forme of enclosure.
And I thinke the force was greater to want the satisfaction of yealding
to so deserving a Friend, then the wanting the seeming of honnour of so
great a gayne and advantage. When in the great esteeme and applause of
the Duke of Baviere his Court the Bishop of Brunderwoot wou'd have
put his Ursilians, with divers belonging to them to the number of 300
under her care and government,[261] his and their Confessour and [92r]
Directours esteeming it a disparagement not to have them admitted in
grosse without proofe or Noviship, without which condition she wou'd
admitt of noe treaty, which they though Priests and Religious Men tooke
so heynously and turned into so bitter Ennemity as to protest to her
Face they would leave her never a Friend in Bavaria, nor Austria. To
the which she with a smile answered. God forgive you. And to begin
their designe they urged the Duke to be so much of their party, as that
our Mother persisting to deny their proposition, his Highnes shou'd
take from her his House, rents, grace, and whatsoever he had given or
professed to her: Which she fore saw before she heard it, and resolv'd
with all the equality in the World to embrace, rather then relent in her
resolution. As she tould the Duke when he recounted what they had
importuned him unto: and that he had answered, God forbid he shou'd
meddle with her affaires, God had given her Light and [92v] Prudence
sufficient to guide them. She gave him humble thankes, and withall
assured his Highnes had he done otherwise she had made him a low
reverence and quitted all his favours with as much content as ever she
embraced them. The passages of her Life afforded a number of these
examples so farre more excellent, then heere expressed so poorely and
sorrily as with impatience done, and leaving to doe more. But must not
omitt some little of the much may be sayd of this nature in matter of
spiritualityes and what was wholy devine, which though so, had noe
further power or effect with her then conduced to God's honnour and
Service in an ordinary way, and conforme to her state and vocation. In
this particular some knowing persons, have seemed to condemne her

as too much neglecting in certaine passages and favours, which had
of the extraordinary, and wou'd have beene highly cherished by such
as had beene very [93r] spirituall, but had not learned that totall quit-
ting of them selves and their owne contents though devine, and as this
blessed Servant of God lived most, where herselfe was least, and that her
greatest advantage was to give, of receaving she had assurance. Of this
followed the great courage where-with she boare two yeares of excessive aridity[262] and this in the time when her busines was in the height
of treaty in Rome. She found herselfe disrobed of all that cou'd either
please or fortify her Soule in the sensible part, wholy uncapable of any
practise, but to believe and hope in God, exposed to the most horrid
apprehensions of being abandoned and forsaken by God Allmighty, even
to the apprehension of being possessed by the divell, which wrought so
strong, as she was faine to use force to continue her daily Communions.
She communicated this with some one whom she thought to purpose,
which was done with [93v] such light and signes of God Allmighty his
guidance as litle remayned to be taught her[b], but much to be admired in
her. In all this time who was most about her and neerest her, never saw
change in word or Looke, or least appearance of conflict or trouble.

a–a C: qui se devoit observer en nos maisons | b B: to her

---

259   AIM Letter 8, 1 July 1622, to Mgr Lorenzo Campegio. The Oblates of the Torre de
Specchi in Rome, founded by St Frances of Rome in 1413, lived under the Benedictine
rule, with a mitigated form of enclosure.
260   Although Mary Ward would not accept enclosure, her Company observed the propri-
eties which were usual for women at that date. Peters p. 229, with archival reference.
261   In 1627 it was proposed by the Bishop of Basel that 200–300 Ursulines from
Pruntrut, members of the branch of Ursulines founded by Anne de Xaintongue in 1606,
should merge with Mary Ward's foundation in Bavaria, despite their different aims and
constitutions, and without any form of probation or noviceship. Mary's refusal to accept
this unconditional merger aroused hostility among the secular clergy and some Jesuits.
Grisar *MW*, B II, Ch. 1, and Chambers II, pp. 264–266.
262   Probably the years Mary Ward spent in Rome, 1629–1630, just before the Suppression took place. The identity of her spiritual guide at this time is not known.

Asceticism and self-control.

The weake and confused putting downe of these devine passages, will
not prejudicate them in the opinion of the wise and vertuous, and may
prove helpfull to the lesse knowing, falling in Love with the pleasing,
and thereby les apprehensive of the sharpenes whereby it was gayned.
Her mortification which did preceade, accompany and conclude all her
actions, and in that regard not out of due ranke in this place, which
interiourly (as by what beene saide will appeare) was very great. For
the exteriour, when she was in our owne Houses, and her occasions
permitted her, she never fayled to take her turne to doe the accustomed

[94r] Pennances in the Refectory, serve the Table, wash dishes etc. Nor did her so many Yeares of Infirmity exempt her from her frequent Disciplines, and such like pennances, with particular fastings on occasions in which she dyed, to witt the Munday fast in honnour of Saint Anne: oblidging herselfe in extreamity of weaknes to kneele daily for such a space. As for her Senses though the carriage of her Eyes was wholy free from all fixion or formality, yet so as not to see but what tended to her immediate employment, and importing God's service; which brought her to that passe, that she saw not persons or things immediately before her: which was cause she gave allwayes order to her Companions when she went abroad, to tell her when she mett of acquaintance or Quality to the end she might not omitt the due correspondance: In briefe her care and vigilancy in the carriage of her Eyes was as if but a Novice in the way of vertue, her Senses of taste and smelling were so wholy dead, [94v] as they neither served nor mis-served her Body nor Soule, and this to such a degree, as when in great Sickenesses, losse of appetite and weakenes of Stomacke, she endeavoured to please her taste, cou'd not though she wou'd. The same likewise in smelling, which was in such measure as a Rose which of all smells most pleased her, was to her like a sticke. Her practise in these particulars was as followeth, sweet but strong and constant, when either sense found pleasure in somewhat she wou'd turne herselfe from it, and as a pressent to God Allmighty, honnouring some mistery of Christ or our blessed Lady, and continue it for a yeare or so.

Her complexion being sanguine enclined her more to the cholericke then flegmaticke, yet that even naturally was free from all violence, or aptnes to give displeasure, but as hath beene sayd, to be hers was enough to seeme needy of an expulsion, wherefore when in herselfe she found an inclination [95r] of speaking quicke, were it in answering ordinary matters, or in reprehending what was reprehensible, she made a stoppe till that little kind of eagernes was over, which she wou'd tell, when for the councell and helpe: of passionate People, what was to be their helpe the great profit she had found in that practise, and that the following passage in the beginning of her Life, had as it were made a conquest in this particular, and was as followeth. One that by her charity was exceedingly obliged to her, and she out of her tender goodnes loved very much, having indeed in her what was love worthy, but without sense, or reason passionatly cholerike, tooke occasion without the least given her, to vent herselfe against this Servant of God, who so rationall and of so delicate a Nature felt very neerely this passage, and on the point to make a reply, but over-taking herselfe by consideration, resolved not onely not to answer [95v] but with inward, and outward peace and Silence to heare all she wou'd say, then with humility and charity endeavoured by word to give her satisfaction, which latter part was as great or greater then the first, the leaving wholy to speake hath of the contempt and revengefull which to corrupt nature is pleasing, in fine this passage she was wont to recount for a proofe of the good that was gotten by this manner of practise.

20. Mary Ward's spiritual life. Her manner of prayer; graces received; special devotions.

Apostolic spirituality.

There is nothing out of the devine nature it selfe to be conceaved so ample, and[a] yet[a] compendiously encluding all that can be delightfull, as to see the operation and effect of God Allmighty his graces in his selected Soules. And how by conquest and power of grace there becometh an union and devine harmony betweene the spirituall and corporall which in some are such as needs a totall overcoming, some others seeme to need but a [96r] Reforme, or as one may say information as if in some degree from the generall curse, and hath an extraordinary power in giving a visible proofe of the inward excellencyes and generall amiablenes of vertue. Wherein this Servant of God excelled, and did as she was wont to say, there were some who living in God carryed all that conversed with them thither not in an absorpt and abstract way, but as if God descended to them and not they ascending to him, which former renders them capable to make humane actiones devine, the Later uncapable of other then devine, which was not proper for our State ayming to serve our Neighbour:[263] To this effect, she was wont to speake of fowre kinds of Loves, Celestial by which a Soule was carryed wholy in Heaven uncapable of ought on Earth; Saintly which made one live holily not onely in our selves but in the assistance of others both spiritually and corporally,[264] sensible [96v] which had so much of the Earth as left one hardly capable to do things in themselves excellent, without mixture; for the sensuall it was wholy bad and therefore not worth the speaking of.

a–a *yet* repeated in B

---

263   PL No. 30.
264   See letter to Roger Lee SJ, known as the *Vision of the Just Soul*, 1 November 1615. '… not lyke the state of Saints, whos holynes cheefly appeares in that union with God, which maketh them out of them selves'. AIM Letters 1. PL No. 25 and 27.

Graces received, mainly in Rome during the Jubilee Year 1625.

The devine Liberality gave this his blessed Servant strong graces, conforme to the great and hard proofes she was to passe, and so much a disinteressed Love as made her not know how to esteem devine Lights

and graces as they had relation to her profit, and content. And that this
was not onely her election, but his devine conduct, will appeare by some
few Lessons given her, and through her charity to us for our profitt.
Importune on a time with Allmighty God, how to satisfy for her sinnes,
she had answer intellectually but distinctly: To[a] beare well all that shou'd
occure in doing his will[a].[265] On an other time begging to know what was
the best use she was to make of sufferance, she had the answer [97r] in
manner as afore sayd, that to be pleased with them was to please God
by them.[266] Likewise desirous to know what her Love to God should be,
she understood in the same manner, that her Love shoud be to part easily
from all that was lesse pleasing to him.[267] She resolved for one whole
yeare and punctually observed it, to visitt daily the Quarant hora.[268]
In which time she receaved many great Lights and favours, particularly in the Church called Madonna Sanctissima dell'horto,[269] where
she passed divers howers with so great union and transformation into
God, as with great difficulty for some time after cou'd she recover her
sight and forces. In the Time of prayer, there was something visible in
her face of the extraordinary and devine. Omitting many others, I must
not leave what is so profitable to us present and future. Considering and
commending to allmighty God the state and difficulty of our Course
of Life, it occurred with most great clarity, that our happynes, security,
and progresse [97v] was not to be in Ritches, greatnes, and Favour of
Princes, but in having our way open and free to God Allmighty whence
our strength Light, and protection must come,[270] which grace filled her
Soule with extraordinary Light and vigour, with great addition to her
allready little valuing of what in this world is esteem'd great and high.
In the last yeares of her Life many seeming occasions occurring, wherby
God might singularly be served, our Course of Life subsist and many
needy soules holpen and all this unfactable for want of money, great
Losses having been caused by the Bull, and the infatigable endeavours
of her adversaryes. In some little anxiety she put her selfe to prayer to
aske a considerable summe of money which she thought necessary what
occurred in the height of her petition was, as it were sayd to her by God
Allmighty is such a summe better then my Providence?[271] Which had
such effect in that devine Soule of hers, as nothing but the [98r] Devine
Providence seemed Ritches to her, nor cou'd she looke on temporall
meanes but with a certain disdayne her mind being filled with the sight
and knowledge of that heavenly treasure. She had in high esteeme that
holy and profitable maxime that who wou'd gayne much, must esteeme
every Litle, which was cause that in all her actions she kept her first
manner of practise, and this in manner as if her poverty needed them
and herselfe uncapable of sublime wayes and high prayer, but observed
posture and manner ordinarily taught.

a–a underlined in A

---

265 Retreat of April 1618. AIM VP IV.2/34.
266 Retreat of April 1619. Meditation on the Nativity. AIM VP I.20/26 and PL No. 39.
267 Retreat of April 1619. 'The comparinge Christ with an earthly king.' AIM VP
I.19/24.
268 In the Jubilee Year 1625 the Quarant' Ore devotions (Exposition of the Blessed Sacrament) were celebrated in each of the Churches of Rome in succession. Mary Ward visited
and prayed in these churches daily, and the special graces she received are recorded in the
Painted Life.
269 PL No. 40. 11 April 1625 in S Maria dell' Orto in Trastevere.
270 PL No. 38. 2 August 1625, feast of St Peter in Chains.
271 PL No. 47. This grace is traditionally connected with Mary Ward's final years in
Heworth, and her wish to found a school in England, in London or elsewhere. This desire
was fulfilled by Frances Bedingfield, who received £450 from Sir Thomas Gascoigne. In
1686 Frances founded the Bar Convent, York, in addition to the previous foundation she
had made in Hammersmith, London, in 1669. Kirkus pp. 1–7.

Prayer for others and favours received.

Her prayer generally was a cleare sight, and freedome to aske. She
was wont to say she guessed by the Audience given, wither she was to
speak or no, and when graunted or not to be graunted, her prayer was
very efficacious for the obtaining of health of which nature besides what
hath beene sayd of Cardinall Trescio,272 what heere followeth happened
in the same place of Monte Giovino273 [98v] a Servant of hers inoc-
ently wounded, but so as held by all in danger was brought home, very
weake and in a great feaver, the place wholly unprovided of remedy
or Cirugian.274 She first making her prayer to our blessed Lady tyed
up his wound with her owne hands, having nothing to apply but the
white of an Egg and flaxe, sent for a Cirugian who cou'd not come till
morning in regard of the distance though the Messenger went all night
with order to bring him speedily away. She bespoake all the Masses to
be said for her Intention and gave order though the Cirugian came the
wound shou'd not be opened till the wounded had heard Masse, which
over night there was litle apparance he cou'd doe, but by morning he
was quite an other Man. His devotions ended and the Cirugian come the
wound was opened, and nothing found but like the scratch of a pinne.
The Cirugian with a certaine impatience, Doe [99r] you make a Foole
of me to send for me for this? But all present with great admiration
assured him of the condition it was in over-Night, upon which all gave
glory to God and the blessed Virgin and deeply conceaved the efficacy
of that blessed Womans prayers. Omitting very many both of our owne
and externes I will onely putt downe three. Mistress Keyes275 one of
our owne, then in Perugia so despayred of by the Doctor, and the most
knowing in that famous University, as that he coming to visit others

the next morning wou'd not believe she was alive. In Rome Doctor Alphonso Ferro[276] in a violent feaver and other accidents which depriv'd him wholly of all sleep which he had suffred three Nights togeather, our dear Mother visiting him and finding him in this case tooke her Leave and went directly thence to Madonna di Scala (where the Quarant hora was) and she applyed her selfe with great instance to begg this Mans health, and as a motive to encline our Blessed Lady to graunt her petition, she added give him my sleepe [99v] I will be content to want it. After some two howers of prayer in her way home we asked her (her benignity and charity permitting us) if she had hopes he wou'd recover, she answer'd yes for she had found accesse and had importuned so and so, which was found to have the effect, for he within an hower after her leaving him, fell a sleepe, which sleep lasted 3 or 4 howers. In which he dream'd that he saw our Mother kneeling before our Blessed Lady of the Rosary (which was kept that day[277]) begging instantly his health, and in particular that he might sleepe, on which condition gave her owne rest, at which he cry'd out: O Signora o what charity, which words he uttered so distinctly as that his Wife and all in the Chamber heard him, and thought he had beene awake, but found he was a sleep: when awaking a Man out of himselfe for joy, I am cured, I am cured, I have noe more head ache, noe more feaver, noe more drought, and [100r] de facto so it was. In Viena Count Altham[278] a Man famous for all respects, birth, vertue and employments, even at the last gaspe with paynes of the gout, which had so possessed his head as the meere want of sleepe was held sufficient to kill him very speedily, he being a Person as hath beene said of so much meritt, with the addition of singular respect to her and hers, she found great sensibility to see him in that case. So as returning home she called all Ours togeather tould them what she felt, and that she desired Prayer shou'd be kept all Night, which herselfe began. Next Morning (which she longed for to know how he did, having in her selfe an assurance he was either dead or recovered) at 4 of the Clocke (which he knew was the hower we used to rise at) the good Count sent word it seemed long to him, till he cou'd acknowledge the grace of his health receaved by her prayers, the manner of which he recounted [100v] to her, she that day going to see him, which was as followeth. Lying in his extreame paynes he fell a sleepe, and dreamed he saw two grave Matrons of gracious and pleasant aspect, having two little Children with them coming neere to him asked what he ayled, and that he answer'd, he had nothing but paynes and out of possibility to sleepe, they tould him they wou'd make his Bed, which they did with so much charity as greatly edifyed him. He asked them what they were, they seemed as if those little Children shou'd expresse what their state of Life was. Noe sooner was he laid in the Bed thus charitably accomodated, but all his paynes left him, they went away, and he fell a sleepe, and sleept

5 howers, waken'd not onely cured of his corporall infirmity, but filled
with spirituall joy and devotion, called for his Confessour etc.

---

272 See above, ff. 28v–29v, and PL No. 36.

273 See above, f. 29r.

274 Surgeon.

275 Elizabeth Keyes, an important member of the community in Rome. In 1642 she was
the recipient of Mary Ward's last extant letter (see note 210). This incident in Perugia
would have taken place c.1624.

276 Doctor Alphonso Ferri was Mary Ward's physician. In September 1631, after
Mary's imprisonment, he put down 500 scudi as bail for her final journey to Rome, and
in February 1634 he provided a medical report for the Cardinals of the Inquisition. Wetter
pp. 95 and 174.

277 The feast of the Rosary is celebrated on 7 October and on the following Sunday.

278 Count Michael Althan was appointed by the Emperor Ferdinand II to assist Mary
Ward in Vienna and then in the attempt (unsuccessful) to make a foundation in Prague in
1628.

Devotion to Our Lady and favours received.

Her devotion to our blessed Lady was very great and tenderly deare,
confidently in all occasions she made her recourse to [p. 101ª] her. It
was not a devotion in formality tyed to this or that particular devotion,
but as a deep apprehension of her most high Quality of Mother of God
etc. and that all else were as lesser tytles needfull to our small capacity
to make us capable of the highest. She allways gave her the Tytle of
blessed. She had an admirable manner to bring those she conversed with
to use the same. In fine her honnour as hath beene said was what she
greatly desired to give her Life for, and was once very neere the pinch of
so doing, reprehending most undauntedly one of the Justices in Guild-
hall[279] for blasphemy spoken against the sacred Virgin of whose many
singular and visible protections I will onely recount two. Returning to
Rome from Mont Giovino[280] passing by a little Image of our blessed
Lady which is on the high way, at the foot of the hill called Tavernella,
when as is sayd passed by, called upon all her Company, [p. 102ª] who
were on horsebacke, as herselfe also was, and said Lett us returne backe
and say Sub tuum to our Blessed Lady, that she will please to protect
us in all the dangers we may chaunce to come into this day, which done
went on her way, but had not past two coytes cast, when one of her
Companions Horse stumbled and cast her into a ditch, fell himself upon
her, what with force to gett up and his owne malice, beate with his Feete
at her Head, so as all assured themselves her braines were beaten out,
though she had not beene crushed with the fall of the horse upon her.
Neither durst any approach for feare of doing rather hurt then good. The
blessed Servant of God beheld all this in silence, without any expression of feare, by looke or gesture (which was her usuall in all passages

of greatest horrour). The horse of itself gott up, and the party without any least hurt, but what was on her head full of hoales made with the Nayles of the horse Shoe.[a] [103r] The other was at Egre in Bohemia,[281] where she was to drinke those waters: importuned one a Day to walke into the woods out of Towne, though she found aversion went, but as she went along, had as it were somewhat that drew her backe. At length when on the rampers, over against the Franciscans Church she said Lett us kneele downe heere and say our Ladyes Litanyes, to begg her that she will vouchsafe to blesse us from all evill encounters, for my part I have noe inclination to goe, but still importuned by others went on. When in the thicke of the Wood her Companions began to be afraid hearing the hummering of Men's voyces, and beheld presently three comming with great fury with hatchets and bills, the formest having his lifted up in posture ready to knocke one on the Head, upon a Sudden stopped as if one had frightned him, whereas there was really nothing but a poore dogg that by chaunce was come abroad [103v] with us, belonging to the Landlord of the house where we lodged. By that time the fore most had turned his backe, the Men that belonged to us appeard, which made them all returne to the thicke of the woode, and our dear Mother with her Company giving thankes to God returned home. Not onely of this nature alone, but in matter of health, supply of moneyes etc. great were the favours this dear Servant of our Blessed Lady receaved of her faithfull protectrice[b].

a–a in A these pages have been incorrectly numbered, in another hand, as 101 and 102 | b in A protectrice correcting the underlying protectione; B: protectione

---

279 On Mary Ward's visit to England in July 1618. Chambers I, pp. 435ff.
280 Returning from San Casciano dei Bagni October 1634. See above, f. 54r.
281 Eger, near Prague, where Mary Ward went to drink the waters in August 1628. AIM Letters No. 52.

Devotion to the Angels. Concern for priests. Prayer for the souls in Purgatory.

Her devotion to her Good Angell and all Angells in generall, was very great, particularly to Saint Michaell, Saint Gabriel, and Saint Raphaell whom she served daily with some devotion, and 28 Angell Guardians besides her owne, the Popes his, and some other Princes theirs. She served an Angell to have a care of her Letters much importing her busines, their safe passage, and the danger there of, a certaine Prelate [104r] having offred a great sume of money to stoppe all her Letters, an other to have care of her journeyes. A 3[d]. to prevent the misservices of God by the indiscretion of ours. A certain Priest brought out of danger of loosing himselfe eternally, by her meanes which charity of hers was accomplished by her perpetuall and continuall care of him, daily serving his Good Angell: One Night in particular[282] apprehending him in more then ordinary danger, with great anxiety (which was not ordinary with her) praying for him, presently she beheld his Chamber and Bed with him in it, and his Angell Guardien with an unexpressable diligence hovering over him in posture of deffence, turned to her and with a loving reprehension expressed these words, doe you not see the care I have of him? The roome was so perfectly discovered to her, as she putting downe what she saw, it was found to be so conforme to the reality, as there was not the placing of a Stoole [104v] found different. This Angell seemed to her of such beauty, as she was wont to call him the fine good Angell, and the grace done her heerein of high conse-quence: Employing about that time a Painter, and willing to make the abovesaid good Priest in Love with his good Angel, made the Painter draw him by her description in his posture etc. which had in it so great incitation to reverence and devotion, that the good old Painter then 60 Yeares old began to say daily a Pater and Ave to his good Angell, which he never had done before. When any of her owne or deare friends dyed with whom she had had correspondance in and for God Allmighty his service, she made Masse be sayd if she cou'd, at least communicated for the party, and the same in thankesgiving for the good Angell, then tooke him into the number of those she served, imploring his assistance in some particular concerning Gods Service, which she did with as [105r] much facility and confidence, as one can doe recurring to some deare Friends. Her devotion to the Soules in Purgatory was so great, as to make all that conversed with her in Love with the same: her prayers for them went a long with all her recourses to God and his Saints, neither passed there a day wherein they had not their part, besides thousands of Masses, Communions, Beades, and Diriges[283] said and procured by her.

---

[282] PL No. 29.
[283] The opening antiphon of the Office for the Dead before the revision of the Roman Breviary in 1970.

Journeys: Mary Ward's order of the day and pattern of prayer while travelling.

What she observed in her journeyes was thus when determined, next to our Blessed Lady and her good Angell, she commanded it to some one Saint her Patron, as also to the Saint or Protector of the place wither

her journey tended, when begun, at first setting out, sayd our blessed Ladyes Litanyes all answering, then the Itinerarium in the same manner then to each of the following a Pater and Ave, her and her Companions owne good Angells, Saint Michaell, Saint Gabriel, and Saint Raphaell, the Angell of her voyages and [105v] the fine good Angell, the two Saints above named, Saint Joseph, Saint Ignatious, and Saint Anne, then made her hower of prayer, which done, she recreated herselfe with some profitable and cheerefull discourse; if there were seculars with her of Quality, she applyed it to their capacityes. If occasion of rokes, falling of waters and other things high Pine trees, Meddowes, or pleasant Brookes, she wou'd dilate herselfe in admiration of God Allmighty his Power, Providence, Wisdome, and goodnes. What had of melancholy and solitary, suited exceedingly with her disposition, sometimes she wou'd complayne that such things distracted her in her prayer such content and recreation she found in them. If she had time and oportunity she did allwayes eate before she sett forth, and that was allwayes provided over Night. At noone she nor her Companions never made any Meale, but her Servants, she was carefull shou'd. In the [106r] afternoone she tooke time for her devotions, saying her beades etc. Neere the place where she was to lodge she said the Te Deum in thankes giving for her preservation that day, a Laudate Dominum omnes gentes etc.[284] for the graces bestowed on the Saints to whose protection she had commended herself. When arrived and in her Chamber, she sought out some Picture before which kneeling downe, she made an offer of her selfe and all her actions to be done in that place to the greatest honnour and glory of God. When order was given for Supper and Linnen had for the Bedds etc. she had a Saints Life red, that of that Day if there were any, if not some other, and for this end carryed allwayes with her the Saints Lives and Romane Martyrologe which was also daily readd. The time of meale she tooke occasion to say something that might edify and profit those of the Inne that waited. She was carefull to spare their Labour and that things shou'd be left in the manner [106v] as they were found, which did so much edify and oblidgge them as they not onely remayned slaves to her, but it was enough to have relation to her passing the wayes she had, to find all duty and service, which was the same in effect with Coachmen, Victorins[285] etc. amongst whom there was none so wicked, whom with her Prudence and goodnes she did not overcome.

---

[284] Ps. 117. Praise the Lord all you nations.
[285] Providers of food at inns (victuallers).

Liturgy. The Divine Office. The Word of God: scripture, sermons, catechetics. Care of books. Sacramentals. Reverence for the Priesthood.

Great was her respect to the Devine Office, and infatigable her diligence when we had Churches to have all belonging thereunto compleate, the musicke, the manner, and order of observance, and all conforme to the Romane rubrikes. Which was so punctuall as in Liege the Canon Churches wou'd vouchsafe to say, they might and did learne of her. When the Prince Electour[286] came thither to Masse, wou'd not heare his owne Musicke, but ours as surpassing, as he sayd etc. [107r]

Noe les great was her reverence to the word of God, preaching, Catechisme etc. She knew well to distinguish the good from better, but reverenced all, and wou'd say, she heard none she found not profit by, wou'd goe amongst young People and Children to Catechisme with as much reverence and attention as if truly needy, and wou'd returne still with profit and satisfaction as herselfe tould us. In a place where we had a House, she observed great defect in this particular, neglecting Sermons, so as to make it an ordinary thing to goe to Confession in Time of Sermon which she extreamly disliked, and strictly forbad ours ever to doe it, let the occasion seeme never so urgent, which so much edifyed and took with Externes, as many reformed themselves in that point.

This respect of hers extended it selfe to Bookes, and her observance so exact, as she wou'd have as a marke of who was hers [107v] never to fold Leaves of the Bookes, or crumple up the corners, or warpe the covers, when one readd to hold them so as not to force the binding, never to lay them on the bare-ground, never to cover any thing with them or make any use of them but with reverence to reade them and lay them up, and this respect she boare in a degree to Bookes of Historyes and Morality.

Her reverence was great to Agnus Dei,[287] Relikes, Pictures, Medalls etc. and this not in an ordinary and generall manner, but exemplar edifying and impressionating others. Of Saints Bodyes she wou'd say, by contempt they came to that honnour their power to interceade for us, their certainty for ever to be united to God, for Agnus Dei, holy water, and Indulgences, she wou'd say, who dares dispute their vertue which is grounded on the merits of Christ.

To conclude how profoundly great was her Reverence to Pope and Prelats of holy Church, [108r] Priests and least of the Cleargy, neither could there be any so bad in matter of Life which she know not how to separate from the meritt of his Caracter, which was above any particular vertue. Religious Men were all in great esteeme with her, but the caracter of Priesthood above all, and amongst Religious her private and particular devotion to some did not lessen what was due to all, and where most need there she applyed her selfe with most ardour and devotion.

---

[286]　Ferdinand von Wittlesbach, Prince Bishop of Liège.
[287]　Wax image of the Lamb carrying a flag or cross, as in the book of Revelation.

21. Final paragraphs: value of knowledge; influence on others; instructions for her own members. Devotion to the Holy Name of Jesus.

Importance of knowledge and education. Influence on others.

She was a great ennemy of Ignorance, did not love to see People of litle meane Spirits, much les endured what was vile and base. She was wont to say she cou'd not find out a reason, why knowledge shou'd be domageable but many that it might be advantageous,[288] knowledge though but morall, was a preservation from vice and an encitement to vertue. Sublimity though but in naturall things kept at a distance vice. Her Soule and [108v] mind thus ritchly adorned, rendred her conversation most profitable and pleasing, and was cause that a great devine and Persone of extraordinary breeding and birth was wont to say, he never made visitt to her but he returned with encrease of knowledge both devine and humaine. But what? The effects rested not there, her very presence, and the onely beholding of her gave Light and admiration and such as never knew her Person or Quality, at the first sight found themselves surprised with somewhat that was heavenly, and never seene or immagined by them before, breeding in them a confussion for the passed, and beginning to love what yet they knew not but at a great distance. Even her dead picture had greatly of the moving to devotion and heavenly thoughts. Persons of Learning and Religion seeing it, said it expressed much Sanctity and Majesty. A Protestant, but a Man of great parts [109r] and highly honnouring her wou'd say, that never any Creature had that power to conferre graces as she had, which was as excellent in the manner as the matter, having as it were a peacefull infusing manner, conforme to the rule she was wont to give to witt, not with violence to seeke to breake ones affection and inclination,[289] but first lay before them what in it selfe was truely lovely, then the deformity of what was naught, saying it was too great a violence to take away what one did possesse, without giving somewhat in place.

---

[288]　Cf. Mary Ward's *Three Speeches*, December 1617. AIM Libellus Ruber pp. 216–234. Quoted in Chambers I, pp. 408–411.
[289]　Cf. AB 6, note 20.

Various maxims and instructions.

An other of her documents was, that ours should never be ambitious to be feared, but deserve to be loved. To doe charityes and curtesyes freely for the contrary she said was to sell them. To ayoyd all manner of formality or fixion as well in the comportment of the body, as posture in prayer. That in speaking it shoud be in voyce and [109v] manner as not to need to be asked againe, that[a] we shou'd never love to keep people in suspence[a], to be free and speedy to give all satisfaction, to be unwilling to see any need what we can help them in by councell or Labour. For our selves that what we can doe by ouer selves, never to doe by an other, and that we should not make a need where there was none, but if God permitted that either by scruple or ignorance there were need, we should humbly seeke help, and so as not to be ever needing. Never to mixe matter of confession with other discourses, nor make that throne of so high consequence a place of conversation, but if aught occurred to take an other time for it. She was wont to say, once a friend ever a friend, which quality was in her in highest perfection, and with extraordinary grace, Light, and efficacy expressed. She had a singular guift by ordinary Discourses, and in few words to make [110r] marryed People understand the duty of their State, and how to make themselves thereby happy, and blessed in the next, which happened to the great profit of severall, and some of singular quality. She was wont to say, three things pleased her exceedingly, but they were hard to be found, to witt, young People devout, sicke folkes merry, and old folkes patient.

a–a A: insertion in another hand

Conclusion. Devotion to the Holy Name of Jesus.

To conclude she was in Soule and Body so adorned as made appeare somewhat, which when one would compendiously expresse, called it, Goodnes, and in particular the old Lord Evers[290] was wont to say, I never knew goodnes till I knew Mistress Ward. Good doth not leave to be good, which produceth a Patience to see so many excellencyes in her with such order and harmony, heere putt downe without forme or order. Yet must be seealed or concluded with her Love to that sacred name of JESUS her first and last word, beginning and ending of all her [110v] Petitions, her refuge in all dangers and protection in all evill. In fine the marke of all that was hers, and this in the auncient forme thus Ihs[291] which she allwayes putt on the toppe of all her letters and Bookes which were for her owne use. The dearnes of her love to the Holy Name of JESUS was as to a thing that had or was to cost her deare.[292][a]

a in A The text is followed by a decorated tailpiece: 1716. A[d]ieu. Lieber Leser. Lebe woll.

William, 4th Lord Eure, or Evers, succeeded to the title in 1617 and was listed as a recusant from 1618. He had estates at Stokesley, near Hutton Rudby, and Malton; the latter were sequestered by the Parliamentarians in 1652. Aveling, *Northern Catholics*.

291 This can be seen in the original manuscripts of Mary Ward's letters and notes.

292 It was only in 2003 that Mary Ward's congregation received permission from the Church to take the full Jesuit Constitutions, and a title which included the name of Jesus. In 2004 the 'Roman Branch' of Mary Ward's foundation adopted the full Constitutions (feminised and laicised) and with them the name *Congregation of Jesus*, fulfilling at last the founding vision of Mary Ward.

The Autobiographical Fragments (AB)

In 1613 or 1614 Fr Roger Lee SJ[1] gave Mary Ward the task of writing the story of her life. At the end of 1615, shortly before his death, he repeated his request, asking her to write before she began a journey which might endanger her life or liberty. Before travelling to England in 1617, Mary Ward began her autobiography. She confesses her negligence in delaying the work, but as well as the pressure of events, she was gravely ill in 1614. She speaks of the difficulty of finding the words to express her life story; she was not a natural author, and the task of writing about herself was evidently distasteful to her. This is clear from the numerous deletions, overwriting, and other corrections to be seen in the original manuscripts, which are kept in the Institute Archives in Munich/Nymphenburg. They give the impression that we are dealing with drafts that were perhaps intended to be put together into a well-ordered autobiography later on.

At the beginning of her work, in a passage which has been described as a remarkable example of the grace of the First Week of the Spiritual Exercises of St Ignatius, she professes her aim, to set down God's leading and the work of grace in her life. Her concern for the formation of those who will join her Institute is also clear in these passages. The Autobiographical Fragments are a rich source for the first twenty-four years of Mary's life, with details which are not found elsewhere. In addition they offer an insight into Mary Ward's own inner world, her motivation and inclinations, and her single-minded search for truth and for God's will.

Autobiographical Fragment (AB) 1

Liège 1617

Original: AIM Autobiographical Fragments No. III. Autograph.

Mary Ward began her autobiography on St Emerantiana's day, 23 January 1617 (new style), her thirty-second birthday. She was then in Liège and was planning a journey to England, which she began on 21 July 1617. There are two introductions to this record of her early life, probably composed at different times; part of the first version is adopted almost word for word in the second, but this is unfinished. For comparison the introductions are printed synoptically in this edition. The original pages were put together and numbered subsequently. In this edition subheadings have been added between sections for ease of reference.

Two Introductions

First Introduction	Second Introduction
	+ Ihs −

[3] I was commanded 3 or 4 years since[2] by my confesser father Roger Lee of the holy Socity of Jesus, unto whom I had on my part vowed obedience, to set doune in writting all that I could remember or call to mind of my life past; but throw sloth, and the dificulty I conceived in finding fitt words for what I would express I neglected to doe yt. Too years after[3] (or their abouts) which happined to be some few days before he blessedly departed this lyfe) he gave me a more absolute charge to doe yt, and that before my going to England or anie other place whear my life or liberty might be endaingered, and that I should leave yt sealed upp with our company hear when I was to undertake anie such iurnay. Since this last command yt ys more then a twelve month and I am now of necessaty to goe for England[4] and theirfore darr no longer deferr yt. Jesus give me grace to sett yt doun [4] truly as yt passed. This St. Emerentiana her day, upon which I began to live in this world and am now of age thurty three, in the year of our Lord 1617.[5]

Ihs −

[1] I beseech all thos (even for our lords love) that shall read thes my falts, and the goodnes of god towards me, notwithstanding my unworthynes, that they iudge not of anie thinge hear according to their owne affections, but determin of all as the truth ys, distinguishing the great and true differance betwext gods preventinge graces, his imasurable goodnes and the meanes affourded me to be wholly his; and my continuall fales, unspeakable negligence, and imperfitt concurrance with all such his favours,

I beseech all thos (even for our lords love) that shall read thes my falts, and the goodnes of god towards me notwithstanding my unworthynes: that they iudg not of anie thinge hear according to their own affections, but determin of all as the truth ys: distinguishing the great and true differance betwixt gods preventinge graces, his imeasurable goodnes, and the means affourded me to be wholy his: And my continuall fales, unspeakable negligence, and imperfitt concurrance with all such his favours.

as your selves will iudge and wettnes with me so shall you doe iustis giveing god what ys his, and me my deserts, who asketh noe other recompence thinge etc. mor accountable of anie thing they could do for me besides those that the readers of thes would endevour thence forward,
to become lovers of truth and workers of justis, which petition who granteth and proceedeth accordinge, verity yt self will free them from errors, rectify their iudgments, perfitt their knowlidg, endue them with true wisdom, make them able to desarne things as they are in them selves, the diferance betwext trifils and matters of importance, what ys to be done, or not done in all. I intreat all my frinds to converse much with such and would to god I had ability in anie thing to further thes to heaven, our lord will not denye me to doe somthinge for them, and all I shall be able to perform in heaven or on earth, they may freely challins as their due, and my promis.
[2: *blank page*]

So shall you doe iustis giveinge god what ys hes, and me my desarts.

O all seeing goodness the lovers of truth, and workers of iustes,

o verity yt self preserve them from errors, rectifie their iudgements, perfitt their knowlidg, endue them with true
[5,6: *blank pages*]

---

1   Roger Lee SJ, 1574–1615, entered the Society of Jesus in 1600, after making the Spiritual Exercises under the direction of John Gerard. He was Mary's spiritual director at Saint-Omer from 1608 until his death in December 1615, and he played an important part during the early years of her congregation. Cf. Vita E, f. 14v and note 56.
2   At the end of 1613. Mary travelled to England in April 1614.
3   1615.
4   Mary made this journey to England in July 1617 and stayed there about a month.
5   23 January 1617, the thirty-second anniversary of Mary Ward's birth in 1585, and her entry into her thirty-third year.

Parents and early childhood.

Ihs −

[7] my parence[6] wear both verie vertuous, and suffered much for the catholyke caus, my father as his charity towards the poore, and commiseration of all in necessaty was such, as I have neiver experienced the

lyke in anie secular person since, so his care of his children espetially
in matters of purity, and that we should neiver tast the poison of hericie
was so great, as I wish the lyke wear to be found in all catholyke parance
now a days; in his howse he would never permitt to be reed or cept
such bookes that treated of sentiall or worldly loves, and I remember
he hath caused my mother (who was noe less emenent in the vertue
of modesty as wittness as well both her owne carridg, and the strict
watch she cept over the men, and the mades in her howse) to turne away
such servants, as wear otherways very profittable, for some such little
signes of lightnes, as now adays are accounted harmless and a recreation convenient to bannish mellincoly even amongst catholikes. And
when by occasion we wear to live for anie little time with such of our
kindred as wear sismitikes[7] I shall neiver forget the exortations he would
give us tuching the necessaty for salvation of catholike religion, and his
inflamed desirs that all his should live, and die children of gods church.
He hated swearers and would not endure this vice in us. I living with
thes my pearance[8] till the age of 5 or their abouts, at which years I had
iudgment to desarne[9] [8] a great ingratetud, I had noe sooner [*space in
the text*] my fathers inclination in divers things being theirfore in a rome
wher him self was writing; playing with one of my companions, that
some time came to our howse, she suddenly swore (by christ his sacred
wounds) and I presently repeated the same her words severall tims in
way of reprehention,[10] with desirs, that my father should hear me and
love me the better, god permitted that he hear me say the words, but
minding not what went before thought I had sworn and coming with this
conceit theirfor in great coller unto me he corrected me him self (which
was unusuall and the first and last time that ever I could learn he did the
lyke to anie of us his children). He afterwards heard me speake;

---

6   Marmaduke Ward (b. 1551) and Ursula née Wright.

7   Schismatics. This refers to some Catholic heads of families who, to protect their property, conformed outwardly to the State Church and attended Protestant services on occasion; for example, Sir William Ingleby of Ripley Castle, with whom Mary often stayed.
They were known as 'Church Papists' by their opponents. Marmaduke Ward remained true
to his Catholic faith, without compromise but at great cost.

8   Parents. From 8 September 1585 Mary Ward's father was appointed estate agent for
Spofforth Castle by Henry Percy, Earl of Northumberland, and went to live there; from 16
November 1588 he purchased and occupied the manor of Mulwith, traditionally Mary's
birthplace, which he had previously been working. Peters pp. 30–34.

9   Discern.

10   Reprehension.

*Five years spent with grandparents, Robert and Ursula Wright, from late
1589 to 1594. The grandmother's care of Mary.*

I was now not full 5 years ould when by whos means or procurment[11]

I know not I was sent to my granfather and granmother (parents of my mother) to be brought up.[12] Who for her great vertue, was much noted, and esteemed, she had in her younger years suffered impresonment for the spase of 14 years togeather in which time she manie tims made profession of her faith before the presedent of yorke, Huntintone,[13] and other officerers etc. She was once, for her speaches to the sayd Huntintone tending to the exaltation of catholike religion, and, contempt of hericy, throust into a common prison[14] or dungan amongst theefs; whear she [9] stayed not long, becaus being much spoken of, yt came, to the hearing of her kinred, who procured her speedy removall to the prison whear she was before, at her enterance into thos dongan, the malifactors iudged she had bein commited for theeft, or murder (for such wear all that came to that place) sayd unto her that she must either give 6 pence unto their comon purs as the coustom of all that came their at their first enterance was, or els she should not eat of their common meat, which was that which good people of charity would give, all sorts of meats put togeather in one vassell, and so given them in at the presin door; to thes their words my granmother made noe other reply then that she would willingly give them the 6 pence and so she ded. When I came unto her she had bein releaced some few years and had leave to live at home, I remained their near 5 years, the most of all which time I lodged with her self, for the howse being great she was very carefull least by idoll or ill companie I should be drawn to offend god, (and although my granfather wear livening yet for holy respects they lodged in severall chambers) and so great a prayer she was as that I doe not remember in that whol 5 year that ever I say her sleep, nor did I ever awake, when I perceived her not to be [10] at prayer. She used to provide much almiss[15] to catholike presoners, which she sent them secretly at severall tims of the year, once I heard her give order (amongst other things) for the killing of certaine pullon,[16] some of which I called, and accounted mine, loving them as children will such toys, I was sorie but made noe sing[17] to have understood of anie such thing; soon after I askeed my granmother (which apeared sing of devotion when she would send anie almiss to the preson: she bed me tell why I asked, I answerd becaus I was desirous such poullan which she had before given me should be so bestowed, this seemed to pleas her much, and I sayd yt only to gaine her esteem.

---

[11] Mary spent much of her childhood and youth with relatives. This was the common practice of the time, but the reason for sending her to her grandparents so early in her life may have been the conviction of her parents as recusants, and the imposition of heavy fines from 1590 to 1592. See Peters pp. 34–37 for this and the following sections.
[12] Robert and Ursula Wright (née Rudston) of Ploughland, in Holderness, East Yorkshire.

13 Henry Hastings, 3rd Earl of Huntingdon, 1536–1595, President of the Council of the
North, a fierce persecutor of Catholics, who enforced in full the strict laws of 1580/81
against recusants.
14 Conditions in the notorious Blockhouse prisons in Hull and in the Ousebridge and
Castle prisons in York were very severe.
15 Alms.
16 Poultry.
17 Sign.

*In the company of a frivolous relative, Alice Wright. Mary's account of
her own lack of prayer and virtue at this time, with thanksgiving for God's
protection.*

Their lived in my Granfathers howse a neer kinswoman of mine,[18] whom
god had endued with many exelent gifts of nature, though she used them
not to hes honour nor her owne good. She had alowed to attend [11] her
a young gentilwoman, who though in show modest, yet was she indeed
light of carridg, and the cause as I saw of her utter perdition. This kinswoman of mine was not much elder then I, she loved me much, and I
bore her exeed her great affection when I could without blame be from
my grandmother, I was for the most pert[19] in her company, I saw her
with the help of her woman doe many things which I knew to be not
well, she lykewyse made me of her councell in most of her intentions,
and desires which yf gods goodnes, and providence over me had not byn
so very great might have done me much harm. I accompanied [12] her
in severall actions which wear not good. As such, and such, I cept her
councell in all, for so she often intreated me, and so farr as I can iudg I
was naturally inclyned to do so; yet this was the caus I fear of her furder
falls. I never saw her doe anie thing, that since I understood the Divels
malice better I could iudg to be dishonest, only once I saw a man in her
Chamber whear I knew her mother a lowed none to come, I conceived
that to be a miss, yet made known to none who spoke what I had seen;
this silence of mine I fear was the cause of her furder fale, and wilbe
occation of her eternall perdition, for being not prevented in thes beginnings [13] she committed afterwards great abuces in this kind, to the
publicke scandell of many,[20] and still as I have cause to doubt remains
mesirable in severall respects. I want both time and words to express the
manie and great daingers I so narrowly escaped in thos 5 years whyll
I lived whear she was but I now see they wear such (all considered) as
none but god who can doe all things, could have preserved me, from
falling most greevously into that, which once begon would by all lykelyhood have bein my eternall ruine, I was not then adicted to anie one
vertue, when my grandmother commanded me to pray, I sat in the place
but spent my time in sports. Yet I wanted not witt to seeke cunningly
my owne esteem and to lye some tims in owne excuse, or other wyse to

have my will. This my lacke of vertue disposed me yf occation had byn offered for [14] vice, and the company of my kinswoman might have afforded means, and supposing my fale my bashfullnes, was such as that in all lykelyhood I should have committed a greater sinne then before by concealinge what was done and past. O my God in what state had I now bein yf you had not don all.

---

18   Alice Wright, Mary's aunt and her mother's younger sister.
19   Part.
20   See note 22 below.

Marriage of Alice Wright to William Readshaw. Superstitious practices while staying with the grandparents.

This kinswoman went once to see my mother who was very near her in blood, though unlyke in condition, and their living at my fathers howse one whom he intended to mach with me when I should come to years of concent,[21] god so disposed as that before my kinswomans retourn to me again, this party and [15] she wear maried,[22] hear once more our lord prevented what would have hindered my greater good; what was their my god in me worthy your self, why was she forsaken and I chosin, she exceled me I thinke in all good gifts of nature, and I had then noe inclination to vertue, neither affection to practis anie thing that good was. Let not thes and other your favours, o frind of frinds I humbly beseech be to my greater condemnation, whylst still receiving I concur not with all, and remains so ungratefull. In this 5 years my fortune was asked, and tould severall tims, once or twice I thinke I procured yt, at the least as I remember [16] I was glad to hear yt and according to my capacity beleeved what was sayd.[23] I once intended and ded till I gott my self seized with hunger to fast sant Agnes fast,[24] for the fowlish[25] end accustomed, moved as I remember by the speech, and example of my afforesayd kinswoman. I thinke I once procured that unlawfull practis of sive, and sheers[26] to be done excercised, and holp to doo yt my self, for the finding out a triffle of mine that was lost; and I am morrally sertain that in the excecution of thes 3 last things I had some fear and understanding, that they wear sinne. Yf thos years I remembered anie one act that wear good I would faithfully set yt down; for I am to tell all.
[17] I was now almost 10 years ould when my father sent for me home, to his howse,[27]

---

21   Canon Law at that time prescribed a minimum age for marriage of twelve years for girls and fourteen for boys. Betrothal often took place much earlier.
22   In 1593 William Readshaw of Oulston was married clandestinely to Alice Wright in the house of Marmaduke Ward of Mulwith, Ripon. In 1599 Alice was accused of adultery. Peters p. 35 and Aveling, *Northern Catholics*, p. 186.

23 Superstition, fortune-telling and magic arts were widespread in England in the seventeenth century.
24 On the eve of St Agnes (21 January) girls who wished to get married fasted in order
to see their future bridegroom in a dream.
25 Foolish.
26 To find a guilty person people consulted 'sieve and shears'. A sieve and a pair of shears
were held in balance, and after a prayer-formula the name of the suspect was spoken. If
the sieve began to move, that person's guilt was considered to be proved.
27 The death of Mary's grandfather, Robert Wright, on 18 July 1594, may have been the
reason for her return to her parents' home later in that year.

Autobiographical Fragment (AB) 7

Vienna 1627 October 11
AIM. Various Papers VI. 2/42: A. Original. Autograph; B. Copy (incomplete).

This fragment was written in Vienna in October 1627, following the foundation
of a house and school at the request of the Emperor Ferdinand II. Although the
date of composition is later than the other pieces of autography, it has here been
placed in its correct chronological order, February or March 1695, not long after
Mary's return home to Mulwith. This is the only reference to the incident, which
is not found in any other written source.

The fire at the family home, Mulwith near Ripon, North Yorkshire, 1595.

Ihs

I had great confidence in the powre and help of our blessed lady, when
I was yet young: when I was but att tenn years owld, and so much as
betwixt St. Emerentianas day in January and the feast of the purification of our Blessed Lady the lent following upon which day my father
had great loss by fire.[1] I being present, and seeing the danger callid
earnestly upon our Blessed Lady beseeching her to extingush the fire,
often repeating with great confidence that yf yt wear not her feast Day I
should fear the worst but being hers I had noe doubt but she would help
us etc. and perceiving by the noices of people the danger still to continue
I tooke tow of my younger sisters[2] (both which wear after so happie
as to live and dye of our Societie[3]) and went into a lower roome of the
howse where stood a trunk or cofer filled with littning damaske which
I had heard some say my mother layd a part for me which coffer with
the help of my two sisters I drew into the chimnye of the same roome,
and then we sett our selves to pray the mother of god that she would
not permitt the howse to be burnt etc. and this with great earnestnes
and confidence in which prayr we had all 3 byn burnt but that our lord
provided by the entercession of his Blessed Mother as I veryly believe,
that my father (whos love for his children was boundles) seeing the case

erimediable, the whol howse of one flame, and all in yt to be lost, called
for his childred and missing us 3, him self entered the howse a gaine

---

[1]   Mary Ward kept her tenth birthday on 23 January 1595. The fire took place on 2
February, the feast of Candlemas, or the Purification of Our Lady. PL 4 assigns this accident to 25 March (feast of the Annunciation).
[2]   Elizabeth and Barbara Ward, b. 1591 and 1592.
[3]   Only Barbara Ward was already dead in 1627. The date of Elizabeth Ward's death is
not known, but there is evidence in Mary Ward's letters to show that she was still alive in
1633.

Autobiographical Fragment (AB) 2

undated

Original: AIM Autobiographical Fragments, No. II. Autograph.

This episode is difficult to date. It is likely to relate to Mary Ward's stay
in the large Babthorpe household in Osgodby (1600–1605) and probably to
some time after her vocation to religious life ('religious vertues'). See Peters
pp 47–48.

*Behaviour in a case of conscience: fear of slandering or belittling someone,
and the hidden motive – not to lose the confessor.*

Ihs –

yt might be indeed I was a caus of some hurt in this sort manner perticuler. First living some years in one howse[1] whear some lived that I
had suffitient caus, to thinke affected me in such manner as was not
lawfull, and yet neither removed my self from the place nor discovered
the busines to such as in lyklyhood might have procured remedy without
inconvenience.

The preist that was confessor[2] to us both, was a learned discreet
and pious man, and one who besyds his so great zeall that all under
his charge should offend God little; and pleas him much, tended on
my progress in all (espetially religious vertues) [*manuscript damaged*]
perticulerly. This so holy man (upon what grounds I never understood)
inquired of me once or twice very seariously yf ever that party showed
anie such carrage towards me. I answered confidently that I knew noe
such thinge by him, either towards my self or anie other which was
false, for he used besyds uncoomly famaliaryty to an other young
woeman[3] in that howse unto whom though I gave the best councell
I could (becaus she made only me aquainted and asked what to doe
in such a case) without discovering anie known hurt of the party she
blamed and that I am moreally certaine shee failed not while I lived
with her, yet perchance her confessor might more have strenthned her
soule and discreetly prevented in both parties anie further harm which I

trust howsoever happened not for she left the place soon after wheather upon advice or noe. This only might in some sort make my falt[4] in consealinge what [3] perchance had byn [*manuscript damaged*] [bet]ter to have tould [*manuscript damaged*] though I had not byn asked, was an ignorant fear, that by telling the truth I should committ the sinne of detraction[5] in a matter of mortall sinne: thinking yt therfore a better deed to conceall then otherwise, which fear was cheif yf not all the caus why I answered thus: ther might be [*manuscript damaged*] some self love in this which I did not then perceive (for I think I would not in thos days have offended God seriesly [*manuscsript damaged*] fear I doubt not perfict love for anie humaine respect or whattsoever comfort could have byn had in this world) for my confessor, when he asked this sayd that yf the aforesayd party wear so disposed he would leave the howse and yt may be I was the willinger to [*manuscript damaged*] fourth of fear to lose him:

---

1   Probably Osgodby or Babthorpe, near Selby, Yorkshire.
2   Probably Fr John Mush; see AB 3, note 11.
3   This young woman is unnamed and unknown.
4   Fault.
5   Detraction: causing injury to another's good name by revealing behaviour which, though true, should not be made known. Mary's motive in this was similar to her earlier reserve during her stay at her grandparents' house. Cf. AB 1.

Autobiographical Fragment (AB) 3

Liège 1618/19

Original: AIM. Autobiographical Fragments, No. I. Autograph.

The dating of this fragment comes from the information that Mary Ward went to the Babthorpe family nineteen years earlier. Her parents sent her there at the end of 1599, or at the latest at the beginning of 1600. The last section may be part of Mary's recollection of preparation for her general confession.

Life with the Babthorpe family in Osgodby. Thanksgiving for God's grace and protection. Lady Grace Babthorpe as a model. Attraction to the spiritual life.

Ihs–

[1] Beinge about 15 years owld, so neer as I can gess, my parence had occation to remove[1] to a much coulder clement[2] then that whear ordenarily they lived. And I being very sickely, they feared least that ayre might endanger me and therfore sent me to a kinswoeman of my mothers, a Catholyke lady,[3] on whom I was to attend, till either my parence retourned, or some means of preferment should happen. Which

they hoped I would be sooner drawn unto, living abrode then I had byn at home. (Though I refused not thos they offered[4] fourth of anie desirs to be religious, nor other reason but becaus I could not affect them). This latter – as I have since thought – was the cheef caus they sent me from them though I remember the first was espetially aleaged: and both might well be for they loved me dearly. But o parent of parence, and frind of all frinds; thy intent in thus disposinge was different from thos: for hear – without intreaty – thou tookest me into thy care, and by degrees ledd me from all els, that at lenth I might see, and settle my love on thee. What had I ever don to please the? Or what was ther in me whearwith to serve thee? Much less could I ever deserve to be chosin by thee. O happie begun freedom, the beginninge of [2] my good, and more worth me at that time, then the whol world besyds. Hadd I never since hindered thy will, and working in me what degrees of grace should I now have had. Yt ys more then 19 years since, and whear as yet am I? My Jesus forgive me. Remember what thou hast done for me, and wheather thou hast brought me; and for this excess of goodnes, and love let me noe more hinder thy will in me.

This lady was of more then ordenary vertue, and all things in her howse so well ordered for the service of God,[5] as led me by degrees to begin to serve him. And with in a little time I hadd some such taste of his love, as made all that tended not som ways to his service, of little value with me. I hadd much sensible devotion, and sayd many vocall prayers, was carefull to come with due preparation to the sacraments (accordinge to my scill at that time) very carefull of modesty in which both then, and for divers years after I was severall times solicited to falle. (But for this [3] noe thankes to my self for I had naturally a great avertion from that vice; and was besyds so bashfull, as that I could neither drinke, nor be drawn [manuscript damaged] unto by speake or look, upon anie man, without so much blushinge as ma[de] my carrage rather disgracefull, then gaininge. Nether could I without extreem mortification, be in a room alone, for anie time, or when others wear not lykely to come in, thouge the party wear spiritual

1   Probably to Alnwick, to stay with Thomas Percy (married to Martha Wright, a sister of Ursula Wright), who was steward to Henry Percy, Earl of Northumberland. After their conviction as recusants, Marmaduke and Ursula Ward moved frequently, and Mary spent very little time in the family home. We do not know whether the other children were sent to relatives or stayed with their parents.

2   Climate.

3   Lady Grace Babthorpe, wife of Sir Ralph Babthorpe; daughter of Grace Birnand (née Ingleby) and thereby second cousin to Ursula Wright.

4   PL Nos. 2, 5 and 8 name three suitors, Redshaw, Shafto and Eldrington.

5   See Peters p. 46 for a contemporary description of the Babthorpe household (1604–08) by James Pollard SJ. Pollard (alias for Sharpe, b.1576 in Yorkshire, ordained priest 1604, entered the Society of Jesus 1608) was in Osgodby between 1604 and 1607/8. He

writes that two or three priests were often lodged in the Babthorpe house. Morris III, p. 467; Foley II, pp. 617–625. From time to time these included Richard Holtby SJ, Jesuit Superior in the north of England; Mary Ward was well known to him. Peters pp. 48 and 84.

Conversation with a maidservant, leading to love and admiration for the religious life and desire for God

I lyked to keep company most with thos of the howse that I thought to be most vertuous; amongst whom ther was espetially one, a maide[6] of great vertue, (and in years) who looked to the Chappell, and such lyke businesces, with whom I loved to be, and was much [manuscript damaged] (and I trust in Jesus she hath a great croune in heaven for the good my soule gained by her means) for by some speeches of hers I found my self first moved to love a religious life. She never knew so much while she lived, but now my God reward her, with that which ys truely good, and ys never to have end. And wherin [4] yt may be avallable to her let her have a part in all that little I doe that ys good, who by thy permition gave a beginninge to yt.

Once as we wear sewinge togeather in one roome shee speakeing of God, (which was her ordenary talke) amongst other good stories, she tould one of a religious Nunn, who violating her virginity and beinge found with child, was therfore by the lawes of her religion injoined daily, and for divers years togeather, to lye prostrat without the Chappell or quir door of her monnastary, for all the other Nunns passinge by to tread upon. This so great a pennance made the falt seem extreem and withall I reflected that the lyke was nether rare very disgracefull nor much punished a mongst worldlings: by which I emediatly conceived a singuler love, and esteem of religious life, as a santuary whear all might, and must be holy. And haveing throw[7] Gods meer goodnes as yett noe prepossession of worldly affections, he gave me at that instant [5] such a desire never to love anie but him, as I doe not remember that ever since that time I have had the least inclyning thought to the contrary: but on the other part, have very manie times seriously reflected and as me thought certainly perceived that yf one man should, or could be indued with the excelences of all men togeather; yt wear unpossible for me to content my self with the election of so little a good: which light, and love came wholy from him; unto whom I trust all that thinkes this was a benefitt will give the prays,[8] for what belongs to me, I that should best know finds cause to fear, that yf God had given less, I should have left him; or at least the best way to serve him: and so either lost my self (being forth of my right way) or els by my many falles, and much misiry come home at lenth: yet so as for ever, and that infinittly less happie, then that goodnes intended me, who of his mercie hath heathertoo kept me in that perfitt way in which this holy woeman holpe[9] to putt me.

And I am perswayded one principall means of my continuance hath byn the little satisfaction I could take in anie worldly contentment (somtim by a sight that thes wear insecur, uncertaine, and short, but for the most part, without anie reasons why; only that I could not effect them, nor find [6] repose in them). For yt will hearafter appeir by the disposition of mind which in severall occasions God diversly gave me, how great a lover I am of my owne content, and how needfull yt was for anie thinge should be don by me, that God gave me first a feelinge affection to yt: and in what I should fly the contrarie.

---

6 Margaret Garrett. Her name is known to us from PL No. 9.
7 Through.
8 Praise.
9 Helped.

Various spiritual exercises. General Confession: lack of moderation in eating; unsuitable choice of company; lack of charity towards wrongdoers; inordinate desire for praise and esteem, but this combined with drawing others to good.

With this desire to be religious, my devotion to prayr and the excercise of severall other vertues: after some time I begun to thinke of a generall confession, which I had reed in some bookes (for I had little other instruction at that time than what I gott by readinge[10]) was very profittable to ones self; and pleasinge to God: and so I was resolved to make one, (though as I remember yt was more then a year and half before I could bringe my self to doe yt (espetially becaus all such preists as came then to the howse wear strangers, made noe stay, the ordenary confessor[11] being then at roome[12] about some differances risen amongst the Clergie of England etc.)

After this was made, with the best preparation I could (for I examined as I remember divers howrs every day, from Saint Thomas his day before Christmas till Easter Eve[13]) my longinge to be a religious increased.

But how much good shall I say of my self: havinge forgott the badd I ded in this time. Thou knowest o lord my hart, and that I doe this by commandment; and that my only care ys to tell true, and to sett down all I can call to rememberance good, and badd.

I stayed in this place 6 years and some monthes[14] (so neer as I can gess) [7] whear as I have sayd by reading and the example I saw; I learnt the excercise of divers vertues – how I corrupted the use of thes after some years, and more, some twelve month or more before I came over as to place severall Saints in such roomes of the howse,[15] as I had most often occasion to come into: which I ded, and indevoured to practis the vertue most eminent in the same Saint very often. I failed most in the dininge roome whear the vertue was abstinence: for my appityd was

good, and my disiesture[16] very badd: so as I usially confessed eatinge
too much; and not with so little caus as some may thinke for though the
quantitie wear not much, yet too much for me; and very many times of
that which pleased my tast, though I knew before yt would make me
sicke: and thus I veryly thinke many hundreds of times, I eat against
my contience some times too much, and other things not agreeinge,
fearinge at the same time that I sinned by so doinge: and yt ys lykely
that some times (my much scruple, and little scill considered) I might
be fearfull that the sinn I should by this committ might be mortall: I
doe not remember this certainly; nor that ever I ded determin yt to be
mortall sinne, and notwithstandinge ded yt.

Some 3 or 4 times I remember I surfitted so as distempered me for
divers days. And 2 or 3[is] fourth of greedines, rashly eate flesh [8] on
fastinge days, so much as might breake my fast, and perhaps twenty tims
without anie need, and at unfitt tims: as the evinnings when all should
have byn in bedd: and twice, or trice in the company of men, and once
espitially, in company of one whom I had rather caus to suspect was
lyght of carrage then otherwyse: yet he discovered noe badd at that time:
and so farr as I remember I ded not occation his being ther: at least I am
sure neither the presence of this, nor ever anie man els for anie bad end.
(Nor after twelve year ould ded I ever see anie that I ded, or, for any
ought I know, could affect, even in way of marrage) but against sinfull
affection my bashfullnes, and the avertion I had naturally from this vice
holpe me so much as next to what god ded without my knowlidg, this
was all.

And hear my God in place of gratitude for such a defence: I often
offended the (even with what thou hadest given me) in the other extreem:
for yt was ordenary with me not only to hate the sinne, but the partye
or practice that used yt, in such extremity (espetially when the wronge
was offered to myself) as could not stand [9] with Christian charity:
and towards severall, and for divers years togeather. But my God gave
not I some just caus (though without intention of hurt to either part)
that some of thes might seperate them selves from the; loose thy grace;
their place in heaven; and so becoming thy enimy, committ many other
sinns, to thy dishonour, and ther owne greater damnation, at least eternall loss (becaus though all may be forgiven yet what ys once done
cannot but have byn? Ther was nothing more hatefull then that anie
should effect me so; but I was so desirous to be estemed, and loved
by all, that I sought this of every one good, and badd. My carrage,
speach, and attire was ever noted for more then ordenary modest: so as
I never by lyghtness in anie kind, gave occation to anie ones hurt: but
thes wear so mixed, and tempered with other perfections, of nature, and
helps by grace, as gained more even of some that wear wicked, then
ever the contrary could have done. (But hear was wantinge (through

my only want to the my God) that grace that so graceth all thy giftes, as excludeth badd affection, (what caus so ever the badd may find of esteem) and all hopes to prevail. And therfore such never hurt them selves by attemtinge[17]) [10] God almighty knows I never intended to hurt them, or sought anie thinge that was bad in this, but inordenately to be though worthy the prays, and esteem of all, nether wear thos goods of my procuringe, much less gained by me: this only was mine, that in the use of them, I thus offended him, that gave them, not only – as yt may seem – for my owne help to heaven: but (which causeth extreemest confution) that many seeinge thes, might love them, and by this lynke of affection, be more inclined to hear and observe her, whom he, that goodnes, thus requited intended to make a means of ther salvation.

---

[10]   Despite the penalties of the law, Catholic books were constantly printed secretly in England or imported.

[11]   Fr John Mush, c. 1554–1613, born in Yorkshire and active as a priest in the York area, was Mary Ward's confessor. He had been confessor to Margaret Clitherow, and after her martyrdom in 1586 he wrote her biography. In 1601 he went to Rome to appeal against the appointment of Blackwell as Archpriest. John Mush was highly respected by the English secular clergy, and on his return to England in November 1602 he became assistant to the Archpriest.

[12]   Rome.

[13]   Mary made her general confession to Fr John Mush on Holy Saturday 1603 (23 April Old Style, Julian calendar). Cf. AB 6.

[14]   From c.1599 to c.1605.

[15]   Cf. AB 6.

[16]   Digestion.

[17]   Attempting / in their attempts.

Autobiographical Fragment (AB) 4

undated

Original: AIM. Autobiographical Fragments, No. V. Autograph.

This fragment contains two notes which in content relate to Mary's description of her vocation to religious life (Cf. AB 3). Pages [5] and [9] contain other pieces of information.

Conversations with a maidservant, leading to vocation to religious life at the age of 15.

[1] My first motions to religion happinned so near as I can remember about the 15. year of my age, occatined partly as I thinke by a devout womans[1] speech who amongst pieous other discourses happined upon a true storie which fell fourth in our countrie before the faile of religion, a Nune sayd shee having violated her virginity in such sort as the thinge was verily apparent and commonly known was first bannished

the monasterie till she was disbordened, and afterwards admitted again
[2] (becaus they could not dismiss her she having made vows); their she
suffered much confution, sheam, and pain amongst her other pennance
this was one that for manie years she was allways at the time of prayer
to lye at the threswould of the quire that the religious as they passed too
and fro might tread upon her; this exact punnishment of that vice gave
a splendor to the contrarie vertue, and as I thinke on at that instant, my
loving lord ded so tuch my hart with a longing desire [3] to dedicate
my self to his divine service, as that I do not remember since anie one
moment in which I had not rather have suffered death then betaken my
self to a worldly life.

O my lord and saviour permitt me not to be proud of that which ys
not mine, for yf your maeistie had left me to my self whear had I now
beine, nay how have carried myself this grace notwithstanding. O how
much importeth good example and holy conversation, and how great
harm have I caused by my contrarie proceedinge. But to goe [4] forward
as I am commanded, my desire to religion dayly encreaced, in such sort
as that I tooke noe delite in anie ons companie except such as wear good
nor ded their conversation pleas me except yt

*Vocation to religious life though no knowledge of the various religious
orders; telling this to her confessor on Ascension Day 1601.*

[5] croune, 5. Mrs. Moors children[2] Father Prov:[3] Tal:[4] Flack[5] and all
our benefactors
my oune life and health, yf yt to be the greater glorie of god.

betwext 15 and 16 years of my age so near as I can remember yt
pleased our loving lord to inspire me with a desire to lead a religeous
life, in generall for I had noe instructions tuchinge anie perticuler Order,
nor means to inform my self in that living in a cuntrie infected etc. nether
had I the curredg to aske anie one the difirence betwext them never
somuch as to acquaint my confessor[6] with my desirs, for a year and
half after, about which time he perceived my inclination rather by some
tears which I could [not] [6] forbear by the occation of some speaces
which then he uttered, in commendations of religious women in thos
cuntries where such piety was permitt: O goodnes of god I can neiver
give thankes suffitient for this benifit nor am able to express the ioy of
spirit which then I felt after I had oppened my mind and perceived him
inclyned to further me in that cours, this discoverie of my self happined
upon an assention day[7] after supper, [7] before which time for the space
of ten weks togeather I had noe means to come to the sacrements, in
which space the devill tempted my exceedingly and I perceived not his
drift, I remember I used extriordenarie preparation for the space as I
think of ten days before the sayd assention, but what devotions I used

in perticuler I have forgotten except some short speaches of desire of
his presence; [8] but with what confusion may I thinke upon this, when
being now permitted to communicate daily I remain notwithstanding
such as I am known and iudged to be by as manie as hath a quaintance,
or converceth with me.

[9] to aske questions of all tuching that obedience

---

1   Margaret Garrett
2   Perhaps expenditure for the children of Elizabeth More (née Gage, related to Anne
Gage, one of the first companions of Mary Ward) who had died in 1610, leaving three
children. Elizabeth's husband, Cresacre More, suffered very much as a recusant.
3   Provincial. Fr Jean Heren SJ was the first Provincial of the Franco-Belgian Province
of the Society of Jesus, founded in 1612.
4   Probably to be read as Talbot, referring to Sir George Talbot of Grafton, Earl of
Shrewsbury, who was a benefactor of Mary Ward's community.
5   Fr William Flacke SJ, founder and first Rector of the English Jesuit College in Saint-
Omer.
6   Fr John Mush.
7   Ascension Day 21 May (old style) 1601.

Autobiographical Fragment (AB) 5

Perugia, 1624 August 19
Copy: AIM. Parchment Book pp. 147–153

Mary Ward had founded a house at Perugia at the beginning of 1619. Between
15 May and 23 July 1624 Mary Ward took the waters at S. Casciano dei Bagni;
this fragment was written after her return. It covers her departure from England
and arrival at Saint-Omer, 1609.

*Entry into religious life; journey via Canterbury to Saint-Omer. Received by
the Poor Clares as a laysister.*

[147]   August 19. 1624
The Whitsuntyd following that Christmasse wheron I was twenty one I
happily begun my long desired iourney from England towards Flanders
there to become a religious woman. Upon the Thursday before whit-
sunday in the year 1606 I parted with unspeakable content from London
towards Canterbury where I stayed whitsun holy dayes[1] in company
of Mrs Catherin Bentley[2] in whos passe I was putt to goe over sease
[148] as one of her daughters;[3] our stay in that Citty was in Mrs. Bently
her Mother her howse called Mrs Roper,[4] etc.; from thence we went to
Dover a port towne of England: then passed the seas in fower or five
howers arrived at Callis, and from thence to the Citty of St. Omers.[5]
Wheather when I was come before I would take time to putt of my riding
safegard I went to a Colleg of the fathers of the Society of Jesus which

is in that towne commonly called the English Seminary there to deliver
certaine letters of commendation [149] given me by Father Houltby[6]
an English father of the said Society a man of speciall note which then
lived in England to a father in the aforesaid seminary called Father
William Flacke[7] for whom being entered the porch I called: immediately came to me one called Father Georg Keyns,[8] who tould me that
I was, and had bin for some time expected at a Monastery of the poor
Clares in that towne, wherin wear, and had lived divers years severall
Gentilwoemen [150] of our Nation, commending much the place the
discipline observed amongst those Religious and perticularly the witt,
good quality spiritt, and perfection of those of our Nation that wear
amongst them: and of their Order adding that this Monastery was now
so full that they wear resolved to admitt noe more English within their
inclosure or to be of the Quire, as was experiensed some few months
before in a Neece of the Lord Lumlos[9] called Mrs Anne Campian,[10]
who said he, desiring to be of that holy Order and wanted not friends to
intreate [151] her admittance they utterly denied to receave as one of the
Quire, but offered to admitt her for a lay Sister which she accepted and
there she lives with much content: her only difficulty is that by reason
of her years she is unapt to learne their language which impediment said
he is not in you, being young etc; he added that the Abbes and some of
our Nation had many months expected my coming, that my place was
allready granted amongst the lay Sisters, more being not to be obtained
for any [152] English; that Mrs Campian her Cloathing was deferred so
long as the Abbes could, though with some inconvenience, so desirous
she was we should have taken the habitt togeather. That the state of lay
Sister was indeed held amongst worldlings more abiect, and of lesse
renowne, otherwise he did assure me the lay Sisters and the Quire of
those of that Monastery wear of one and the same order,[11] and equall
meritt in the sight of God. And verily quoth he I iudge it the will of
God you should be there, and enter as lay [153] Sister. While this good
father was in this discours came into the portch Father William Flacke to
whom my letters wear directed; to him I gave them, who retiring aside
redd them and after gave eare to Father George his discours observing
as it seemed some change in my countenance, or signe of lesse gratfull
acceptance: wherupon he spoke these very words: nay Gentilwoman,
(for he knew not my name)

---

1   According to the Julian (old style) calendar Pentecost was celebrated on 8 June in
1606.
2   PL No. 15. Catherine Bentley, née Roper, was a descendant of St Thomas More. Her
husband, Edward Bentley, was imprisoned several times for his Catholic beliefs, and the
family had moved to Flanders.
3   Rigorous legislation allowed English Catholics only a limited freedom of movement.
Travel to the continent was only allowed under certain conditions.

4   Catherine Roper, mother of Catherine Bentley, was married to Sir William Roper, great-grandson of St Thomas More.

5   Saint-Omer, about twenty-two miles south-east of Calais, then in the Spanish Netherlands. The English Jesuit College in Saint-Omer had become a centre for Catholic refugees. Peters p. 74.

6   Richard Holtby SJ (1552/3–1640) born in Yorkshire, ordained priest at Douai 1578. In 1583 he entered the Society of Jesus; after theological studies he returned to the north of England, where he was Superior of the Jesuits serving there. Following the execution of Henry Garnet in 1606, he was appointed Superior of the English Mission until 1609, after which he returned to Yorkshire to continue his energetic work until his death at the age of eighty-seven. Foley III, pp. 3–17.

7   William Flacke SJ. See AB 4, note 5 and Peters p. 74.

8   George Keynes SJ. See Vita E, note 36, and Peters pp. 74–77.

9   Probably Lord John Lumley (1533/34–1609) from Yorkshire.

10   Campian was a popular alias among English Catholics. Anne Campian (real name unknown) later transferred to the Gravelines convent founded by Mary Ward in 1608.

11   This was not correct. The choir nuns had the strict rule of St Clare, while the lay sisters were tertiaries, following the Third Order of St Francis. Peters p. 76.

Autobiographical Fragment (AB) 6
The Italian Autobiography

undated

Copies: AIM A. Autobiographical Fragments No. VII; B. Autobiographical Fragments, No. VI (incomplete).
AIY English translation by M Campion Davenport IBVM (Roman Branch, now CJ) c.1965.

Autobiographical Fragment 6, covering the period 1600–1609, was written in Italian, and is sometimes known as Mary Ward's *Italian Autobiography*. In this edition it is presented in an English translation, with subheadings added for clarity.

This text focuses on Mary Ward's religious vocation. The early part appears to be a compilation of the previous fragments, expanded and followed by a continuation until 1609. It is therefore likely that it was written after August 1624, probably during the period of Mary Ward's first stay in Rome; this would give a dating between 1624 and 1626. Though unfinished, it is the longest and most unified piece of writing of the Autobiographical Fragments.

Vocation to religious life – proposals of marriage – life in the Babthorpe household – spiritual exercises – general confession – 'The Spiritual Combat' – too many spiritual practices – desire for martyrdom.

IHS

When I was about 15 years old I had a religious vocation, which grace, by the mercy of God has been so continuous that not for one moment since then have I had the least thought of embracing a contrary state. My parents though otherwise extraordinary pious would not for any consideration give their consent, for I was the eldest child and much loved, especially by my father. I was therefore obliged to remain in England six years and some months longer. During that time many of what the world esteems fortunate opportunities[1] happened me, against which when nothing in me could prevail, God himself took the matter in hand, and freed me by means considered, by many, more divine than human.[2]

In those six years and as many months or more, living in the house of a relation[3] of my mother (in great measure because the retirement was more to my taste) I practised much prayer, some few fasts, and some austerities and internal and external mortifications (as far as I recollect on all occasions that served) and acts of humility, such as that to those who did not know me, I appeared to be one of the domestics of the house. I showed much respect to my confessor[4] and used daily to thank God for having given me such a one, but from excessive bashfulness (which at that age and for many years after prevented me from having any communication with men, even ecclesiastics) I did not confer with him on these things, not even on my religious vocation for a year or more after I had it.

I delighted in reading spiritual books, particularly those which treated of monastic life, and I spent much time by day and sometimes by night in this employment. The divine goodness (perhaps to prevent in me a less useful exercise of the affections, with which I abounded) gave me at that time such light as to the beauty and perfection of the religious state, that in all that I have since seen or read in this kind, I have never seen anything exceed, if it equalled, the same. But this affection to the religious life was in general, for I had no inclination to any Order in particular, only I was resolved within myself to take the most strict and secluded, thinking and often saying that as women did not know how to do good except to themselves (a penuriousness which I resented enough even then) I would do in earnest what I did.

In a certain book called the Rules of Christian Life I found a way of distributing the days of the week for the exercise of the divers virtues, and of dedicating the rooms of the house to various saints. I applied myself so punctually to this practice, that many years afterwards returning to England for certain affairs, and coming to the said place to visit some relations etc. the house appeared to me like a paradise, the same devotions and exercises presenting themselves at every step as I had before used them, so that I had not freedom of mind sufficient to perform certain civilities and other things more fitting to the time and the occasion, which sentiment caused me confusion in remembering what I had done when I was less obliged.

Of all the virtues to which I was drawn with the greatest affection was chastity, but I did not aspire to take the vow then fearing lest the devil should tempt me extremely and I should not have the courage to consult upon it or ask advice. I frequented the Sacraments with extraordinary fervour, Confession alone was rather difficult to me, no otherwise than from my too great bashfulness and extreme repugnance to hear myself speak against myself, although in those years I did not find much to say.

My confessor having gone to Rome for the settlement of certain controversies between the secular clergy and the Religious in England: in his absence I asked leave of another who knew me but little to prepare myself for a General Confession, (thinking I ought not to undertake such a thing without leave of some priest) and I did not intend to make it to whoever I should propose this, that it might not be expected, but that I might remain at liberty until the last to make it, or not make it, fearing that when the time came I should not have courage to proceed with it. But this Father[5] (who was of the Company of Jesus, a person much spoken of for sanctity of life) denied it to me, saying that it would not be useful to me then (fearing perhaps that I was scrupulous) although afterwards I had leave from another, and from the feast of St Thomas before the Nativity of our Lord, until the Vigil of the Resurrection, I prepared myself, according to my little knowledge, and I made it (I think with profit) to my ordinary confessor, who had then returned from Rome.

The above-named Father, who refused me this leave, gave me and recommended me to read, instead of making a general confession, a certain book called 'The Spiritual Combat'[6] which book was, so to speak, the best master and instructor that I have had in spiritual exercises for many years, and one perhaps of the greatest helps, which until now I have enjoyed in the way of perfection. From what I found in this book and sought to follow, I was, so to speak, almost always actually in prayer (which I did not confide to any one for the reason above said). After some time of this fervent practice, there occurred such a multitude of manners and ways of producing various acts of virtue, and this with such eagerness, that what at first was easy and pleasing became on a sudden difficult and wearisome, and with the additional scruple that I did not obey good inspirations, not doing all which were presented to my thoughts as good, (a thing impossible from there being so many and so different). And here I found myself in some perplexity, not being inclined to confer on these things with others, and the way I naturally went was rather with latitude than strictness, but God compassionated my simplicity, and in this anxiety gave me courage to reason in this manner with myself: These things are not of obligation but of devotion; and God is not pleased with certain acts made thus by constraint, and to acquire one's own quiet, therefore I will do these things with love and freedom, or leave them alone. And this I began, sometimes doing, at other times omitting the said devotions directing both one and the other to the better pleasing God, which doing, in a short space my usual peace of mind returned, and the easy use of these exercises, an experience which has much helped me since in other occurrences of this nature.

I had during these years burning desires to be a martyr[7] and my mind for a long time together fixed upon that happy event; the sufferings of the martyrs appeared to me delightful for attaining to so great a good, and my favourite thoughts were how? And when? And notwithstanding my many sins, infinite ingratitude, and most evil correspondence to so many graces received from that time until now, the same boundless goodness grants me yet the hope of attaining one day to that happiness. But through certain occurrences it pleased God for the present to moderate the vehemence of these aspirations, in order, as I believe, that I might take breath and apply myself to follow the Religious Life.

---

1   The final suitor for Mary's hand, Edmund Neville. PL No. 13 and Peters p. 49. Cf. Vita E, note 28.
2   PL No. 14 and Vita E, notes 32–33.
3   Lady Grace Babthorpe.
4   Fr John Mush.
5   Probably Richard Holtby SJ; possibly John Gerard SJ.
6   *Il Combattimento Spirituale* by Lorenzo Scupoli (d.1610), a Theatine priest. Translated into English as *The Spiritual Conflict* by John Gerard SJ. The first edition was printed secretly in England, 1598 under an Antwerp imprint, the second in 1603 at Douai. Allison/ Rogers II [273] No. 759.
7   PL Nos. 10 and 11.

Opposition from family, friends and confessor; overcoming the opposition.

From my exterior and my application to the exercises most fitting for that state, it was generally known that I was resolved to leave England for that purpose. For this reason my father came in person to the place where I was, and most peremptorily prohibited me from departing out of England without his leave and express order, to which command I made no resistance either by word or sign (for I loved him extremely, and had not the heart to say anything to him which would grieve him), but at the same moment I was most firmly resolved to observe nothing less than this precept, but to set out immediately, and never see him again, which God did not permit that I should do.

Of all my relations and friends, both secular and spiritual, there was not one, as far as I recollect, who did not more or less dissuade me from taking up that state of life, being wont to allege among other reasons that my complexion was not fit for such a way of living, especially in a severe order, upon which they knew I was bent, and the danger that I might be forced to return to the world through the failure of my bodily powers, was the only thing among all they said which made any impression on me. Being in some distress for this reason, there occurred to my mind that sentence: Quaerite primum Regnum Dei,[8] etc. when suddenly the burden was raised from off me, and I had as one may say, a certainty, that if I did my part in embracing the better portion, and preferring before all the honour and service of God, his divine Goodness would supply for every deficiency of mine. This same sentence in the sense which I then understood it, has encouraged me at other times in certain things to all appearance impossible.

My confessor, to whom I had confessed for seven years or a little less, was also of opinion, that in no way ought I to leave England nor make myself a religious. His words truly were of weight, and on this occasion caused me inexpressible distress, because I did not dare do what he prohibited as unlawful, nor could I embrace that which he proposed as my greater good. His motives were pious, prudent; regardful of the service of God and the common good.

But the same God deigned to behold and have regard to me in particular; and through the many merits of this his servant, and the true desire he had for my good, he would not permit that I should be hindered through his means, so that finally he caused him to change his opinion, at least so far as to leave me to myself in this matter, which was sufficient for me.

In this conflict I prayed much and had little repose, forcing myself as best I could to put my mind into a state of indifference and myself totally into the hands of God, entreating him, almost night and day, to do his holy will on this occasion, and not to permit anything in me or in any other person to prevent the same; which truly he disposed for the best and by means customary with his Goodness, when he wills to bestow a favour.

Setting forth then upon the so greatly desired journey,[9] and not yet out of England, a great obscurity darkened my mind and doubts rose up within me, as to where, and in what religious order I should have to settle, and in this darkness and disquiet of soul I crossed the sea and arrived at St Omer in Flanders where I went immediately to the College of the Fathers of the Company of Jesus of the English nation to treat with them concerning the monasteries of the city etc.

---

8   Seek first the kingdom of God [and his justice, and all these things shall be yours as well]. Matt 6:33.

9   PL No. 15.

Advice from a Jesuit – entry to the Poor Clares as a lay sister – exterior and inward resistance – deception practised by the Superiors of the convent – the real reason – advice to leave – change of confessor.

At my first word, one of these[10] said, that the Religious of St Clare of that town had heard of my coming with the intention of choosing a severe order, and were expecting me with much anxiety and had already assigned me a place. This was not within the enclosure, he said, because they could no longer admit foreigners within, but outside with those who spent themselves in the humble duty of begging for the enclosed (according to the custom of that country). The Father added that enclosed and unenclosed were the same order and had the same rule, only the latter added the charity of supporting the enclosed religious with their labours etc. (which I afterwards experienced to be the contrary, the Rules being very different and way of life and exercises quite diverse, but the Father spoke as he had heard). In conclusion he expressed his admiration at the Providence of God in ordaining circumstances to coincide with the great desire of the nuns to accept me so quickly, never having seen me, affirming that it certainly was the will of God and my true vocation. Which words "Will of God" so pierced my heart that I had no inclination to say or think of anything else: I stood silent for a while feeling an extreme repugnance to their offer, but reasoning within myself that the Rules being the same and the place offered me only more abject and contemptible, this disinclination and repugnance could only come from pride. I was at the same time invited to other orders, as those of St Benedict, St Augustine etc.[11] where I should have been received with all love, and as I myself wished, but these did not appear to me to be of such austerity as I sought. In short the fear of my own pride, and the words of the Father, that this was the will of God, so bound me that I did not dare to do anything of myself to the contrary. Turning myself therefore to God, I applied myself to prayer with extreme diligence, entreating that the divine will might be done whatever it should be, without regard to my content and consolation, present or future, and then with all sincerity, I declared both to my Confessor and to the Superior of the monastery the internal suffering which I felt, and the exceeding difficulty which I found in embracing that vocation, throwing myself for the rest upon the Providence of God, to follow whose holy will, I resolved to do whatever should be ordered me of them. The first day after my arrival I was invited by those holy nuns to live with them which I did, remaining with them one month or more before taking the habit as the Provincial made a difficulty about receiving me for the service of the enclosed, judging perhaps that I was not fit for the practices. The people of the city likewise protested at it, asking the Abbess why she did not receive me within. But she answered that my humility was such that I absolutely insisted on serving the enclosed, which devotion, God knows, was far from my thoughts in that mode and manner of living although his divine Majesty made use of this occasion for my great good and to dispose my soul for still greater. The real cause however of the nuns' desire I should be outside was that some time before, some of the out-sisters had given disedification causing dishonour and loss to the Convent so much so that one of the choir nuns had been obliged privately to break her enclosure in order to superintend the out-sisters until someone satisfactory could be found for such a post. And the idea of the nuns was that a person endowed by God with gifts of nature inspired by him to renounce fortune and favour in the world, urged to leave her native land and parents in the best years of her life, and drawn to serve him in retirement and solitude should, and rightly so, give an example in all religious exercises, especially in matters concerning chastity. In fact the reputation I had for modesty was beyond the ordinary.

This conceit the nuns had of me, made them determine, when my noviceship should be finished to give me the government of those outside, which had I known, assuredly I should never have entered, having even then, as I remember, a very different idea as to the qualities necessary to govern well and as to the affection I might have to such an office, I can with truth say that from my first vocation to religion (which was as I have said, about the age of fifteen) until now I was never capable of any, as one might who leaves a position honourable in the esteem of the world, stable as belonging to her state of life, and who could feel an exaltation in promotion to titles, or superiority, and offices in Religion, as if it were a dignity to seek such in a state, where by its very nature they must be common to all, of short duration and subject to change.

But to return to my subject: The importunity of the nuns was so great that at last Fr Provincial consented and I was clothed by the advice and command of my Confessor, the Father of the Company of Jesus, who affirmed that such was the will of God, and this my true vocation and that if an angel from heaven should tell me to the contrary, I ought not to believe him. From this counsel I did not dare to depart, esteeming this to be my sole security, these words coming frequently to my mind, Qui vos audit, me audit, etc.[12] and thus I followed it willingly, but with such an aversion and grief that death by any kind of torment that I could imagine to myself appeared most sweet to me, if so I could escape from that, which nevertheless, I now believe to have been a thing which God willed, and in a fitting way, at least with a view to what was to follow.

I remained in the monastery nearly a year, during the whole of which time the same distress continued, rather with augmentation than otherwise, but through the special grace of God, they did not cause any impediment in the exact observance of the Rules and customs practised there. Many notable things passed during these months too long to state now. For the present I will only say (as well as I can) just what is necessary to understand better what I have said and still have to say. Two months after my entrance the above mentioned Father, my Confessor, declared for certain that this was not my vocation etc. which opinion of his amazed me and forced me to turn to God with increased love, which I did, feeling persuaded that he would not deceive me nor could he be deceived. I saw what the Superiors of the monastery had told me, regarding the Rules and statutes, was quite other than what I found to be the case and such as, had I known before (although good in themselves) I should never have entered, as not being conformable to my aspirations etc. But now finding myself there (and with every requisite disposition on my side) the change in the confessor and the pious intentions of the nuns did not serve in any way to liberate me from that place, but far more to bind me there until God should by some other means give more certain signs, what I was or was not to do.

And so imperfect and human was I, that this, their (to my mind) little correspondence with my great sincerity towards them, much increased my suffering. No other comfort remained to me but to have recourse to God more earnestly than ever. His unfailing goodness had not only given me courage to overcome myself in entering purely to please him, but also to endure extreme distress during the whole time that I was there, and that with such observance of the holy customs of the place, that I may venture to say the year, allowing for human frailty, was passed well.

The two first months being ended, I was commanded to conform myself to the other nuns and to confess to their Confessor, who was a Franciscan monk of the French nation, I knowing at that time but little of that language. Yet notwithstanding this additional trouble, I enjoyed great quiet of conscience, finding on this occasion, and much more in the occurrences of the following years, that when God is sought sincerely, the way to him is always open, and the pardon of defects committed through frailty easily obtained.

---

[10] George Keynes SJ, who became Mary's confessor for the first two months spent as a lay sister. See Vita E, note 36 and Peters pp. 74–77.
[11] The English Benedictine Convent founded by Lady Mary Percy in Brussels, and the Augustinian Convent of St Ursula in Louvain, where there were many English nuns.
[12] He who hears you hears me. Luke 10:16.

St Gregory's Day 1607 – the General Visitor's advice – desire to found
a Poor Clare convent for the English – illness of the novice mistress
– question of spiritual direction – God's leading – novice mistress' decision
– departure from the Walloon Poor Clares.

Towards the end of this year of probation, on the feast of St Gregory the Great[13] (my particular advocate) sitting in silence at work with the nuns, I recited privately certain prayers in honour of that Saint, entreating him that as on earth he loved and helped the English, so now in heaven he would help and protect one of that nation, betaking myself to him that I might live and die in the will of God, and in the state which should most please his divine Majesty etc. which short devotion I had not finished when I was called with the others to receive the blessing of the Father General[14] of that order who happened to be there (as I remember to have heard accidentally) who after having given me his blessing, spoke to me in private and counselled me, with demonstration of great affection, to think well what I ought to do, that the time of my profession drew near, that I was still free and fit to serve God in any state or religion, but having once made my profession I should be obliged to remain, and should have to content myself with the means of perfection which I found there; to which as far as I recollect, I did not say a word in reply, but making my reverence, and showing signs of gratitude, I took my leave, returning to my work and devotions to St Gregory, when I found myself full of astonishment at the words of the Father General, never having spoken with or even seen him before. Suddenly I was enkindled with a vehement desire to procure a monastery for the English of this Order; but not being able otherwise to moderate this vehemence and place myself in indifference before speaking or doing anything for that purpose, I retired myself alone, and earnestly entreated our Lord God that nothing I might do in this business should have other success than that which he willed and which should be the most acceptable to him, praying our most Blessed Lady and other Saints to be witnesses that my desire were no other but to do and have done his divine will. And so not being able further to restrain myself, I went in all haste to entreat the said Father General, that in this visitation of his, he would put two monasteries into one and give one of them to the English; but I could not find the Father who had returned to his convent. And this my simplicity appeared not to displease God, who afterwards showed me more appropriate means, and concurred with them to the entire fulfilment of the good desired.

Some weeks previously and after the event just related the Superior[15] of the extern Sisters, the one whom I before mentioned as having had to leave the enclosure to govern those outside, was seized with a malignant fever and returned to the Enclosure where those outside did not and might not enter. There this holy religious remained ill for about two months; finally her life was despaired of by the doctors; but our Lord gave her back her health, on account of her great merits and intelligence she was elected first Abbess, of the English Monastery of that order as I shall say later.

This illness of hers was a cause of very great grief to me, both from the great affection which I bore her, a grace which God has always done me, and without my endeavour, of loving well my superiors, because such they were) and from her being the only person to whom until then I had communicated every circumstance and difficulty concerning my remaining in the place, and from whom I expected in time the decision whether I ought (that is whether God willed me) to make my profession there or not, not having language enough to confess upon these things with the confessor of the monastery, and there being no custom of calling spiritual persons from without for that purpose. And to speak the truth it was always a most difficult thing for me to discuss my personal affairs with several people at the same time, both because of the difference of their opinions and the confusion and uncertainty that arises therefrom, and because of the imperfection of my nature, feeling it like death to be ungrateful or to displease anyone seeking, or taking pains, to do me good. (And to say still more of what I know about myself in this matter, if there is anything not good may I be told of it, both in every particular already said, and in what is to be said. This I desire with all my heart and humbly beg.)

I do not remember ever having spoken of the affairs of my soul, through form, to please others, to be esteemed good or intelligent, or for similar unworthy causes, disliking ever every kind of deceit, and, more than all others, to deceive myself. To hear spiritual persons discourse of the things of God, or to treat with them of such matters is to my taste, but to talk in a certain way, as if I sought or desired their counsel upon things already known and by fitting circumstances determined, and when there is not the wherefore for following it, I neither do nor can do, being a deceit too distasteful to myself, and to my mind a certain injury to whoever does it. I have never chosen a person on whom to depend and to whom to confide my soul (of which sort I have had very few, but those such that for every reason I am obliged continually to be grateful to God for them), solely or especially through inclination, however great were their merits and the affection that I bore them, but I have been always led on in such choices by the rule of reason, a peculiar Providence of God, or by some divine ordering still more marked, and with such as these I have ever treated with all sincerity, without any reserve, as well in matters of detail and of minor moment, as in greater and in the entire government of my soul. For matters appertaining to morals I could never find satisfaction in the answers of those whom I knew were not well acquainted with the subject treated of; much less should I have felt it in matters spiritual under the same circumstances, because these are in themselves far more important and more likely than others to be prejudiced by ignorance. And more so, so greatly have I from the first loved integrity (proportionate to the occasions) that unless I had gone against my nature it would have been impossible to me to act half-heartedly in things of the soul, where all is intended, and should be full and entire. From much which has not caused me to judge otherwise, I should say that the above dispositions are special gifts of God to whatsoever person, but particularly to those of our sex who seek to walk in the way of the spirit, as one who can with perfection express them better. And for me, as far as I can judge, they have been of extreme use, and have brought me great peace of conscience in so many changes and various accidents as by Divine Providence have happened in my poor life and past years.

But I have strayed again from my subject. Being through this illness and absence of the said mother deprived of all human aid I turned to God, my only help, who without delay, and as if he had awaited a similar privation, favoured me with frequent and clear lights, accompanied with peace and strength of soul far more than I had ever before experienced, showing me that this was not my vocation, and that I could, without scruple, depart from there, with various particular circumstances to assure me of their truth, which now I do not recollect so minutely as to venture to put them in writing. But I remember well that the manner which God employed on this occasion was not to command me, or divinely to force me, but as if, compassionating my labours, he would with Fatherly affection propose the means to solace me, leaving me the liberty to use them or not. But not having experience in similar favours, not knowing how to proceed in them, nor having, as I said, anyone to teach me, I wrote down from time to time what happened to me concerning them, to show afterwards to the above named Mother if God should grant me to see her again; and having thus noted them down, I took pains not to think any more of them, fearing that if they absorbed my thoughts I should be less observant of the ordinances and exercises of the place where I was.

These papers, when she was a little recovered and had come out to where I was, I gave her, praying and conjuring her that as she would answer for my soul at the last day, that she would tell me what she judged with regard to my profession there, yes or no; resolving to depend upon her decision, who, by her office, was assigned to me as an aid in such things.

After some days the Mother returned me my papers, and assured me decidedly that to be there outside, where the Third Rule of St Francis only was observed, was not my vocation, but I was to take that observed

within: the First of St Clare, an austere and secluded Rule, conformable to my mind, was for certain that which God willed for me. While
I listened attentively to her discourse, various sentiments passed within
me as to the divine permissions in things touching so nearly the salvation of the soul, and how his divine Majesty makes use of things less
good to arrive at the end determined by him. I, to have given pleasure
to that holy Mother according to my natural feeling, would willingly
have lived all my life a slave; and she, at all times and on all occasions,
appeared to have the least possible regard to me in particulars, I treated
with her in all sincerity and submitted to her judgement, and she, having
to determine that which so greatly concerned both my soul and my
life, promoted, as if for my welfare alone, that which she sought (quite
lawfully) for the consolation of others. At entering she told me that
within and without the Rule was the same, and now she explained how
much difference there was between the one and the other. Then if an
angel from heaven should tell me that my vocation was not with those
outside, I ought not to believe him, and now such could by no means
be, but my vocation was within, etc.: all (perhaps through my defects)
appeared to me too human, and very unsuitable to my mind and way of
acting.

Feeling myself, during this silent listening, like a person deprived of
the help and counsel necessary in such a conjuncture, it occurred to me
that on my side I had done disinterestedly all that was possible to know
and to walk in the way pre-ordained for me by God, and that what the
mother now said to me was the only guidance which was granted to me,
therefore I would embrace it with all affection as the will of God, which
only, only I desired. A few days later I left the convent.[16]

---

[13] St Gregory the Great, Pope 590–604. In 596 he sent the first missionaries to England.
His feast was kept on 12 March at that time.
[14] The Spanish Franciscan Andreas de Soto. As General Visitor he bore the title of
General, customary in his Order for this office. Cf. Vita E, note 40.
[15] Mary Stephen Goudge. Cf. Vita E, note 38.
[16] Mary Ward left the noviceship of the Walloon Poor Clares in late April or early May
2007.

*Foundation of the Poor Clare convent at Gravelines for Englishwomen –
spiritual dryness through being led on the way of fear – temporary housing
in Saint-Omer – the full Spiritual Exercises of St Ignatius – postponement
of profession.*

Putting on a secular dress, without further delay, I applied myself to
secure a habitation and all else to found a monastery of St Clare for
the English. In that work, God knows I did little, but his divine Majesty
supplied all my deficiencies in such a manner, that in the space of two
years,[17] a little more or less, a convenient site was found, a spacious

monastery and church built, English nuns of that order taken out of other monasteries to preside in it, and then persons of fitting qualities and talents admitted to probation.[18]

During these two years I suffered extreme aridity without any intermission, not knowing the cause, but I believed most firmly that, through some unknown negligence of mine in the divine service, I had wholly lost the spirit of devotion and the sensible sweetness that I used to feel, which thought caused me great grief, and sometimes fear whether I should be saved or not, but this never with doubt or mistrust in the divine mercy, only I feared myself, lest I should thus fall away for ever. By an especial grace this fear was nevertheless always accompanied by a firm resolution, followed by acts when the occasion occurred, that although I might never see God, yet I would serve him until death; and especially I would do all that was possible to me to carry out the work which it appeared to me he had placed in my hands. And from these sufferings and the above-named acts sprang great love and desire to labour without reward, that giving me most satisfaction which was done unseen.

And because God's co-operation was great, and the success beyond expectation, all gave me generally too much commendation and attributed to me what was not mine, (for no one better knows how little is given of their own in the accomplishment of such works than they who to the world appear to have done most in them). But I being, as above said, otherwise interiorly disposed, did not in any way care for such praise, nor do I even remember that they gave me any disturbance, appearing to me only as the guesses and conceits of men, beside the truth and without reality.

At that time I confessed to that Father[19] of the Company through whose advice I entered the first monastery, as it appeared to me ingratitude, and in a certain way derogatory to him personally, to take another when I came out and was free, there being no further need to treat of my vocation, as therein I was following precisely what the above-mentioned Mother had said to me. This Father was truly of great goodness of life and no less solicitous for the progress of my soul, but he guided my conscience entirely by the way of fear; for instance that I ought to hate myself, to fear the judgements of God, to tremble at the pains of hell, in all of which I was most inapt. As to the first I could not sensibly hate the enemy of all good, much less myself, whom I loved far too well. To labour through love even death appeared to me to be easy, but fear with me made but little impression. Hell I was resolved, by the assistance of God's grace, never to merit, and of the doings there I could form no conception as vivid as the Father wished. Finding myself so differently disposed from what he required, and which I therefore with all diligence sought to be, was, I believe, in a great measure the cause of that aridity and those doubting thoughts. Perhaps he did this that the good success of the business I had in hand might not cause me injury, and whichsoever way, through his merits it proved, as I hope, for my profit.

Through this occasion I have sometimes thought (perhaps I am deceived) that there are some souls not the less fit to arrive at more than ordinary perfection, who in their commencements it would be well to treat with great generosity giving them better things before taking from them that which is less good,[20] changing the object not destroying the nature, especially if their defects are produced by extreme self-love or less well-ordered affections, proceeding from that part of the soul. I could easily enlarge upon this, and perhaps not without reason, having experienced much in this particular, but there is no need.

To return to our subject. Towards the end of two years the new monastery was finished but too damp to be inhabited and many English having already come out of England with the resolution of entering the monastery, that time might not be lost, a large and convenient house was fitted for the interim in the city of St Omer, and so arranged that they might observe therein all religious discipline and live in full observance of that holy rule, so austere in itself, and carried out in that monastery with entire rigour and perfection.

As a beginning both the religious taken from the other monastery[21] to govern the new one, as well as those still seculars,[22] made the Spiritual Exercises each for the space of a month. Which, that they might make them with more profit I procured that Father Baldwin[23] of the Company of Jesus, then Provincial of the English Mission, should assign some father in the College of that nation in the city to aid in grounding them in spiritual things; he nominated Father Roger Lee, of happy memory (a man truly apostolic and much illumined and favoured by God) who charitably accepted the burden, and when the said Exercises commenced, I among the rest began also to confess to him, whose aid to the great profit of my soul I was so happy as to have for ten years together.[24]

The recollection being ended, and all desiring to put their hand to the work, it was settled that the seculars should take the probationers' habit, but not formally nor in public, as that solemnity was to be celebrated in the new church. The Bishop, Mgr Jacques Blaes, a prelate much celebrated for learning and holiness of life, of the Order of Friars Minor, under whose jurisdiction I had placed that monastery, wished in every way that I should make my profession immediately, without waiting, or another noviciate. This he proposed from the affection he bore me, as a particular privilege and a certain sort of reward for the little labour I had in the commencement, etc. But the Abbess[25] who was the same who had been my Superior in the other monastery inclined greatly to the contrary alleging that the said Monsignor would come in person to consecrate the church of the new monastery (which was in the city of

Gravelines, a day's journey from St Omer) and give the habit to all who were to enter, if I waited until that time, but that otherwise he would not, and therefore to defer my profession would be more for the service of God and the good of that foundation.

And here may be seen the greatness of my obligation to God, who willed to make use of every occasion for my greater good. If the designs of this holy Bishop had taken effect, the happiness which I now unworthily possess would have been prevented; and the pious desire of the Abbess for the common good served most perfectly to advance mine in particular. Fr Roger Lee, my Confessor with the Rector, and other Fathers of the College were all averse to my longer waiting. But they were actuated by a certain reputation of mine, of which I had already had too much, and more than I cared for, and, therefore, to diminish it, and to atone in earnest for whatever I had lost during that time of negotiation in which I remained at my own disposal with God alone for a guide and instructor in the said matter; and now as I had the opportunity of an entire subjection, I adhered to what the Abbess judged for the best. And so I put on the habit with the others,[26] continuing in exact observance of that Rule until all were about to go to the other monastery to be clothed solemnly, which was a year or thereabouts.[27] Which austerity and retirement were extremely to my content, and so far as I remember nothing then could have disturbed me, or given me cause of temptation, except to hear that there was some order in the Church of God, more austere and more secluded, in which two virtues I had, at least in theory, placed all perfection. I followed the order of the day eagerly and lovingly, ashamed sometimes to find myself before the others at the sound of the bell, fearing thus tacitly to accuse them of tepidity. And so full was I of human respect that I was obliged to do violence to myself in performing that which was my duty, and was more to my taste, and to write down as a good resolution to be observed, that as God through his goodness had called me with the first, I should not show myself so ungrateful as to be among the last in due observance.

Everyone had half an hour in the day to spend as she liked, in resting, praying, writing, reading etc. which time I used praying for the prosperity of Holy Church, and especially for the perfection of Religious Orders and for the advancement of new foundations among them. God was liberal in inspiring me with other similar little devotions, and in giving me grace to correspond with them, of which there is no need to write.

---

17   The time between departure from the Walloon Poor Clares and the provisional beginning of the English Poor Clares was about a year and a half.

18   Cf. Vita E, ff. 11v–12r and Peters pp. 83–93.

19   George Keynes SJ.

20 'Take from no one what he loves unless you give him what he loves still better.' (From Mary Ward's *Maxims*.)

21 Pope Paul V gave Bishop Blaes of Saint-Omer permission to transfer three choir sisters and two lay sisters from the Walloon Poor Clares to the new house on 7 November 1608.

22 Mary Ward, her sister Frances, who later became a Carmelite, several Englishwomen, and two candidates who wished to enter as lay-sisters. Peters pp. 88–92.

23 It was Mary's wish that Jesuits should take on the spiritual guidance of the new Poor Clare foundation. William Baldwin SJ (1563–1632) was Vice-Prefect of the English Jesuit Mission 1600–1610, not the Provincial. The English Province of the Society of Jesus was not created until 1623.

24 Eight years, including the year 1608, when the Exercises took place (probably November/December). Roger Lee SJ died in December 1615.

25 Mary Stephen Goudge.

26 The clothing of the postulants took place on 5 February 1609.

27 The solemn clothing took place on 3 November 1609, by which time Mary had left the Poor Clares.

Feast of St Athanasius – Fr Lee's attitude – departure, having made a vow of chastity – concerns about the effect of Mary's departure on the reputation of the new foundation.

Having passed four or five months in this place and at these exercises and enjoying great peace of mind and interior consolation, I was sitting at work among the other nuns on the day of St Athanasius, the second of May, about 10 o'clock in the forenoon, being employed making cords of St Francis for the use of the religious, and reciting privately, as I was accustomed to do at each one that I made, the Litanies of our most Blessed Lady, that whoever should wear that cord might never commit mortal sin, when there happened to me a thing of such a nature that I knew not, and never did know, how to explain. It appeared wholly Divine, and came with such force that it annihilated and reduced me to nothing; my strength was extinguished, and there was no other operation in me but that which God fulfilled in me; the sight – intellectually – of what was done, and what was to be done in me, I willing, or not willing, of this only was I conscious. The suffering was great because far beyond my powers, and the consolation was greater to see that God willed to make use of me in what pleased him more. Here it was shown me that I was not to be of the Order of St Clare; some other thing I was to do, what, or of what nature I did not see, nor could I guess, only that it was to be a good thing, and what God willed.

The bell for examen was rung as usual before eating, which was to my content, for thus I had time to be alone and return to myself, in order that the others might not see any difference in me, etc. But what I say bears no proportion to what passed on this occasion, and is in no way to my satisfaction, nor will it be to those who read it: may God supply what is wanting as far as it will be to his service.

The next day, the Feast of the Finding of the Holy Cross, I sought to speak to the above named Father Roger Lee, upon whose counsel I then depended, and begged him to receive what I had to tell him under the seal of confession, but he would not be content to do so. I argued, and would by all means tell it thus, saying that the things were of that nature that he could not properly keep them from his Superiors if not thus heard, and that once known it would immediately follow that, where now I was loved and praised by all, in one half hour I should not have a single friend, nor would there be a person who would not condemn and despise me, and more – (which I believe I also felt the most) – he himself would have his part in this suffering, (as afterwards most minutely happened). But with all this he would not yield, so that I related to him what had passed in the manner he desired, which from prudence, and for my greater trial, he appeared to disapprove, and to oppose with a certain severity unusual to him, exhorting me to a more than ever exact observance of the rules and regulations of the place where I was, which I did with a very good will. I loved what I possessed most sensibly and before all things that I knew, so much so that when I was left to my own nature and human defects, I wept to remember that I was not to be in that order. And so desirous was I of a quiet life, and so good for nothing, that I found myself already wearied out with the little labour taken in that foundation. At the same time I was in every-thing too human, and sometimes even fearful of being deceived, and of believing that to be good which was not so. All which were motives to cause me to remain there with all content for further trial, and so six or seven months passed. In this time many things happened, which, not to be tedious to the one who reads it, I omit.

The time drew near when all those not yet formally clothed were to again put on their secular dress, and to appear in their own rank and condition at the new monastery in the city of Gravelines,[28] and there solemnly to receive the habit. Among whom I was to be one. But in those seven months I saw more and more that God did not desire this, though I remained entirely ignorant of that which his Divine Majesty willed from me; and seeing that I had to return to live in the world, to prevent the deceits of the devil, and to dispose my soul entirely for the divine service, on Palm Sunday[29] I made a vow of chastity, with the leave and approval of the above mentioned Father, and then took leave of these dear friends with much feeling on both sides. To the end that this foundation might not suffer on account of my departure, the conceit of the people being more placed in me than was fitting, the report was spread (with my consent) that my constitution was too weak to support such austerity, (which nevertheless was not in the least the motive of my leaving). There was, however, some appearance of its being so to the public, and to those who did not know the contrary.

In that monastery they live with great strictness: they never eat meat even when ill, their food is poor in quality, and they never eat more than once a day, except on the day of the Nativity of our Lord. They sleep on straw mattresses; instead of linen, rough, coarse cloth is worn; what may be called continual silence is kept; they rise at midnight, say the Divine Office, and always make an hour of mental prayer after Matins before returning to rest. For my part, during the whole of that year, I slept rarely more than two hours during the night, from the hunger I felt.

---

[28] The move from Saint-Omer to Gravelines took place on 15 September 1609, with the solemn clothing on 3 November 1609.

[29] Cf. Letter to the Nuncio Antonio Albergati, L 2. The Palm Sunday dating for this private vow of chastity causes difficulties; it may have taken place before the revelation on 2 May. Palm Sunday remained a special day of devotion for Mary: cf. Vita E, f. 49r and notes 174–175.

Uncertainty about God's will – vow to enter an order – return to England and activity there – Gloria vision.

To the sorrow of parting was added the displeasure and condemnation of many, and the opprobrium of those who shortly before had expended themselves in praises of poor me. All these were trifles, not to be felt in comparison with the interior suffering caused by the uncertainty of my vocation and of that which God willed with me. Those holy religious went to Gravelines to their monastery, and I remained for some weeks at St Omer, still in suspense as to what the Divine will for me could be. The pain was great but very endurable, because he who laid on the burden, also carried it. Notwithstanding I could believe that there is no suffering greater than the uncertainty as to the Divine will, to one who is resolved to seek above everything to serve God, yet I would not have attained the knowledge of it at a less price, nor can I be surprised at the imperfections of those who acquire it cheaply. But the offences and ingratitude of those who arrive at it with greater difficulty are exceedingly great, and what are they in the sight of God?

At that time I made a vow with the consent of my Confessor to be a religious, but not of any order in particular, not being able to incline towards one more than another, and finding in none of them anything which appealed to me. Then in obedience to my confessor without any inclination on my part, I made another vow to enter the Order of St Teresa should he so command me.

Afterwards for good reasons and with his consent, I returned to England for some months with the intention of trying to do good to others, and, as far as I can judge, I did not spend that time ill, nor did I neglect to do as much as possible for the cause I went over to serve.

My few labours were not altogether in vain, divers now living holily in various religious orders say that they left the world in great part through my conversation. Various other good things happened then, which it appears better to omit, because I do not know how to explain myself without so many words, and those unapt. The following, nevertheless, I ought not to leave out.

One morning making my meditation coldly, and not at all to my satisfaction, at the end of it I resolved to assist a person to be accepted in some convent who much desired to become a nun, but, wanting a portion could not otherwise enter. And then going to dress myself according to the fashion of the country and other circumstances, whilst I adorned my head at the mirror, something very supernatural befell me,[30] similar to that already related on the day of St Athanasius, but more singular, and, as it appears to me, with greater impetuosity, if greater there could be. I was abstracted out of my whole being, and it was shown to me with clearness and inexpressible certainty that I was not to be of the Order of St Teresa, but that some other thing was determined for me, without all comparison more to the glory of God than my entrance into that holy religion. I did not see what the assured good thing would be, but the glory of God which was to come through it, showed itself inexplicably and so abundantly as to fill my soul in such a way that I remained for a good space without feeling or hearing anything but the sound, "Glory, glory, glory". By accident I was then alone, therefore what external changes this and similar things cause I cannot say, but from the internal feeling and bodily disturbance, they must be remarkable; my knowledge fails as to their continuance; all appears to last but a moment, even at those times when afterwards I made a computation, and found it to have been about two hours.

On this occasion a good deal of time passed before I recovered; but returning to myself I found my heart full of love for this thing, accompanied by such glory that not yet can I comprehend what it was. And seeing for certain that I was not to be of the Order of St Teresa, remembering also the vow which I had made being of that order if my confessor should command me, I felt great fear of offending God in these two contraries, or of adhering to one or the other side. To resist that which had now been operated in me, I could not, and to have a will in opposition to the vow, I ought not. In this conflict, giving myself to prayer, I protested to God, so liberal that I had not and would not admit on this occasion any other will than his. As a testimony and sign that my mind and will were totally to do his without exception, I put on a haircloth, which I have forgotten for how long a time I wore, but I believe for some continuance, for I well recollect through this and other corporal penances done for this end during the months that I remained in England, I did not little injury to my health, especially being occupied at that time with some fervour in winning and aiding others, observing (according to my knowledge) the circumstances requisite and suitable to the said business and to my condition. Such a labour is only too honourable, but nevertheless painful enough, if not undertaken for him to whom we owe all, and through the help of whose grace alone it is fitly and perseveringly feasible.

30 This inner experience, known as the 'Glory Vision', took place in 1609: see PL No. 21, Vita I, and Letter to the Nuncio Antonio Albergati, L2. In Vita E, ff. 18v–19r it is incorrectly attributed to the stay in England in 1614.

Selected Letters and Documents

L 1. Mary Ward to John Gerard SJ (alias John Tomson) Rector of the Jesuit College in Liège

[Liège] 1619 [April]

Copy: AIM. Parchment Book pp. 39–45.
Printed (with modern spelling) in Chambers I, p. 452–454.

From the words of the introduction, it is clear that this is a copy, prepared at more or less the same time as the original. John Gerard SJ (1564–1637) is well known for his *Autobiography* in which he describes the eighteen eventful years he spent on the English Mission, and his imprisonment and escape from the Tower of London. From 1614 to 1621, using the alias John Tomson, he was Rector of the Jesuit house of studies in Liège, which he had himself founded. He was Mary Ward's confessor and a strong supporter of her enterprise. In 1619 Mary Ward made two retreats under his direction, in April and October. The place of this letter among the copies of her April retreat notes in the little Parchment Book, and the observation in the *English Vita* (f. 24r) that Mary Ward discovered the difficulties with Sr Praxedis on her return from England, suggest an April date for the letter.

Mary Ward returned from England in April 1619 to find unrest and disunity among the community in Liège. A certain faction led by Praxedis, a young lay sister from the Ardennes who claimed visionary insights, and supported by Mary Alcock (the Mother Minister) and others, was pressing for the foundation to become a more traditional type of religious order. Mary Ward did not enter into conflict, but went into retreat and allowed her plans to be questioned. The immediate situation was resolved by the sudden death of Praxedis, though the unrest continued.

The significance of this letter lies in Mary's account of her inner experience of 1611, which is otherwise only reported in the letter to the Nuncio Antonio Albergati. For her this was the crucial revelation, her God-given commission on the nature of the Institute she was to found, described in her letter to John Gerard exactly as she 'heard' and instinctively responded to it.

For further information on the Praxedis incident and the part played by John Gerard at this point in Mary Ward's story, see the *English Vita* f. 24r and Peters pp. 258–266.

To Reverend Father Tomson (alias Jhon Garett) of whom she tooke now the Exercise and in it wrott the letter following in the year 1619 at the time when Sister Praxedis[1] busines was about our institute and the manner of Subordination[2] she said ours were to have which was wholy different to that our Mother had understood from God etc.

Reverend dear Father,

As I was to day in a sea of uncertainties, and full of fears, forth of my owne inability to doe any thing how little soever, without some powerfull, and extraordinary help, calling to God for his, as my last, and best refuge, and receaving him to that purpose: this came to my mind to propose (wherby I found some ease, without any reason why this should ease me, except I doe what god would, in propounding it, for it seemes if this have any effect, it will be that which yet I know not.) Might not Sister Praxedis sett down what she hath seene, with what els she can obtaine of God touching that matter in forme of an Institute?[3] What if she wear bid by your selfe, or Father Burton[4] to draw an Institute with as great care as she would, if she wear in my place, and I in an other world so as this busines rested wholy upon her.[5] She may likewise know, what I had from God touching this, if that be thought fitt, or would further her: which was as follows (understood as it is writt without adding, or altering one sillable) Take the same of the Society. Father Generall will never permitt it. Goe to him, these are the words, whos worth cannot be valued; nor the good they containe, too dearly bought: these gave sight where there was none; made know me what god would have don; gave streingth to suffer what since hath hapned: assurance of what is wished for, in time to come: and if ever I be worthy to doe any thing more about the Institute, heather I must come to draw: I could say a great deale of thos words but never all; but she will farre better see what God intended by them: if she will but aske him what he meant by them: except he that can doe all that he will, and all what he doth is well, give her some other ground to worke upon. Twice doubting what kind of Subordination[6] should be, I was sent home (I meane to your Institute) and bidden doe, as there was don.[7] Some other things I have some times perceaved, about Subordination which is not to purpose for her. Once I thinke I saw a Generall of yours, who said nothing, but his countenance promised all concurrance with us. This was I thinke to comfort for some of yours at that very time would needs that the Generall of the Society[8] both could, and would hinder such a thing as I did beleeve to be Gods will in us. The first I could never beleeve to be in the power of man: for the second this sight gave confidence: the same I saw likewise in those words goe to him, that when the time should come, neither would he have a will to hurt us, but the contrary.

What els I have had, hath bin in generall; or generally; and in perticular, such an understanding of your Institute, and such a neernes of affection to it, as he can only worke, who aloane is able to make without my disposing or indeavour: One thing of two so farre differant as is your order of life and my perverce will. I doe not propound this for her with desire to leave any thing that lies in me undone: God forbid. I will doe my best, and all I can. Doe in this what pleaseth you.

Your blessing.

Your Reverances ever
Ma[ry] Ward.

1619

---

1 Cf. Vita E, f. 24r and Peters pp. 263–266.

2 Praxedis' faction proposed subordination to a religious order of men, or to the local Bishop. Fridl I, pp. 142–144, 179–182. See note 7 below.

3 Institute (Institutum). In St Ignatius and in the documents of the Society of Jesus this term is used to sum up everything constituting the Society: its nature, spiritual principle, constitution and activities. It is in this sense that Mary Ward uses the word, which occurs five times in this letter.

4 Edward Burton SJ (1584–1623/24), procurator in Liège, and one of the confessors to Mary Ward's Society. In 1617 he had written a treatise in defence of Mary's foundation, but he later turned against it. Peters pp. 214ff.

5 The place of this letter in the Parchment Book shows that it was probably written during the retreat, following a meditation ('On Death') in which Mary reflected on the importance of her presence to her new foundation but, towards the end, was ready to leave its future completely to God.

6 This aspect of the manner of life was evidently not clear in the insight of 1611.

7 Not dependence on the Society of Jesus but, following the SJ model, self-government by a Superior General and subordination to Papal jurisdiction alone. (*Rationibus quibus* ... Brussels. Archives SJ Gallo-Belg. Carton 32a. Summarised by Peters pp. 305–306.) A long time elapsed before this was allowed for women's congregations, because the Council of Trent had laid special stress on the subordination of women religious to episcopal authority, or to the superior of a corresponding religious order of men.

8 P. Muzio Vitelleschi, General Superior of the Society of Jesus 1615–1645. His correspondence shows that despite his regard for Mary Ward personally, he felt unable to support her plans. Peters p. 247.

L 2. Mary Ward to Antonio Albergati, Papal Nuncio at Cologne

[Probably from Cologne or Trier, 1621 May/June]

Copies: A. Staatsarchiv, Munich, KL fasz. 432/1, ff. 16r–18r (handwriting of Margaret Horde); B. AIM Parchment Book pp. 123–141. Additions to the two manuscripts: A. Marginal in another hand: A Mon B. At the head: Written to be given to the Noncio Apostolico of Lower Germany, Monsignor Albergato[1] etc. Ihs omitted.

This letter, so important as a source for Mary Ward's aims and life story, exists only in copy. It consists of a preparatory draft for a Latin document to be addressed to Antonio Albergati, the Papal Nuncio in Cologne. The draft was probably prepared by Mary Ward herself; the Latin document is no longer extant.

Antonio Albergati had supported Mary Ward's foundations in Cologne and Trier, but it appears from the letter that he had warned her against adopting too fully the Constitutions of St Ignatius. In this document Mary Ward explains why she kept so tenaciously to the part marked out for her, outlining the most significant events that had led to the climax, the definitive revelation at Saint-Omer in 1611 which had finally impelled her to choose the Institute of the Society of Jesus as her model.

Albergati left Cologne in August 1621 to return to Rome. As his sister was married to the Pope's brother, Oracio Ludovisi, he could be an important facilitator there. It is thought that this letter was given to him in about May 1621, when his coming departure became known. Other letters of support were being canvassed by Mary at this time, in preparation for her journey to Rome.

Through an account of her spiritual journey and God's guidance in the formation of her community, Mary Ward wishes to dispel the Nuncio's doubts. She asks for support for the approbation of her foundation, and encloses a copy of the outline plan of her Institute.

Ihs:

Illustrissime ac Reverendissime Domine,[1]

In that other paper[2] is contayned the Summe of what we doe desire as the same which God in a perticuler manner hath called us unto; if I had language to expresse my self by speach, I doubt not but your Illustrissime would alow of those reasons I could yeald why this may seeme to be Gods ordination in us; and that I may not seeme to contradict without the greatest cause your Illustrissimes proposition and pleasure[3] I will say a litle of the much might be sayd to this purpose:

At 15 I found my self called to Religion, after which time I could take noe content in any worldly estate; hindered by parents, and other worldly incumberances, I could not gett into these partes, till the age 21. I had noe perticuler vocation to one order more then another, onely it seemed to me most perfection to take the most austere that soe a soule might give her self to God, not in part but altogether, since I saw not how a Religious woman could doe good to more then herself alone: To teach children seemed then to much distraction, might be don by others, nor was of that perfection and importance as therfore to hinder that quiett and continuall communication with God which strict inclosure afforded, which inclosure and the perfect observance of poverty were the tow especiall points I aymed at in whatsoever order I should undertake, being (as I sayd) I could doe noe good to others, which if it could have bin, I valued above all, though I found a farre more sensible content in solitude, and abstraction from the world, and therfore never soe much as thought of that other (in way of practise) till God (as I trust) called me unto it in a manner against my will.

What hapned in the first 4 yeares after I came over, would be too tedious and troublesome for your Illustrissime to read; in which space, a Monastery was erected for such of our nation, as desired to render themselves poor Clares, in which holy Order, I intended to live and dye, for the reasons aforesayd.

The busines of the Monastery ended, but the place not yet habitable, the Religious that were brought out of another Monastery to begin that were placed in a seculer house by, and we that were to enter, with them who altogether observed the Rule of Saint Clare in full perfection, in which practise, I found singuler content; and now began to feele a great tranquility of mind, often comforted to think that after a 11 yeares withhoulding and turbation, the rest of my days should be spent in quiett, and with God alone. This quiett lasted many weekes, in which space, upon the Eve of the Invention of the holy Crosse,[4] setting at work with the rest (reciting privately the litenies of our Blessed Lady, that she that should ware that I was then working might never committ mortall sin) came sodainly upon me such an alteration and disposition, as the operation of an unexpressable power could only cause; with a sight and certainty that there I was not to remayn, that some other thing was to be don by me, but what in perticuler was not showne; the chang and alteration this wrought for half an houre or more was extraordnary; I saw not any thing, but understood more clearly that this was to be soe, then if I had seen, or heard it spoken. To leave what I loved soe much, and inioyed[5] with such sensible contentment, to expose my self to new labours, which then I saw to be very many; to incurre the severall censures of men, and the great opositions which on all sides would happen (appearing at that time as afterwards I found them) afflicted me exceedingly; yet had I noe power to will or wish any other then to expose my self to all these inconveniences, and putt my self into Gods hands with these uncertainties. By the advice of my Confessor I continued the practise of that austere life half a yeare longer, the better to discover from whence that light came.

When the rest were to be clothed I departed from them (my Confessour telling me I might be saved ether going or staying which was all the encouragment or assistance any alive gave me at that time). I made a vow of perpetuall Chastity, and another to obey my Confessor in this perticuler, that if, or when he should command me to enter into the Teresians I would obey, this they councelled me unto, and though I found noe perticuler vocation to that order, yet hoping God would not leave me, nor forbeare to dispose me to his best will, for, leaving my self for him, I did as they advised me, which caused me great trouble afterward many wayes, though all turned to my best in the end.

I made a third vow to spend some months in England to doe all the litle I could for God, and the good of those there, not to be idle in the meane time, and the better prepared for whatsoever God should call me to.[6]

Being there, and thus imploied, I had a 2[d] infused light in manner as before, but much more distinct,[7] that the worke to be don was not a Monastery of Teresians, but a thing much more gratfull to God, and soe great an augmentation of his glory as I cannot declare, but not any perticulers, what, how and in what manner such a work should be; which after this light was past I reflected upon with some sadnes, for though in that instant of time, my understanding was clearly convinced that the thing then putt before me was truely good; and the same which reason it self would have effected, and my will soe possessed as left without pouer then, or ever after to love or elect any contrary thing, yet to have still all denied me, and nothing proposed in perticuler seemed somewhat hard, and besides I was anxius how to governe my affection for the present in these tow contraries, as not to have a contrary will to what I had vowed (which was to enter into the Teresians when I should be commanded), nether to be unanswerable to that which then seemed to be God Allmighties determination (which was not to be Teresian but some other thing). God holpe[8] me in this, as I trust he will in all.

My purposed time of stay in England expired, I retourned to Saint Omers; diverse followed with intention to be Religious where I should be, living together there;[9] great instance was made by diverse spirituall, and learned men, that we would take upon us some Rule already confirmed; severall rules were procured by our frinds, both from Italy and France, and we earnestly urged to make choyce of some of them; they seemed not that which God would have done, and the refusall of them caused much persecution, and the more, because I denied all, and could not say what in perticuler I desired or found my self called unto.

About this time in the yeare 1611 I fell sick in great extreamity, being somewhat recovered (by a vow made to send in pilgrimage to our Blessed Lady of Sichem), being alone, in some extraordinary repose of mind, I heard distinctly, not by sound of voyce, but intellectually understood, these wordes, Take the Same of the Society,[10] soe understood, as that we were to take the same both in matter and manner, that onely excepted which God by diversity of Sex hath prohibited, these few wordes gave soe great measure of light in that perticuler Institute, comfort and strength, and changed soe the whole soule, as that unpossible for me to doubt but that they came from him whose wordes are workes.

My Confessor resisted, all the Society opposed; diverse Institutes were drawne by severall persons,[11] some of which were approved and greatly commended by the last Bishopp Blasius of Saint Omers, our soe great frind and some other divines, these were offered us, and as it were pressed upon us; there was noe remedy but refuse them, which caused infinitt troubles, then would they needs, that at least we should take the name of some order confirmed, or some new one, or any we could think of, soe not that of Jesus: This the Fathers of the Society urged exceedingly (and doe still every day [more] then other), telling us that to any such name we may take what Constitutions we will, even theres in substance, if otherwise we will not be sattisfied, but by noe means will they that we observe that forme which there Constitutions and rules are writt in, which say they, are not essentiall or needfull; the neglect of these offers did, and doe cause extreame troubles, especially for the first 7 yeares, while my Confessarius (whom I had tyed my self to obey) lived[12] they urging him in many things to say as they sayd, though against his own iudgment and knowledg, as after I understood, nether could he yeald unto them in all; one time in perticuler they urged him soe much about the name, as that he made answere to diverse grave fathers, that if there case were his they durst not urge any change.

Concerning the name,[13] I have twice in severall yeares understood in as perticuler a manner as these other things I have recounted, that the denomination of these must be Jesus. And thrice, I think more often, of the inconveniences would happen to both partes if ours should have any dependensy[14] of the Fathers of the Society.

The severall great effects of those former words were to many to recount: The continuall light God gives in litle, and great, appertayning to the true practise of this Institute, is such as cannot easely be declared: And the progresse of soe many soules as are now of this Company; if your Illustrissime knew the perticulers of there proceedings soe as some other lesse intristed[15] might recount them; together with the miraculous calls of severall of them; it would manifestly appeare that Gods hand were in the worke and that his Majestie is well pleased with the manner hithertoo observed; which is noe other, then what in this other paper, I humbly heer present.

And begge for the meritts of Christs passion your Illustrissime will approve if soe in our Lord it seeme to you convenient.

---

1   Antonio Albergati (1566–1634) from Bologna, was Papal Nuncio of Lower Germany, including Liège and Cologne, from April 1610 to April 1621. An active reformer in the Church and in religious houses, he supported Mary Ward's foundation in Cologne in 1621. On 4 August 1621 he left Cologne to return to Rome. Note the Latin address in preparation for the translation of the document into Latin. Peters pp. 307–310.

2   Probably a copy of the *Institutum*, the *Formula Instituti* of the Society of Jesus, adapted for women by Mary Ward and her companions, which Mary took to Rome with her petition to the Pope. BV, Capponi 47, ff. 56v–63v. Peters pp. 615ff.

3   It appears that the Nuncio Albergati had raised objections to the form which Mary Ward's Institute was to take. Mary's aim in writing this letter is to show that her decision was not the fruit of her own judgment, but of a revelation from God.

4   Feast of the Finding of the Holy Cross, 2 May 1609.

5   Enjoyed.

6   PL No. 16.

7   Known as the 'Glory Vision'. See AB 6 for a full description; also Vita E, ff. 18v–19r with note 73 on the date, and PL No. 21.

8   Helped.

9 Vita E, ff.15r–15v and PL No. 22.

10 In Mary's letter to John Gerard the insight is repeated word for word. Here the essential content is stated, followed by further explanations.

11 Of these, only the *Scola Beatae Mariae* is extant. Peters pp. 124ff.

12 Roger Lee SJ died in December 1615.

13 PL No. 27 shows a meditation on the words 'You shall call his name Jesus' in which Mary Ward in London was granted a sight of the beauty of the way of life to which God had called her.

14 Mary Ward intended her Institute to be modelled on the Society of Jesus, but governed by its own Superior General. In any case, the Jesuit Constitutions prohibit responsibility for an Institute of women. Peters p. 247.

15 Interested (i.e. concerned, involved).

L 3. Mary Ward's Petition to Pope Urban VIII and the Cardinals

Rome. 1629 March 25

Copies. Italian: Vatican Archives, AV Misc. Arm. III, 37, ff. 213r–215r (signed by Mary Ward, handwriting of Elizabeth Cotton); Archives of the Discalced Carmelites, Rome, Documents of P. Dominicus a Jesu Maria, f. 106v (unsigned, handwriting of Winefrid Wigmore).
German translation AIM. Documents up to 1645, No. 15.
English translations AIY. CJ Provincial Archives.

This text, composed in Italian, has never before been printed in its entirety in English. Josef Grisar SJ admired its sincerity, clarity of thought, and power of expression, and considers that the signed original was intended for the Pope himself. (Grisar *MW* pp. 390–391 and note 181.) The *English Vita* (f. 37v) relates that it made a great impression on the Cardinals.

On the advice of Giovanni Battista Pallotto, Nuncio Extraordinary in Vienna, that there was a possibility of confirmation for Mary Ward's foundation if she had another audience with Pope Urban VIII (see Vita E, note 144) Mary left Munich for Rome on 2 January 1629, arriving in Rome in early February. Her state of ill health and the rigours of the journey are described in the *English Vita* ff. 36v–38r. On arrival in Rome in early February 1629, she was forced to keep to her bed for three weeks. She spent this time dictating a long petition for distribution to the Pope and Cardinals, the text of which is printed below in an English translation. In May 1629 Mary Ward was granted an audience with the Pope in Castelgandolfo, and at the end of 1629 a new Special Congregation of four Cardinals was appointed to re-examine the whole matter. Early in 1630, at the invitation of the four Cardinals, Mary was received in audience by them, and presented the case for her foundation once more. This audience is described in the *English Vita* ff. 38r–39v, but there is no report of it in the documents of the Congregation of Propaganda Fide. This may be because it was not considered necessary to record an unusual audience with a woman, especially as a decision had been made (though not yet published) on 7 July 1628 by Propaganda, in the presence of the Pope, for the suppression of the whole Institute.

The long sentences of the original petition, with their elaborate periodic construction, have been modified in this translation, and the text has been divided into paragraphs.

The petition contains a memorial of the history of Mary Ward's Institute from its foundation in 1609 till 1629. This is followed by a plea for an open and full examination of the long-standing accusations and slanders against the members. If they are found guilty, they will accept punishment, but if proved innocent, as they know they are, they will ask the Pope to bless their Institute with full confirmation.

A number of Englishwomen who had been called by God to a state of perfection that could not be put into practice in their own country, so unhappily tainted with heresy, crossed the sea and reached Flanders, willingly giving up all the consolations that homeland and family might grant them, to seek in foreign countries the greater honour and service of God.

In the year 1609 they began to live [a life subject to] regular religious discipline in the city of St. Omer under the patronage of Her Serene Highness Donna Isabella Clara Eugenia, the Spanish Infanta, and to the great content and satisfaction of the Bishop of that city, the Reverend Monsignor Jacques Blaes, as is testified by letters of his now in Rome. For some years they gave themselves to prayer and other efficacious means of getting to know the Will of God more exactly about their best way to serve His Divine Majesty and Holy Church. God Himself is witness that his Divine Will is and has always been their only end and object in electing this their way of life.

As Divine grace supported them to the complete satisfaction of their souls and the number of persons who esteemed their Institute and way of life increased, they began to open colleges and noviciates at Liège, Cologne and Trèves, the chief cities in Germany, to which they had been urgently invited by the inhabitants. There they were graciously received by the princes, bishops and apostolic nuncios, as is testified to this day by many letters of the said princes and prelates, especially those of His Lordship Cardinal von Zollern, of their Serene Highnesses the Archbishop and Elector of Cologne[1] and the Elector of Trèves, and of Monsignor Albergati, who was then the Nuncio in that region.

As our Lord God was developing his own work, the above-mentioned Englishwomen, so as not to fail in corresponding on their part, got one of the most important persons[2] in the kingdom of England, a relative of several of them and a highly educated man, to come to Rome in the year

1616 during the pontificate of Pope Paul V of happy memory. He was to present their Institute to the good pleasure of His Holiness, and to offer their persons and their labours to obey him and serve Holy Church for ever. His Holiness deigned to refer the consideration of their business to the illustrious Cardinals of the Holy Council of Trent.[3] When they had weighed the matter well and reported back to him (as is customary in cases of similar consequence), His Holiness gave his approval, promised to consider confirming the Institute, and had letters of recommendation written to the Bishops and Apostolic Nuncios of the regions where they were living at the time. Some of these are now living here in Rome.

The leader[4] of the above-mentioned English ladies was so seriously ill that she could not come in person to Rome to plead for the full confirmation of the Institute, and in the meantime the said Pope Paul V of happy memory departed to a better life. Otherwise he would probably have brought to perfection the work he had begun to favour so highly. But Divine Providence (which always works for the best) did not will to allow that blessing without sending them greater trials and sufferings.

In the year 1621 however, during the pontificate of Pope Gregory XV of happy memory, they came to Rome (with letters of recommendation from His Sacred Majesty the Emperor, from the Catholic King of Spain and from Her Serene Highness the Infanta of Flanders) to seek the confirmation of their Institute. The Holy Father received them graciously and referred their business to the Illustrious Lord Cardinals of the Congregation of Regulars. He also replied to the above named rulers by sending excellent letters that showed the favour he meant to do to the petitioners and their Institute.

But the enemy of all good prompted some ecclesiastical and religious persons (perhaps out of certain interests and envy) to rob them of their good name by spreading lying rumours and saying among other things that the said Englishwomen were preaching in pulpits and squares, and holding public disputations on divine matters. Other similar false charges were made against them, extravagant charges quite contrary to what they really did or thought. However God allowed such lies to be too readily believed, and they caused Pope Gregory XV to make a difficulty about confirming their Institute at that time. Seeing this, the said Englishwomen asked leave to live here in Rome in community, as they had lived elsewhere for many years, so that people might see their activities as they really were and not as they were reported to be. That request was approved by his Holiness and kindly granted by him and by the said Congregation of Cardinals of Regulars. So they led that kind of life here in Rome for about three years, (that is, until the death of the said Pope and for one year of the pontificate of our Lord Pope Urban VIII).

Six years ago they opened a college at Naples with the leave and approval of His Excellency the Duke of Alva, viceroy of that city, of His Excellency Cardinal Archbishop Carafa[5] and of Monsignor Pamphili, the Apostolic Nuncio, to all three of whom they had been recommended by letters from several Cardinals of the Congregation of Regulars. To this day they are well regarded there, and are highly esteemed by the nobility and others. Up to a few months ago they ran schools there, and had boarders and a noviciate.[6]

In the second year of the happy pontificate of our Lord Urban VIII they again offered themselves and the Institute in the aforesaid manner, humbly begging His Holiness to show favour to their way of life and to perfect it with his final confirmation. However, they had not earned that favour yet, as the sequel showed,[7] though His Holiness was graciously pleased to confer other favours on them such as a regular monthly alms, which they still enjoy, etc.

As the lady who was in charge of the rest of them had no longer anything to see to here in Rome she thought it was her duty to go back to their colleges in Germany and Flanders and give instructions there etc., so she set off in that direction two years and a few months ago. Passing through Munich, the court of His Serene Highness the Duke Elector of Bavaria, she found there was a demand there for ladies to educate young girls. After thinking the matter over, as those good and prudent rulers do in all their undertakings, they placed at her disposal a house that was in a good position and very suitable for the purpose. This house they furnished and fitted up as a college, with an endowment of 100 gold scudi per year for each person. They also sent to other Colleges at a distance of many days' journey, for other members of the same Company to live in that house. All this was done with great courtesy and in accordance with the generosity characteristic of their Highnesses when the service of God and the common good are concerned.

And so from the beginning of 1627 schools for day-pupils and boarders were established there, with a noviciate in which are to be found girls from the best and noblest families of various countries and provinces. Up to now all this is going very happily and successfully. As far as can be judged, the affection and esteem of those princes increases day by day, and more favourable conditions than those we have there could not be desired.

A few months after the Munich foundation had been established, the city of Vienna, seat of the Imperial Court, represented that it had even greater need of the same kind of assistance, since it contained many heretics and persons addicted to such vices as always go with consciences in which there is little fear of God and a lack of true faith and of due obedience to the Holy See. The Emperor graciously told the aforesaid English ladies to choose the most apt and suitable locality for their work and when this had been found he bought a new and spacious house, paid down a great sum of money for it, had the ladies publicly installed by his Chancellor and Grand Chamberlain and other officials, and settled a permanent yearly income on them by public contract. About 450 girls of all ranks of society, not counting boarders, attend the schools, and the fruit produced through the mercy of God by the ladies' humble means is much esteemed and recognised by their imperial majesties and by prelates, as well as by the common people of the city and others. They will all undoubtedly testify that this is true, if they are asked.

A year ago Monsignor Peter Pásmány, Archbishop of Strigonia (a prelate rightly reputed cultured and prudent) established them at Pressburg (the capital city of the Kingdom of Hungary). This was a difficult thing for him to do because most members of the senatorial Council were Calvinists and Lutherans, and so were the townspeople, and all stood out against accepting the foundation, alleging with one voice that to do so would soon destroy the practice of their religion. That practice, they said, depended chiefly on the upbringing of their daughters and on good family training (a duty left to women in that part of the world) whereas if their daughters were to be brought up papistically (to quote the word they used) while they were young, [their own] religion would quickly die out. They made an alternative suggestion to the Archbishop, that he should find a place and allow Catholic ladies to run schools there, but as private persons – a suggestion they had always previously rejected. "Those ladies", they said, "will die in time, but a Company so closely united [as the English Ladies] will never come to an end". The said Archbishop will no doubt testify to this and to much more, if there is occasion.

A little later they went to Prague[8] in Bohemia, having been invited there eight months earlier by the Lord Count Altan, who offered to provide them with a house and suitable church and ample endowment to support 30 persons. The Emperor openly favoured the suggestion and the nobility of the realm set themselves with great goodwill to support it. An Institute of that kind for the education and help of women, they maintained, was not only an advantage for that part of the country but an absolute necessity for accomplishing the desired reform in the Catholic religion – a point that is being insisted on to this day. However as the work was beginning, something occurred not only to prevent it but also to do great harm to a number of existing foundations of many years' standing. [This is how it happened:] Cardinal Harrach, Archbishop of Prague, and Monsignor Carafa,[9] then the Apostolic Nuncio, both had the help of several religious, and among them of good Father Valeriano Magni[10] (the Capuchin father who is now here in Rome). With no regard for the concerns of others in his desire to restrain the force of zeal, (or only if they could give him more help in carrying out his own designs) he used to speak very freely against the foundation and the Company to all kinds of people.[11] In these discourses of his he made many statements that were very far from true – a mistake that nearly always goes with excessive zeal on what are supposed to be good causes. He asserted among other things that the Company in question had never anywhere had a church that belonged to their colleges – a statement so contrary to the truth that in the majority of them there are churches, and from the very beginning there have been churches open to the public where the Blessed Sacrament is always reserved, and Masses are said every day, and sermons often preached etc. To this Monsignor Montoro,[12] who is now in Rome, can bear witness. He was the apostolic nuncio in those regions for several years and often honoured the Sisters with his presence on feast days.

But to go back to the point: The aforesaid Lords, the Illustrious Lord Cardinal Harrach, Archbishop of Prague, and Monsignor Carafa, sent certain reports to Rome and these were added to other adverse statements made a few months earlier by the Illustrious Lord Cardinal Klesl,[13] Bishop of Vienna (who was then against the persons concerned and their Institute but now professes to have changed his mind). [All this] caused such a disturbance that a little later Cardinal Boncompagni[14] was ordered (it was said) by His Holiness to close their college in Naples, take away the schools, and command all the members of the community, both the professed and the novices of whatever nation, to return to their own country and parents. This command was obeyed at once in Naples,[15] to the great sorrow of the parents and children.

With this order the said Lord Cardinal Boncompagni received other documents from Rome (as he himself has said) concerning the same persons. There is not a shadow of truth in any of them, for example that the said Company was accustomed to preach, spoke scornfully about his Holiness and prelates of Holy Church, and lived so scandalously that the above named Cardinal declared that modesty forbade him to read two questionable items contained in those papers. And this (it was declared and is still generally believed in Naples and in other places) was the cause of His Holiness' great displeasure with the said Company, and why he ordered its complete destruction etc. The same order was given likewise to the Apostolic Nuncios in all other places where these ladies have Colleges, and the order was repeated again and again, so that the said Company (besides other sufferings) is now slandered everywhere, princes, prelates and the common people believing that such scandalous behaviour has certainly taken place, even if not in their own district or town. In Germany, for example, people say that the scandals happened in Flanders; in Flanders they believe they were committed in Rome (because that was where the directive came from); and in Rome some worthy prelates have seriously enquired whether the said scandals were not committed in Naples, because it was there that the blow fell. And what confirms that opinion everywhere is the fact that of all the Congregations, Houses and Colleges of women (especially in parts of Germany, Flanders, France and even Italy) where they live together as a community and, like these women, without a cloister, these should be the only ones to be punished in this way by having their houses closed and their income confiscated – not only the houses founded by princes but those bought out of their own dowries – and by all members being sent to their own countries, many of them not finding any living relatives to receive them, or anyone to provide them with a new dowry for their support. Besides, those journeys alone would be expensive, since the aforesaid Company has members from many countries and nations: there are Italians, Spaniards, Germans, Flemings, Bohemians, Hungarians, French, Irish and English. It will be the most difficult of all for the English women, because they are the largest number and they come from a native country infected with heresy, to which they cannot return without great danger to their souls; it is not everybody who is given sufficient grace to suffer even unto death. Their parents will not have the courage to keep them at home; few perhaps will even be willing to take them in, still less (considering the unhappy state of their country and the broken fortunes of Catholics) be able to offer them a new dowry, etc. And besides all that, the reproach of having led a scandalous life makes their burden worse in another way.

Therefore all the members of the said Company, since it has pleased the divine Goodness out of his pure mercy to make use of them for 20 years in this way of life for the edification and help of their neighbour (in so many different cities, provinces and kingdoms, favoured by so many prelates, bishops and apostolic nuncios, and under the patronage of so many ecclesiastical and secular princes), now implore our Lord His[16] Holiness not to allow them to be cast out as women of ill repute, but to have their case examined. If they are found guilty, let them be punished, but if innocent (as God and their own consciences testify) then prostrate at the feet of His Holiness they humbly implore that he will deign to bless this Institute with full confirmation. This will be the real remedy, if they may say so, and the only efficacious means of sparing His Holiness many troubles and the said Company unjust sufferings, and also of removing the burdens of conscience from those who in the present uncertain state of things will take the liberty of making false accusations against them. By granting this favour His Holiness will do a deed that will always be remembered. Moreover the said Company will hold itself for ever bound to offer their modest labours and earnest prayers to Him who shed his most precious blood for the souls they strive to help, that he may deign to reward His Holiness abundantly and to grant him a long and happy reign for the greater divine glory, for the consolation and help of souls, and for the universal good of all the faithful.

Quam Deus etc.

Maria della Guardia

Rome 25 March 1629

---

1   Ferdinand von Wittlesbach. Peters p.189.

2   Thomas Sackville. Peters pp. 221ff.

3   This refers to the Congregation of the Council of Trent, set up after the Council had ended in 1563, to oversee the implementation of the Tridentine decrees.

4   La prima delle sopradette Inglesi. The title of General Superior is not used in this document.

5   Decio Carafa, Archbishop of Naples 1613–1626.

6   The short-lived foundation at Perugia (1624–1625) is not mentioned.

7   Following a decree of the Congregation of Propaganda Fide, the school in Rome was closed in June 1625, and the closure of the house followed soon after. Vita E, f. 27v and note 102.

8   Cf. Vita E, f. 35r and Peters pp. 452–460.

9   Carlo Carafa, Nuncio in Vienna 1621–1628.

10   P. Valeriano Magni OFMCap, adviser to Cardinal Harrach of Prague, travelled to Rome in 1628 and won the confidence of the Pope. He fiercely opposed both the Jesuits and Mary Ward's Company. Vita E, notes 139–140 and Peters pp. 453ff.

11   This sentence is obscure in the original Italian, though the general sense is clear.

12   Pietro Francesco Montoro, Nuncio in Cologne 1621–1624.

13   Cardinal Melchior Klesl. Mary Ward's foundations in Munich and Vienna were made at the invitation of the Elector Maximilian I and the Emperor Ferdinand II, without formal ecclesiastical approval.

14   Francesco Boncompagni, Archbishop of Naples 1626–1641.

15   The suppression of the Naples house took place in October 1628.

16   Sua Santità. The formal third person used in Italian speech and writing to address a superior has been retained in this translation.

L 4. Mary Ward's final appeal to Pope Urban VIII

Munich, 1630 November 28

Copies: Italian. ACDF, S. O., St. St., O–3–g, ff. 161rv, 164v; AIM Letter No. 55 (handwriting of Elizabeth Cotton).

The translation of the Italian is taken, with amendments, from Chambers II, pp. 330–331.

Mary Ward returned from Rome to Munich in April 1630. Following her audience with Pope Urban VIII in May 1629 and her meeting with the Particular Congregation of four Cardinals in February or March 1630, she was still hoping to save her Institute, and waiting for the Pope's definitive answer. Rumours reached her about the suppression of the house in Saint-Omer, but the Cardinals of Propaganda communicated directly with the local Nuncios and she received no official notification. Unable to believe that papal authority lay behind these events or that the Pope would take any important step without telling her, she wrote on 6 April to the communities in northern Europe, instructing them, in good faith, to disregard any orders of suppression. By the time this letter reached Liège the suppression had taken place, and the community in its uncertainty showed the letter to their confessor. The letter reached the Nuncio Pierluigi Carafa, who judged it to be an act of serious disobedience and sent part of it, in a Latin translation, to the Holy Office (commonly known as the Inquisition) in Rome.

Hearing the news of the suppression of Liège (30 April 1630) and the imminent suppression of the houses in Trier and Cologne, Mary Ward was still convinced that the suppression was illegal, the Pope having not yet said the final word to her. She sent her closest companion Winefrid Wigmore as Visitor, with full powers, to Liège. By the time of Winefrid's arrival at Liège in September, many members had left the Institute and the houses in Trier and Cologne had also been closed. Winefrid, who was devotedly loyal to Mary Ward but inadequate for the task she had been given, tried to reverse the suppression and fought a losing battle with the Nuncio. Carafa ordered an interrogation of Winefrid and the remaining sisters in Liège, who faced their questioners without any knowledge of canon law or of ecclesiastical procedures, and with no legal representatives of their own. (For a full account of these events see Wetter Chs. II, III, VII and VIII.)

Summer and autumn passed, and Mary Ward stayed in Munich still waiting anxiously for a personal word from the Pope on his final decision. By November the news of events in Liège would have reached her, and on 28 November 1630 she enclosed, in a letter to one of the Cardinals, what was to be her final appeal to Pope Urban VIII. (See Vita E, additional pages and note 156.) There was no response to this letter.

Ihs

Most Holy Father,

All that has been said and done at the present time against Ours in Flanders and some parts of Germany causes me to have recourse to Your Holiness, and in all humility to lay before you what I now write for your paternal consideration. It is now thirty years since, through the mercy of God, I determined to leave the world, and to apply myself to the spiritual life. Twenty-five years since, I left my native country and my parents, the more to please and better to serve His Divine Majesty. Ten years I employed in prayer, fasting and penance, and other things suitable for such a result, to learn in what order of religion, or mode of life, I was to spend my days according to the divine pre-ordination. And that which I now unworthily profess, and have by the mercy of God for twenty-two years practised, was not (God Himself being my witness) either as a whole, or in part, undertaken through the persuasion or suggestion of any man living, or whom I have ever seen, but totally and entirely (as far as human judgement can reach) ordained and commanded to me by the express word of Him Who will not deceive nor can be deceived. Who also gave light to understand and know the said state, inclination to embrace it and love it, clear demonstration of its utility, abundant manifestation of the glory thence to redound to the divine Majesty, loving invitations to labour in the same, efficacious also in giving strength to suffer for it, indubitable promises of promoting and perfecting it, and assurance that this Institute shall remain in the Church of God until the end of the world. By this short explanation I have not the least intention of preferring such lights or inspirations before the authority of Holy Church, nor my interior assurance before the judgement and decision of the Sovereign Pontiff, but only in the present extremity to declare what is the case, where I find myself obliged to do so. Having humbly set this forth, if Your Holiness commands me to desist from such practices, I will not fail to obey. May God in his mercy have no regard on this occasion to my unworthiness, but inspire Your Holiness to do in it what will be most to the Divine glory. Quam Deus etc.

On the 28 November 1630

Below the letter: Alla Santità di Nostro Signore.
Per Maria della Guardia Inglese

L 5. Mary Ward to the Superiors and Members of her Society

Munich, 1631 February 2

Copies: Italian. ACDF, S. O., St. St. O–3–g, f. 158r–v (handwriting of Elizabeth Cotton). There are six other copies (handwriting of Elizabeth Cotton or of Elizabeth Keyes) in the archives of the Holy Office, sent at different times, as this letter was always included, in defence of Mary Ward, with any communication which the companions sent to Rome.

On the back: Copy of what our Mother wrote on the 2nd of this February to be sent to all the Superiors of Ours.

The English translation is printed here by kind permission of Way Books, Campion Hall, Oxford.

The preceding letter shows that at the end of November Mary Ward was still not clear about the decrees made in Rome, and had received no official information. Believing that her foundation was legitimately constituted, she was still waiting for the Pope to make his final decision and to communicate with her personally. By January 1631 she was receiving news from Rome that the Holy Office, which had taken over her case from Propaganda, was calling for the suppression of her institute and for her own imprisonment. She may also have heard that on 13 January Pope Urban VIII had signed the Bull of Suppression, *Pastoralis Romani Pontificis*, though the Bull was not promulgated until May 1631. Understanding from the unofficial information she had received that the Pope had spoken and suppressed the Institute, she wrote the following brief letter to all her companions, a letter 'coming from the soul of the Foundress' as Immolata Wetter says.

My dearest Mothers and Sisters in Christ,

In the event that His Holiness, through Nuncios or other religious officials in the places where you live, forbids you to continue your religious practices and the subordination and dependence one on another, obey at once. And let your reason for thus acting be the same as mine in ordering it, which is, that His Holiness wishes it.

For the rest, love and serve as best you can Him for whose love and service you have left home and family and now endure etc. What other service I can give you in this life and the next is already yours. I warmly commend my failings to your faithful devotions.
Munich 2 February 1631.

Your servant in Christ
Mary Ward

L 6. Letter from Mary Poyntz to Barbara Babthorpe on Mary Ward's death

Hewarth, 1645 February 3 [new style]

Copy: AIM. Documents up to 1645. No 19a.
Printed in Chambers (with coded words retained but spelling modernised) II, 497–500.

This letter, dated 24 January 1645 (old style), 3 February 1645 (new style) was written by Mary Poyntz four days after Mary Ward's death and sent to Rome, where Barbara Babthorpe had succeeded Mary Ward as the second Chief Superior. The custom of addressing the Chief Superior as 'Most honoured' continued until the late eighteenth century. The letter is written in coded terms, as were most of the letters of Mary Ward and her companions after the 1631 Suppression. Coded identities continued into the eighteenth century; keys are kept in AIM and AIY. In this case the perilous situation of English Catholics in 1645 made a cryptic letter even more necessary. The coded words and the spelling of the original are preserved in this edition. Decoded versions can be found in several of the later biographies.

Mrs Poyntz to Mrs Babthorpe

Most honoured,

What is the divine providence? And how great is the Abisse of Gods his secrett Judgments? How profound ought to be our submissions? And that of dutie? Methinkes I can neither speake nor write, what not withstanding you must know, and it will be a maister piece of perfection to resigne to, and the truest act of love and dutie to our Dearest. On the 20. of January[1] 1645 at aleven of the clocke, or there abouts our dearest my father[2] departed this toylesome life at the age of 60 years and 8 dayes. Truely that I live to write it you is noe force of my owne. His decaying began on all Saints day,[3] towards Christmasse complained of great paine in his kidnes, decayd much, and as it wear uncapable of ease, or rest, and according to sence inclining to be content to goe to that sweet rest which through gods mercyes I ame most assured he is in, but forth of his love to his Chieldren, which was above all, but Gods will, was most prompt to doe all both by prayer, and medicines to prolong life. I doe disdaine my penn should pretend to expresse the least part of that love, which truely all the penns of the world can never doe. On the 29. of December he tooke his bed. When I perceaved iust over both kidnes to be swelled like a great roule, in fine all parts downewards swelled, and was so as not able to stirre his legs but with helpe, nor to putt on a rag him selfe, which was not his use, though in greatest sicknes. Will[4] came not home till the 13. This what was there wanting[5] might add to his suffrance, as when we meete you shall hear. On the 15. day changed much, and was indeed agonie. I would aske some times where was his paine, he answered from head to foote, pittifull sore eyes, throate greatly swelled, which we saw not till dead, yet never changed his sweet serene looke, as it were betwixt jest and earnest. Ned[6] said if you dy, we will take packe in lape and away to the Heathen; he answered, if I thought so, it would breake my hart, and in other occasions still insinuated how much it would expresse his Chieldrens love to take his death well, and shew our loves by advancing our Trade,[7] and promises what Marg[ery][8] would with the Lady Blews Sonne.[9] Will begged he would aske of God his owne life, he made signe he would, he had difficultie to speake, againe Will asked if he had don it, he answered, yes intirely, but most resignedly; now we make reflection he had a greater knowledge of his death, then his tender love to us permitted him to manifest not to contristate us, on the 19. not to make it heavy to us said, the chiefe busines is neglected to witt a Silver pinne.[10] we concurred though with hart breaking, and the next morning was concluded one should be sent for, and they are dear things, and not to be had but at dear rates, that was a bitter night, some little times paines, and agonie made as it were an amazement, but on all occasions of speach, most perfect memorie, and understanding, about 7 of the clocke desired us all to be present, Will

said we were all there, he replyed with great feeling, I would you were all, then said I had a resolution to have said other manner of things then now I am able. I forbore it not to contristate you, as also not to send for the Silver pinne in time, which was the greatest thing he had (he said) offended god in, and through gods mercy was the only thing did now trouble him, willed us to aske his pardon, and that we would pardon him, then commended to us with greatest feeling the practis of gods Voc[ation] in us, that it be constantly, efficaciously, and affectionately in all that belongs to the generall and particular of the same,[11] said God will assiste and helpe you, it is noe matter the who, but the what and when god said he shall inable me to be in place I will serve you. Then with greatest love imbracing eache, seemed to mind us noe more, but with eyes and hands gave signes of sweet intrinsicall,[12] intire acts, expressed great heate would noe refreshing but water, never sighed, groaned, nor rutled,[13] nor swett, never turned eye, nor writhed mouth, only inclined his head. He was laid forth as accustomed. About 9. the next day, came the silver pinne, neerer noone with such ease and other circumstances as the friday friend[14] attributed it to Marg[ery] her indeavours with her great Master, which he wondred at, till he saw where she was. 24 howers after his death his swell all fell, and yet noe skinne broke, nor wett seene but one leg runne water when he was alive, and in the same manner dead, the vaines of temples, hands, armes, feete and legs as perfect Asur as ever can be painted, a decaying red in his lippes as when alive, in fine noe signe of dead but cold, was kept from Munday till Wensday, and the last more lovely then the first. And this is all but my humble petition to your selfe, and with your leave to James and Prune[15] to repay that endlesse love with love, which is to live, and remember in your best thoughts poor Will and Peter,[16] who all circumstances considered is poor, yet not to belie her ardent love doth in measure undeserving feele her assistance, who had not had what to buy what she was to travell in, had not Will brought it. Pe[ter] would have lined her Coache[17] as Praxeds[18] was, but could not for more respects then one, did some what that was durable.[19] I know not how to hear from you, patience till God will. Be assured we are in desire as ought.
January the 24.[20] 1645.

---

1   New style would be 30 January.
2   Mary Ward.
3   1 November 1644.
4   Winefrid Wigmore. See Vita E, ff. 70v–71r.
5   Letters from London with good news of the Companions in Rome, which had been held up for over twenty months. Vita I, f. 47.
6   Usually Mary Poyntz herself. Perhaps Catherine Smith here, as Mary Poyntz names herself Peter (her other alias) later in this letter.
7   Continuing our way of life in the hope of ecclesiastical confirmation.
8   Alias for Mary Ward.

9   Jesus Christ, Son of the Virgin Mary.
10 A priest to give the Last Sacraments.
11 'The same' in Mary Ward writings always stands for the founding revelation of 1611 'Take the same of the Society' [of Jesus]. See letters to John Gerard and the Nuncio Antonio Albergati.
12 Interior.
13 Rattled.
14 Probably another term for the priest.
15 Elizabeth Cotton and Elizabeth Keyes in Rome.
16 Winefrid Wigmore and Mary Poyntz.
17 Coffin.
18 Sister Praxedis (1619). Vita E, f. 24r.
19 This is possibly a reference to the heavy tombstone which was originally laid on the grave. Cf. Vita E, f. 73r, note 232.
20 New style 3 February.

TIME LINE FOR MARY WARD'S LIFE

1585, 23 Jan	Birth of Mary Ward at Mulwith, near Ripon, Yorkshire.
1589–1594	At Ploughland, East Yorkshire, with her grandmother Ursula Wright.
1595	Mulwith, the family home, destroyed by fire.
1598	Mary's parents move north to Alnwick, Northumbria. Mary stays with Catherine Ardington at Harewell, West Yorkshire, where she makes her First Communion on 8 September 1598.
1599–1605	With the Babthorpes at Osgodby, south of York.
1600 c.	Receives her religious vocation.
1605 Autumn	Travels to London.
1606	Leaves England. Enters the Poor Clare Convent in Saint-Omer.
1607–1608	Founds and enters a convent of Poor Clares for English women at Gravelines.
1609, 2 May	Shown that this is not her vocation.
Sept	Returns to England. The 'Glory' vision. Apostolic work in London and the gathering of companions.
1609–1610	Foundation at Saint-Omer.
1611	It is revealed to Mary that she should 'Take the same of the Society', i.e. the Constitutions and way of life of the Society of Jesus, but independently governed by one of its own members.
1614–1619	Frequent journeys to England, and the establishment of a small community in London.
1616, April	Provisional approbation received from Pope Paul V in a letter to Bishop Blaes.
Nov	Foundation in Liège.
1620–1621	Foundations in Cologne and Trier.
1621, 21 Oct	Sets out to walk to Rome, arriving on 24 December.
28 Dec	Audience with Pope Gregory XV.
1622	Continued petitions for approbation. Opening of Roman school in the Via Monserrato/Montoro. The first accusations of the English secular clergy against Mary Ward's congregation reach Rome.
1623, 25 Jan	Death of Barbara Ward, Mary's sister.
1623	Foundation in Naples.
1624	Foundation in Perugia.

	Formal recognition by the Prince-Ferdinand of the English Virgins in Liège as Religious.
	Audience with Pope Urban VIII.
1625, April	Decree of the Congregation of Propaganda to suppress Mary Ward's three Italian houses.
June	Closure of the school in Rome.
Nov	Closure of the house in Via Monserrato by decree of the Cardinal Vicar Millini.
Autumn	Closure of the house in Perugia.
1626, Nov	Mary Ward leaves Rome; journey on foot to Munich.
1627	Foundation of the Paradeiserhaus in Munich, at the request of the Elector Maximilian I.
June	Foundation in Vienna, in a house given by the Emperor Ferdinand II.
1628, March	Foundation in Pressburg (Bratislava).
Summer	Attempt to make a foundation in Prague.
7 July	Decree of Propaganda (formal, in the presence of the Pope, though not published) to suppress Mary Ward's Institute.
October	Closure of the house in Naples.
Autumn	Mary Ward makes several journeys between Vienna and Munich.
1629, Jan	Returns to Rome.
May	Audience with Pope Urban VIII, at Castelgandolfo.
Oct	Decision of *Propaganda* to start the suppression of the 'Jesuitesses'. This was communicated to the Nuncios, but not to Mary Ward.
1630, Jan	Suppression of the house in Saint-Omer.
Feb/Mar	Mary invited to talk about her institute by a new Particular Congregation of four Cardinals.
	Rumours reach her about the suppressions, but no official notification.
April	Mary leaves Rome for Munich.
6 April	Mary Ward writes to her companions in the northern houses telling them that the orders for suppression do not come from the Pope and should be ignored.
Apr–Aug	Suppression of the houses in Liège, Cologne and Trier.
5 Sept	Winefrid Wigmore, sent as Visitor to Liège by Mary Ward, tries to reverse the suppression of Liège.
Sept	Interrogation of Winefrid Wigmore and the former members of the Institute in Liège by the Nuncio Carafa. Documents concerning the interrogation sent to *Propaganda* and passed to the Inquisition.
28 Nov	Mary Ward sends her final appeal to the Pope.

1631, 13 Jan	Signing of the Bull *Pastoralis Romani Pontificis* by Pope Urban VIII.
2 Feb	Mary writes to all her communities, telling them to obey the Pope's decree.
7 Feb	Mary's arrest in Munich by order of the Inquisition, with the approval of the Pope. Imprisonment in the Anger convent, Munich.
13 Feb	Winefrid Wigmore arrested and imprisoned in Liège.
14 April	Mary released from prison and ordered to travel to Rome.
21 May	The Bull of Suppression was promulgated in Rome, followed by Cologne (July), Vienna and Munich (August).
October	Mary sets out for Rome.
1632, March	Mary arrives in Rome. Audience with Urban VIII. Cleared of heresy by the Cardinals of the Inquisition, but still under their surveillance. Permitted to live with her companions, but as lay persons.
28 May	Winefrid Wigmore released from prison in Liège; travels to Rome.
1633	House on the Esquiline acquired
1634	Mary stays for six months in Umbria, still under the surveillance of the Inquisition, most of this time spent at San Casciano dei Bagni. On return she is received in audience by Pope Urban VIII.
1635	School re-opens in the Paradeiserhaus, on condition that Mary Ward's companions live and teach as lay persons.
1636, Dec	Mary's health deteriorates. Time spent in Nettuno does not restore her.
1637	Mary permitted to leave Rome for Spa and the north. Five months spent in Paris. Leaves Paris for Spa and Liège: frequent illnesses.
1639, 20 May	Arrives in England. Large household in London with some pupils.
1642	Leaves London. Travels to Hutton Rudby, Yorkshire.
1643	To Heworth, York.
1644, April	Siege of York intensifies. Mary Ward and companions move into City.
July	Return to Heworth after the surrender of York to Parliamentarian forces.
1645, 30 Jan	Death of Mary Ward.

SELECT BIBLIOGRAPHY

Primary Sources

ENGLAND
York, The Bar Convent
CJ Archives, English Province (AIY).
The English Vita. A Briefe Relation of the holy Life and happy Death of our dearest Mother, of blessed memory, Mistress Mary Ward. English manuscript dated 1716.
Two French manuscripts, thought to be seventeenth century copies of Winefrid Wigmore's French translation.

Manchester
IBVM Loreto Archives (AIMan).
The English Vita. A Briefe Relation of the holy Life and happy Death of our dearest Mother, of blessed memory, Mistress Mary Ward. English manuscript, early eighteenth century.

GERMANY
Munich
Archives of the Congregatio Jesu, Munich-Nymphenburg (AIM).
Autobiographical Fragments.
Mary Ward's Letters.

ROME
Vatican
Archivum Congregationis Doctrinae Fidei (ACDF).
Archivio Segreto Vaticano (AV).
Biblioteca Apostolica Vaticana (BV).

Printed Sources

Dirmeier CJ, Ursula, ed., *Mary Ward und ihre Gründung. Die Quellentexte bis 1645*, 4 vols, Münster 2007.
This contains all the Mary Ward source texts up to 1645 in their original languages, with introductions and notes in German. A copy is kept in the archives of the Bar Convent, York.

Published Books

Aveling, J. C. H., *Northern Catholics 1558–1790*, London 1966.

Chambers IBVM/CJ, Mary Catherine, *The Life of Mary Ward*, 2 vols, ed. James Coleridge SJ, London 1882, 1885.

Cover IBVM, Jeanne, *Love the Driving Force. Mary Ward's Spirituality: Its Significance for Moral Theology*, Milwaukee 1998.

Edwards SJ, Francis, ed., *The Elizabethan Jesuits. Historia Missionis Anglicanae Societatis Jesu (1660) by Henry More SJ*, London 1981.

Foley SJ, Henry, *Records of the English Province of the Society of Jesus*, 7 vols, London 1875–1883.

Fridl, Marcus, *Englishe Tugend-Schul ... Maria Ward*, 2 vols, Augsburg 1732.

Gerard SJ, John, *The Autobiography of an Elizabethan*, trans. and ed. Philip Caraman SJ, 2nd ed., Oxford 2006.

Grisar SJ, Josef, 'Die beiden ältesten Leben Maria Wards', *Historisches Jahrbuch der Görres-Gesellschaft*, Munich 1951 (private trans.).

Grisar SJ, Josef, *Die ersten Anklagen in Rom gegen das Institut Maria Wards 1622*, Rome 1959 (private trans.).

Grisar SJ, Josef, *Maria Wards Institut vor Römischen Kongregationen, 1616–1630*, Rome 1966 (private trans.).

Guilday, Peter, *The English Refugees on the Continent 1578–1795*, London 1914.

Hicks SJ, Leo, 'Mary Ward's Great Enterprise', 6 parts, *The Month*, London Feb. 1928 – March 1929.

'Journey into Freedom. Mary Ward, Essays in honour of the fourth centenary of her birth', *The Way Supplement*, No. 53, London 1985.

Kirkus CJ, M. Gregory, *An IBVM/CJ Biographical Dictionary of the English Members and Major Benefactors 1667–2001*, Catholic Record Society 78, London 2001; 2nd ed. The Bar Convent, York 2007.

Littlehales CJ, Margaret Mary, *Mary Ward, Pilgrim and Mystic 1585–1645*, London 1998; 2nd ed. 2001.

Morris SJ, John, *The Life of Fr John Gerard*, London 1881.

Morris SJ, John, *The Troubles of our Catholic Forefathers*, 3 vols, London 1872–1877.

Orchard IBVM/CJ, Gillian, ed., *Till God Will. Mary Ward Through Her Writings*, London 1985; 2nd ed., Slough c.1998.

Peters IBVM/CJ, Henriette, *Mary Ward, a World in Contemplation*, trans. Helen Butterworth IBVM/CJ, Leominster 1994.

Tierney, M. A., ed., *Dodd's Church History of England from the*

Commencement of the Sixteenth Century to the Revolution in 1688, 5 vols, London 1839–1841.

Wetter CJ, Immolata, *Mary Ward under the Shadow of the Inquisition,* trans. Bernadette Ganne CJ, and Patricia Harriss CJ, Oxford 2006.

Wright IBVM, Mary, *Mary Ward's Institute, The Struggle for Identity,* Sydney 1997.

INDEX OF PEOPLE

Number spans may indicate separate mentions rather than unbroken discussion

Abbot, George, Archbishop of Canterbury 21–2
Albergati, Antonio 141, 143–7, 149
Albrecht, Archduke 12
Alcock, Mary xii–xiii, 141
Althan, Count (Altham) 94–5, 152
Alva, Duke of 151
Ardington, Catherine 5

Babthorpe, Barbara 16n, 158–61
Babthorpe family 112
Babthorpe, Lady Grace 112–13, 122
Babthorpe, Sir William and Lady Grace 7–8
Babthorpe, William (son) 7
Baldwin, William SJ 134
Ball, Frances (Teresa) xiv–xv
Bandini, Cardinal Ottavio 28, 88
Barberini, Antonio see St Onofrio, Cardinal
Barberini, Cardinal Francesco 65
Barberini, Donna Constanza 27, 38–9, 58, 65
Barberini, Maffeo see Urban VIII, Pope
Bavaria, Duke of 42, 88, 151
Bedingfield, Frances 66, 93n
Benedict XIV, Pope xiv
Bentley, Catherine 119
Berrington, Bernard OSB 62
Bianchetti, Cesare 60
Blaes, Bishop Jacques 12, 16, 18, 19n, 134–5, 146, 149
Blakestone, Lady 3
Blasius, Bishop see Blaes, Bishop Jacques
Boccabella, Mgr Alessandro 54
Boncampagni, Archbishop Francesco 27, 153

Borgia, Cardinal Gaspare 37–8
Borromeo, Cardinal Federico 30–1
Brown, Joanna (Jane Browne) 16n, 82
Brunderwoot, Bishop of (Bishop of Basel) 88
Burton, Edward SJ 142

Campian, Anne 12n, 120
Capelli, Mgr 61
Carafa, Cardinal Archbishop Decius 27, 151
Carafa, Mgr Carlo 152–3
Carafa, Pierluigi 156
Chambers, Mary Catherine xxii
Constable, John 3
Contzen, Adam SJ 50
Conyers, Thomas SJ 62
Cotton, Elizabeth 37n, 160

de Soto, Andreas 11, 129
Dirmeier, Ursula CJ xv
Dominicus a Jesu Maria SJ 29–30
Dormer, Jane, Duchess of Feria 12

Elizabeth, Electress of Bavaria 32, 52
Evers, Lord William (Eure) 101

Felkirch, Archbishop 31
Ferdinand II, Emperor xii, 33, 151–2
Ferro, Dr Alphonso 94
Flacke, William SJ 120
Fridl, Marcus xvi

Garrett, Margaret 6, 114, 117–18
Gasquet, Cardinal xiv
Gerard, John SJ 141–3
Gimnasio, Cardinal Domineco 28

Golla, Dean Jakob 45–6, 51
Goudge, Mary Stephen 10, 12, 129–32, 134–5
Gräffin, Abbess Katharina 48–9
Gregory XV, Pope xii, 24–5, 150
Guelfi, Isabella 60

Harrach, Cardinal Ernst von (Haroke) 34, 152–3
Hastings, Henry (Earl of Huntingdon) 107
Henrietta Maria, Queen of England 65
Hicks, Leo SJ xxii
Hohenzollern, Cardinal Friedrich von 28
Hollins, Samuel 74
Holtby, Richard SJ 9–10, 120
Horde, Margaret 25n

Ingleby, Sir William 6
Isabella, Archduchess 12, 19, 24

Keller, Jakob SJ 50
Keyes, Elizabeth 93–4, 160
Keynes, George SJ 10, 120, 126, 133–4
Kiesl, Cardinal 153

Lee, Henry SJ (Henry Fines) 25n, 26, 37n
Lee, Roger SJ 14, 17, 79, 103, 134–5, 137
Leopold V, Archduke 32–3
Ludovico, Johannes SJ 50
Lumley, Lord John 120

Magdalena, Grand Duchess Maria 30
Magni, Fr Valerio (Valeriano) 34, 152
Mallory, William (Mallery) 3
Mann, Girolami 60
Margareta, Duchess Regent 30
Maximilian, Elector of Bavaria xii, 32, 46
Medici, Claudia di, Archduchess 32–3

Merry del Val, Cardinal xiv
Millini, Cardinal Giovanni (Melino) 26, 37
Monte, Marques de 55
Montoro, Mgr Pietro 153
Morriss, Lennard (Robert Wright) 26
Mush, Fr John 9, 111–12, 115

Napolione, Bishop Comitoli of Perugia 29
Neuhaus, Lady Katarina von 34
Neville, Edmund 8–9
Northumberland, Duke of 60

Pálffy, Countess Maria (Palvy) 35
Pallotto, Nuncio Giovanni (Pallota) 37n, 42
Pamphili, Giovanni (later Pope Innocent X) 27, 151
Paul V, Pope 24, 150
Pázmány, Cardinal Peter xii, 34, 152
Percy, Henry, 9th Earl Northumberland 3
Peters, Henriette xxi
Piccolomini family 60
Pius IX xiv
Poyntz, Mary xvi, xvii–xviii, 1, 16n, 39, 47, 66, 158–61
Praxedis, Sr 23, 141–3, 160

Readshaw, William 109
Rocci, Nuncio Ciriaco 42
Rookwood, Susanna 16n, 25n
Roper, Catherine 119–20
Rosetti, Count Carlo 65–6

Sackville, Thomas 149
San Sixto, Cardinal (Laudivio Zacchia) 37
Scalia, Cardinal (Deserido Scaglia) 37
Slavato, Lady Lucy 35
Smith, Catharina 16n, 54, 66, 159
St Onofrio, Cardinal (Antonio Barberini) 37–8, 58

Tomson, John *see* Gerard, John SJ
Toole, Canon Lawrence xvi
Trejo y Paniagua, Cardinal Gabriel
  (Cardinal Trescio) 28–9, 93
Trèves, Elector of 149
Turner, Anne 25n, 66

Urban VIII, Pope xii, 17, 27, 37,
  53, 57–9, 148–56

Vitelleschi, Muzio SJ xii

Ward, Barbara 16n, 25n, 85
Ward, David 84
Ward, George 85
Ward, Marmaduke 2–3, 105–6
Ward, Mary
  childhood xi, 2–6, 105–6
  death 73–5, 93–5, 97, 158–61
  devotions 92, 95–7, 101, 115,
    123, 133–5
  education and schools xi, xiv,
    16, 26–7, 33–4, 100, 149,
    151–2
  family 2–3, 105–7, 110–12, 122,
    124–5
  foundations xii–xiv, 19–21,
    27–8, 33–5, 85, 129, 146,
    149–52
  'Glory Vision' 19, 139, 146
  illnesses xiii, 10, 17–18, 28, 31,
    36–7, 43, 46, 50–1, 54, 56–8,
    60, 62, 64, 67–9
  imprisonment xiii, 45, 47–52,
    77

  opposition to xii–xiii, xviii–xix,
    55–7, 122, 124–5, 146–7, 149,
    152–8
  relations with Roman
    authorities xii, xiv, xx–xxi,
    25, 37, 44–6, 49, 53–8,
    148–55
  St Athanasius revelation 13–14,
    136
  travel xii, 24, 26–7, 36–8, 40,
    53, 60–4, 66, 97–8
  virtues 7–8, 15, 35, 75–9, 82–7,
    89–91, 122–3, 137–8, 145
  vocation xi, 6–9, 112, 114–15,
    117, 121–5, 133, 144
  vows 15, 137–8, 145–6
Ward, Ursula 106
Wetter, Immolata CJ xxi
Wigmore, Winefrid xvi, xviii, 1,
  16n, 25n, 26, 37n, 41, 54, 66, 72,
  156, 159
Wittlesbach, Prince Ferdinand von
  99, 149
Wright, Alice 108–9
Wright, Christopher xi
Wright, John xi
Wright, Robert 29, 37n
Wright, Robert (grandfather) 106–7
Wright, Ursula (grandmother)
  106–7
Wright, Ursula (mother) 3
Wright, William 3

Zollern, Cardinal von 149

INDEX OF PLACES

Number spans may indicate separate mentions rather than unbroken discussion

Anger Convent   47–52
Antwerp   64
Augsburg   xiv, xviii, 2, 25, 75

Babthorpe   8–9
Baldwin Gardens   9
Bamberg   2
Baths of Cassiano   28, 54–7
Bohemia   xvii, 35
Bologna   60
Bonn (Bone)   64
Bratislava (Pressburg)   xii, 30, 34–5, 152
Brussels   19

Canterbury   119
Castelgandolfo   148
Charleville   62–3
Citta della Pieva   57
Cologne (Collen)   xii, 23–4, 32, 64, 85, 143–4, 147, 149, 156

Dinant   62–3

Egre   96
England   18, 20–2, 30, 65, 85, 138, 154

Feldkirch   30–2
Flanders   119
Florence   30

Germany   38–40
Ghendall (Givendale)   2
Gravelines   10, 12–14, 121, 132, 135, 137
Grisons   31

Hammersmith   xix–xx, 1–2, 93
Harewell   5

Harewood   5–6
Heworth   xiii, xvi, xviii, 1, 69–71, 158
Hutton Rudby (Hewton Rudby)   66–7, 69, 102

Innsbruck (Innsbrug)   31–2

Lake Como   31
Lambeth Palace   22
Liège
    1638–9   63–4
    autobiography   103, 112
    disputes   23
    foundation   xii, 19–21, 85, 149
    suppression   156
    unrest – Sister Praxedis   141–2
London   xiii, 9, 19, 22–3, 66, 119
Loreto   24, 37
Lyons   61

Manchester   xvi, 1
Milan   24, 30–1, 60
Monte Giovino   28, 57, 93, 95
Mount Grace   66–7
Mulwith   110
Munich (Monaco)   33, 36
    Archives   103
    danger from opponents   41
    departure, 1629   148
    final appeal to Urban VIII   155
    foundation   xii, 32, 151
    illness and grace   43
    imprisonment in the Anger
        Convent   xiii, 47–52
    letter to Superiors and Members   157

Nancy   24
Naples   xii, 26–8, 82, 151, 153, 155

Neptuno 58
Newby 3
Northumberland 5–6

Osbaldwick xiii, 74
Osgodby 9, 111–12

Paradeiserhaus xii, 33, 47, 49
Paris 1, 61
Parma 30
Perugia 29–30, 30n, 57, 119, 155
Piano Castagnano 55–7
Prague 34, 152
Pressburg (Bratislava) xii, 30, 34–5,
 152

Radicofani (Ratiofani) 57
Rome xviii, 50, 65, 151
 1621–2 24–6, 150
 1624 28
 1629–30 36–8, 89
 1632 53–4
 audience with Urban VIII 57,
  148
 closure of school, 1625 27–8,
  155
 confessor in 123
 departure from
  1626 30
  1637 60
 final appeal to Urban VIII 155
 foundation xii, xiv
 girls' school xii, 26
 graces received 91–3
 living under surveillance xiii
 petition to Urban VIII 148

prayers for Dr Ferro 94
 suppression of foundation 157–8

Saint-Omer (St Omer)
 1619 23
 community 146, 149
 departure from 15
 English college 119, 121, 125
 foundation 16, 105, 149
 Poor Clares xi, xii, 10–14,
  119–20
 return, 1616 19
 suppression 155
San Casciano see Baths of Cassiano
Siebenbürgen (Siben Bergs) 35
Siena 57, 60
Spa xiii, 58–9, 63
St Clement's Church-yard 19
Stavelot 64

Torre di Specchi 88
Trèves/Trier xii, 23–4, 143, 149,
 156
Turin 61

Venice 40
Vercelli 61
Vienna
 autobiography 110
 foundation xii, xiv, xvii, 30,
  33–4, 95, 151–2, 155
 prayers for Count Altham 94

York xi, xiv, xix, xxi, 1–2, 69–71,
 93, 108
Yorkshire xiv, xvii, 3, 6, 121